The Ape's Reflexion

Books by Adrian J. Desmond

The Hot-blooded Dinosaurs
The Ape's Reflexion

Adrian J. Desmond

THE APE'S REFLEXION

The Dial Press/James Wade
New York

Published by
The Dial Press / James Wade
1 Dag Hammarskjold Plaza
New York, New York 10017

*This work was first published in Great Britain by Blond and Briggs
Publishers.*

Manufactured in the United States of America

First U.S. printing

Library of Congress Cataloging in Publication Data

Desmond, Adrian J   1947–
The ape's reflexion.

Bibliography: p. 245
Includes index.
1. Chimpanzees—Psychology. 2. Chimpanzees—Behavior.
3. Gorillas—Psychology. 4. Gorillas—Behavior. 5. Mammals—
Psychology. 6. Mammals—Behavior. I. Title.
QL737.P96D47   156'.3   79-13480
ISBN 0-8037-0674-X

Contents

Acknowledgments

The Ape's Reflexion owes much to the ministrations of friends, colleagues and correspondents, some of whom were cajoled into reading an interminable succession of manuscripts. Roger Wescott and Ashley Montagu screened early versions of the typescript, and Leslie Aiello checked the galleys. J. A. Cowie, Barbara Desmond and Nellie Flexner were my mainstay; they followed the entire work through its many manifestations, constantly improving the grammar and the flow of the text. Gordon Gallup and Norman Geschwind carried on a lively correspondence with me on the issues of self-recognition and neuro-anatomy respectively; though I hasten to add that they frequently differed from me on matters of interpretation. Of course, they are exonerated from the blame attached to potential errors in the final analysis. Laura Petitto sacrificed an afternoon to set up videotapes of Nim's signing sessions for me to view. She also let me preview un-published papers analysing Nim's behaviour. In this respect, I am grateful to Herb Terrace for permission to study the videotapes, for supplying me with unpublished progress reports and statistical analyses of Nim's "sentences", and for his constructive criticism. For published and published material, I also thank Roger Fouts, Gordon Gallup, Nick Humphrey, David Premack, Duane Rumbaugh and Roger Wescott. Though I hope we all share similar motives in wishing to understand the human/ape mind and the meaning of evolution, I have no delusions that we will thus reach identical conclusions. I can only crave their indul-gence, and explain that an historian of evolution may perhaps offer a complementary perspective, adding one more vantage point from which we might tackle that momentous subject, the evolution of mind.

I owe a constant debt to the librarians of the D. M. S. Watson Natural Sciences and Medical Sciences Library at University College London; and especially Susan Gove, who constantly comes to my aid in unearthing obscure material. Similar thanks to the librarians of the British Museum (Natural History) and London University (Senate House) Library. Peter Gautrey kindly let me view the Darwin papers in the Cambridge University Library, and Mrs. J. Pingree made available Huxley's correspondence, housed in the Huxley archives at Imperial College, London.

Credits for Illustrations

1, 29: Jane van Lawick-Goodall, *In the Shadow of Man* (London, Collins, 1971). 2: R. M. and A. W. Yerkes, *The Great Apes* (New Haven, Yale University Press, 1929). 3, 4: R. B. Eckhardt, *Scientific American*, 226 (1972). 5: Richard Owen, *Transactions of the Zoological Society*, London, 3 (1849). 6: Drawing by Mary French of a skull cast of Rhodesian man in the author's collection. 7: Gerald A. Tate, Project Nim, Columbia University, by courtesy of H. S. Terrace. 8, 23: Francine Patterson, *National Geographic*, 154 (1978). 9, 10, 34: Drawings by Mary French. 11: Keith J. Hayes and Catherine Hayes, *Proc. Am. Phil. Soc.*, 95 (1951). 12, 13: Philip Lieberman, *American Anthropologist*, 24 (1972). 14: Ann James Premack and David Premack, *Scientific American*, 227 (1972). 15: David Premack, *American Scientist*, 64 (1976). 16: Duane M. Rumbaugh (Ed.), *Language Learning by a Chimpanzee: The Lana Project* (New York, Academic Press, 1977). 17, 19: Norman Geschwind, *Scientific American*, 226 (1972). 18: M. LeMay and N. Geschwind, *Brain Behavior and Evolution*, 11 (1975). 20, 21: Geza Teleki, *Journal of Human Evolution*, 3 (1974). 22: Keith J. Hayes and Catherine Hayes, *Human Biology*, 26 (1954). 24, 25: Ralph S. Solecki, *Shanidar* (London, Allen Lane, 1972). 26: Maurice K. Temerlin, *Lucy: Growing Up Human* (London, Souvenir Press, 1976). 27, 31, 32, 33: Geza Teleki, *The Predatory Behavior of Wild Chimpanzees* (Lewisburg, Bucknell University Press, 1973). 28, 30: Kathryn Morris and Jane Goodall, *Folia Primatologica*, 28 (1977). 35: J. D. Bygott, *Nature*, 238 (1972). 36: Jane Goodall, *Folia Primatologica*, 28 (1977). 37: Emil Menzel, *New Scientist*, 65 (1975). 38: E. Sue Savage-Rumbaugh *et al.*, *Science*, 201 (1978).

Martin Ryan photographed the illustrations, and Mary French was responsible for the line drawings.

"I wonder what a chimpanzee would say to this?"

Charles Darwin, 5 July 1857,
on learning that the anatomist
Richard Owen had raised Man
to a distinct subclass at the head
of creation.

I

Man's Crisis of Identity?

> ... perhaps someday, in order to be logically
> consistent, man may have to seriously consider
> the applicability of his political, ethical and
> moral philosophy to chimpanzees.
>
> Psychologist Gordon Gallup and
> colleagues, reviewing in 1977 the
> erosion of prejudices concerning
> human uniqueness.[1]

Human genes are an embarrassment. This creature who arrogantly styles himself 'man the wise', and who for centuries dismissed his animal body as merely a tabernacle housing the divine spark, must now face an ugly genetic fact: his genes so closely resemble the chimpanzee's as to render them sibling species. The prospect is sobering for an earth creature renowned for its cosmic gall.

The genetic ammunition comes at a timely moment. The man/ape debate, strangely quiescent since its convulsive flare-up in Darwin's day, is once more in full ideological swing. Reformist psychologists are fighting to implement Darwin's long-overdue programme – as they see it – by rehabilitating that anthropoid being, denigrated since the seventeenth century, as a misbegotten freak – the chimpanzee (*Pan troglodytes*). Morphologists today might show a clinical indifference to chimpanzees sullying man's divine reflection. Nonetheless, they too are finding ape genes only marginally less embarrassing, simply because the chimpanzee's too human genetic blueprint palpably fails to reflect the manifold physical differences separating ape from man. We and Washoe's kind do not *look* like sibling species. A chimpanzee complete with cap and clothes strolling down Oxford Street or Fifth Avenue would cause chaos as traffic ground to a halt. At first glance, the genes say this degree of man/ape distinction is impossible.

The flurry of excitement greeting these molecular revelations has scarcely subsided, yet already in their wake come quieter, more profound questions. To the obvious opener, "How close really are the 'sibling' protagonists, man and ape?" – by definition well-nigh impossible to answer fairly because of our distorted *Homo*centric perspective – follows the less obvious but more pertinent corollary, "How are we to measure the distance?" What yardstick gives an objective assessment? This is still trickier to answer; it is certainly suspicious that every criterion we choose places us squarely on top. A problem so multi-layered and of such overriding importance to man – and chimpanzee – deserves no snap answer, nor the slightest concession to traditional sensitivities.

In 1975 the California biochemists, graduate student Mary-Claire King and Professor A. C. Wilson, attempted a direct comparison between human and chimpanzee genes by the process of DNA hybridisation. They mated a strand of human DNA to its chimp counterpart. Since nucleotides in human DNA will only adhere to their exact complements in the chimp strand, the strength of the hybrid union will be a gauge of the structural match. A mutation, however, will fail to be recognised by the other strand and remain unbonded. To test the strength of the resulting DNA hybrid (effectively the basis for a manchimp), the chain was heated and the temperature at which the individual strands peeled apart reflected the number of originally unmated nucleotides. The result was astonishing: man only differs from the chimpanzee in 1·1 per cent of his genetic material. King and Wilson immediately set about confirming this; but in comparing the proteins for which DNA coded, they discovered to their amazement a still smaller (0·7 per cent) difference between the species.[2] Man/ape protein structure is practically identical – which explains why Tulane University surgeons have managed to transplant chimpanzee kidneys into a human recipient, and thus sustain the patient for a number of months[3]: a feat which opened up the distinct and distasteful possibility of cannibalising the living chimpanzee body for makeshift human components.

King and Wilson's result means that since man and ape evolutionarily departed one another's company, only one-hundredth of their once common DNA has subsequently suffered any mutation. We should be sister species, twins of creation: not merely *Homo sapiens* and *Homo troglodytes*, but recently diverged and still closely tied species. We should act alike, look alike, feel alike and think alike. But likenesses are not *that* striking; in fact, considering the intellect, Victorian moralists actually had little trouble opening a gaping chasm between man and the rest of brute creation. More than once apes were relegated along with mice, pigs and elephants to a rag-bag taxonomic bracket marked "others": as distant from us mentally, the evolutionary biologist St. George Mivart insisted a century ago, as the dust of the earth. In one stroke, the towering anatomist Richard Owen pushed aside the sorry and spiritually benighted ape claimant, and officially elevated man to a special (but short-lived) subclass at the head of creation[4]; and there the earth's only 'sapient' animal sat in splendid isolation. Such extremism, broached in the idological heat of the moment, was mercifully tempered by Darwin; but it highlights – one per cent genetic difference or no – man's need to see himself as a creature apart. It also emphasises that there is no immediately apparent psychological identity between chimpanzee and human. Even on bodily criteria alone, men and apes are today split into separate families, hominids and pongids.*

Not so, say the genes: we are sibling close. Hence the paradox. King and Wilson confessed in *Science* that chimpanzee and human DNA are simply too alike to explain in any straightforward manner the visible differences between these would-be Siamese species. Certainly, two frogs so genetically similar would appear to us practically indistinguishable. Aha! came the enlightened reply, perhaps from an amphibian vantage point we *do* look virtually identical to chimpanzees. Having an insider's perspective, might we not distort morphological reality, subjectively distancing ourselves from our nearest of kin?[5] One way existed to detect an inbuilt bias and that was to take a frog's-eye

---

* From "pongo", the native Angolan name for an anthropoid ("man-like") ape. All apes, back to the extinct Miocene *Dryopithecus*, fall into the family Pongidae. Humans, living and ancestral, comprise the family Hominidae. Apes, humans and gibbons are tied together in the superfamily Hominoidea.

view of creation; this is precisely what King, Berkeley biochemist Lorraine Cherry and American Museum herpetologist Susan Case did in 1978. To safeguard unfairly discriminating against frogs, they took just those traits (from head width to toe length) used to distinguish frog species and applied them to man and chimp. The results showed no change: chimpanzees and men looked for all the world (even to a frog) like distant beings – in fact, relatively further apart than frogs of distinct suborders. Yet genetics still insisted that the cage-bound chimpanzee and his human captor were brothers under the nuclear skin.

This widely reported anomaly led to a re-evaluation of evolutionary processes. King and Wilson themselves proposed an ingenious resolution of the biochemical twin paradox. According to the figures, men and apes are marginally more alike in their proteins than underlying genetic material. Perhaps, then, it was the genes *not* directly responsible for protein building which mutated during human history; genes, say, which critically regulate the speed and timing with which other genes manufacture protein. The slightest fluctuation of gene expression could crucially rebalance the subtle equilibrium of foetal growth, retarding some systems and accelerating others. The upshot could be a radically resculpted body. It is notoriously true that the baby ape's physiognomy seems created in a tastelessly comic impersonation of mankind's. Seeing in the 1830s one of the first *adult* chimpanzee cadavers shipped from Africa, Richard Owen fairly gasped his relief that it had a muzzled, small-brained, altogether more brutal face (human-apeing offspring were too man-like for Owen: he feared that they presented heretical evolutionists a god-sent opportunity). In a sense, the infant ape was not mimicking man so much as man cultivating an infantile ape look. Humans are probably neotenous – retaining the foetal ape face, with its big brain, shortened jaw and hairless skin. What apparently happened during our ancestry is that the critical genes regulating embryonic timing mutated and severely slowed aspects of foetal growth, leaving modern man a Peter Pan, a baby with adult abilities. Hence the striking physical dissimilarities between adult apes and men, yet their near genetic identity.

But which – chromosome structure or its architectural and mental consequences – paints the truer picture of man's proximity to the chimpanzee?

Foetal exaggeration, in particular the billowing brain and lengthening childhood, accompanied an exponential growth in human social relations, of learning to cope with customs and rituals, social etiquette and mores. The repercussions of this evolutionary stratagem were enormous: enter the baby-faced creature with the cosmic arrogance, eager to deny his humble birthright and disown his 'poor' chimpanzee relations in their rude state. Such acts of supreme self-deceit have a cruel way of backfiring in our faces, traumatising mankind into revamped rationalisations of its earthly purpose. To many it now seemed that the tale told by the genes added one more nail to the coffin of human uniqueness, a coffin in which man-the-anomaly lay outstretched awaiting interment. Funerary preparations were completed by comparative psychologists – professional voyeurs of the chimpanzee mind – during an unprecedented upsurge of activity in what was until a decade ago a science in the doldrums, if not actually its death-throes, for want of direction. The result is a wholly new and sympathetic understanding of the human and chimpanzee minds, and their relationship; an understanding at loggerheads with the lop-sided metaphysics of Victorian moralists, which to this day overshadows our thoughts about life on this lonely planet. But it is lonely only as long as mankind stands in Victorian indifference to the teeming forms of kindred life about him; after all, species alienation with its attendant neuroses stems primarily from a manifest inability to assimilate Darwin's message. One hundred years without Darwin really are enough.

Pulling together the diverse strands of evidence against human uniqueness, a team of psychologists led by Gordon Gallup of the State University of New York at Albany proposed a radical move. Their review paper, mischievously titled "A Mirror for the Mind of Man, or Will the Chimpanzee Create an Identity Crisis for *Homo sapiens?*" was published in 1977 in the eminently respectable *Journal of Human Evolution*. Light relief it was not; in fact, it was a synopsis of the flood of recent revelations which have apparently placed in peril man's mental hegemony. The punch it packed was this: over the centuries man has talked himself into feeling a world removed; now he suddenly finds himself hard pressed to come up with a single, substantial self-definition which excludes the encroaching chimpanzee – despite the perplexing fact that we look such unlikely bedfellows. Gallup's team picked its way through the plethora of new insights in search of the roots of man's "Identity Crisis"; and perhaps none was more important than Gallup's own elegant experiments, designed to convince even the sceptics that chimpanzees share our crowning possession – self-awareness.

It is the ultimate biological irony that man's closest and homeliest relative has in history been the most vilified of all creatures: the wretch of creation. Gallup's remedy might cause traditionalist shudders, but it is hardly wrong for that. The team prophesied "that perhaps someday, in order to be logically consistent, man may have to seriously consider the applicability of his political, ethical and moral philosophy to chimpanzees". So strident a call to arms deserves full and fair consideration. The evidence on which it rests is at first sight impeccable, and it does seem the ultimate benign act which evolutionarily aware man can perform. But does it best express our "sibling's" interest? Or is it – paradoxically – the definitive expression of a medieval dream which should have collapsed with Darwin's coming?

2

Do Ape Words Make Sense?

Washoe's first signs were a signal start to the loudly heralded 'ape breakthrough'; not on account of a few baby words, nor because apes have usurped something preciously human (if they have), but because language has opened up a brilliant new exploratory corridor to that boundless inner space we call "mind" – in man a vast, microcosmic galaxy defying space and time, infinite yet mysteriously lodged in a hemisphere of grey neural matter. But this is man's mind, what of the ape's? How are we to explore an alien galaxy with its possibly unfathomable reality when we are still strangers in our own? The short answer is "impose language on the chimpanzee mind and see how it copes".

The ape *mind*, not his body (as the Darwinian evangelist T. H. Huxley was lampooned for allegedly thinking) is the real issue. Darwin recognised this; his *Descent of Man* was a tactical strike at the imponderables of human mental evolution, an attempt to make the natural emergence of a moral mind plausible to a sceptical Victorian age. His ammunition plundered from nature was barely adequate for the job; but he did bequeath one priceless gen – the evolutionary key. Slowly we are turning that key. So-called ape language is just the tip of the iceberg; momentous it may be, nevertheless it is only a visible tip hinting at the submerged might below. The breakthrough is more subtle and profound than a cursory glance at chimp 'language' might suggest. It has left us invaluable insights into the ape's reality and perhaps the preconditions for the emergence of a symbolic universe.

After television made Washoe a star, ape 'language' risked becoming passé, its impact lost in the inevitable trivialisation by the media. Yet not so long ago, the 'brutish' ape's capacity to comprehend symbols would have seemed laughable, were not the prospect so damnable. Such heresy uttered in the last century, even after the shock of Darwin's *Origin of Species* and *Descent of Man*, would have been slammed as wildly irresponsible. It was man's prerogative to symbolise, to fashion a mental fantasy-world where moral laws jousted with natural ones. One has only to witness the pounding Huxley received in the press for his uncompromising *Man's Place in Nature*, which in 1863 riveted a staunch Victorian society already recoiling from the *Origin*. Huxley concentrated on man's frame; under the circumstances there was little else he could do. His book fell open at a remarkable illustration – "a grim and grotesque procession" of skeletons, an irate Duke of Argyll styled it – with skeletal man leading gorilla and chimp in a stately but rather pointed procession.[1] The anatomical similarities were striking: but then no one denied them. What ruffled the Duke's feathers was the unwritten assumption that human and ape minds followed in similar evolutionary procession. Others were equally shaken. As the *Edinburgh Review* concluded, pitching into Huxley:

> We believe that all the higher faculties of human nature – all the powers that make us MAN – are visibly independent of that mere structural organisation in which, as we have seen, many of the animals surpass us. Take an animal gifted with the nicest sensuous faculties, and he will not approach in mental capacity the lowest of the human species. Take a man deprived or destitute of all his senses and animal powers, there is still something in his capacity immeasurably superior to the whole brute creation. There is the gift of articulate language, – the power of numbers, – the power of generalisation, – the powers of conceiving the relation of man to his Creator, – the power of foreseeing an immortal destiny, – the power of knowing good from evil, on eternal principles of justice and truth.[2]

This strikingly Victorian vision was trotted out with alarming frequency in the wake of *Man's Place*. Perhaps the jocular *Athenaeum* stole the last word. Conscience, reason and right lifted man out of kinship with apes. "To these is added the gift of articulate speech which, though mechanically organised, imparts supreme value to them all; which makes man a communicative being; which gives to a lecturer, such as

Prof. Huxley, that power to instruct, amuse and illustrate [his heresy], by which he is raised immeasurably above the cleverest ape which ever climbed a tree . . ."[3] Victorian moralists *were* right to stress language: it is marvellous. And Huxley did of necessity give it short measure.

Washoe is beginning to change that. But while heresy, as Huxley might have said, begins its long trek towards superstition, I think we are in mortal danger of missing the point no less than the psychological underpinnings of Washoe's achievement: those aspects of the "ape breakthrough" omitted from the headlines, but which seem to make sense of Washoe's words. Ultimately, only the faculties of abstraction, conceptualisation and human-style sense association can explain the ape's comprehension of symbols – and these faculties in man ultimately permitted self-conceptualisation, perhaps the hallmark held most tenaciously as human. Yet even here, Gallup argues, the ape holds "A Mirror for the Mind of Man".

Stepping out of the Firing Line

Academic psychology has predictably split like a chromosomal strand on the vexed issue of ape 'language'. Strongly partisan positions have already coalesced (dictated as much by prior theoretical bents as the evidence), and a good deal of head-banging is now in evidence. From the resultant sparks, one might imagine a world-shattering principle at stake. Of course, for the protagonists there *is*: one side vehemently defends human language as unique, while the other claims (on behalf of apes) to have stormed this allegedly impregnable bastion. The two sides seem intent on throttling each other with such gusto that language must clearly be a point of honour. But the issue – do or don't apes 'have' human language? – is to my mind a bogus issue, and always has been. We are standing like shell-shock victims in the midst of a philosophically unsound if not positively preDarwinian battlefield, one into which Huxley would never have strayed. Stepping round this psychological charnel-house is something of a frying-pan-and-fire move, since we are immediately plunged into a hotter, if more profitable, dispute. Of course, I'm not exactly neutral on the ape question (one can't be), and it pays to admit one's prejudices from the start. I believe apes can use symbols creatively and purposefully. But they don't therefore use HUMAN words, which may sound confusing. Words mirror *our* 'reality', which is simply a mental construct anchored in our unique social and conceptual framework. To put it bluntly: human words have peculiarly human meanings because they are interpreted exclusively from our vantage point. If words meant the same for chimpanzees, their 'reality' would be ours; we would all be chimpanzees – or humans. I suspect we're not.

If apes can use our words, then they might invest them with different meanings. Surely a cat is a "cat" for both chimp and man, but is "sorry" (a word in all ape vocabularies)? Even though "cat" might describe the same object, it is equally possible that our two species conceptualise the animal differently. It is, however, in ethically loaded words like "sorry" that the real crunch comes, since their human meaning presupposes a human social structure. And finally, just to introduce a piece of interpretive pandemonium, what about "think", a word used by the first symbolising gorilla? How can two species whose brains differ come to the same understanding of a word which describes brain states?

The early partisan positions on ape 'language' can be cannibalised to pinpoint the common ground, one on which both protagonists might be happy to stand. When Washoe first signed, a chorus of ideological ecstasy rang out loud and clear. The issue was henceforth closed, wrote W. C. Watt of the University of California; by which he meant that the linguistic chasm between man and ape was bridged:

> To put it as baldly as possible, chimps can "talk". They have now been shown to have an ability so irrefragably on a continuum with our own speech that the chimps' ability cannot well be denied the adjective linguistic.[4]

This would be fine and rousing, but for the next paragraph, where Watt admits there exists no consensus on how exactly to define language in man. He escapes the difficulty by following established practice and insisting that whatever a child can say, so can a chimp sign. (Meanwhile, linguists were busy pulling the plug on this apparently unimpeachable practice.) Watt concludes with the sobering thought "that the history of our planet will be obliged to record that the first species to learn the language of another, to the degree possible given intraspecies limitations, was not man but chimpanzee". Notice the two salient features of the clarion call which mark out this partisan position. First: as a snub to humanists, it seeks to champion the evolutionary underdog. I hope, by putting the argument on a new footing, that even if humanists want to play the chauvinist game, there will no longer be any need for pongists to follow suit – precisely because there is no evolutionary underdog, philosophically speaking. The whole notion of apes as *sub*human is as ludicrous as humans being subdolphin. Secondly: it accepts a linguistic continuum across nature, something vehemently opposed by psycholinguists. For them, man cannot learn the chimpanzee's language because it has none! Language is human; its structures are programmed into man's cortical circuitry. What *we* have to do in our revised formulation of the key issue is to ask: "Why do apes have this capacity for wielding words when they have no natural language?" Only this might give us some clue to the preconditions of the emergence of language in man.

Diametrically opposed to this pongist position is the psycholinguistic fortress. Child psychologists and linguists are adamant in rejecting the wilder claims of their ideological opponents. Says John Limber, a linguist from the University of New Hampshire, whose speciality is the child's first utterance:

> With increasing frequency, widely read journals such as *Science* publish reports of the transmutation of base primates into noble ones. It is no wonder there is a growing belief among students and scientists alike that modern behavioral science has in fact succeeded in teaching human language to apes.[5]

And in a damning critique Limber fairly demolished that claim; "hardly compelling" was his verdict on the evidence that Washoe was using human language. Setting aside Limber's specific criticisms for a moment, there are positive concessions in his paper. Although the two sides seem implacably opposed, they can agree that the issue is human language. Treat this battleground like a mathematical equation: subtract the polemical issue, human language. Neither side concedes to much being left; after all, the ideological fire has been removed from the hearth. I disagree. After cancelling out the common language element, we are left with this: linguists like Limber admit that "apes can indeed be taught to engage in an extensive amount of symbolic communication", even if it has few properties of human language, and the pongists for their part see Washoe's symbol-wielding as creative.

These two points have still to be proved and are by no means free of contention. Still, a poll of psychologists and anthropologists would probably show overwhelming support for these basic assumptions (not that this is any criterion of their validity). So let us swing away from human language which, with all its syntactic sophistication and semantic idiosyncrasy, has probably taken untold millions of years to evolve. Moreover, it *might* well be genetically preconditioned in man – this has the added attraction of explaining the child's generation of a seeming infinity of complex sentences, none of which it need have heard before. There is no reason to expect apes to master this in all its subtlety over a decade; it would be a staggering jump. Not only is it unnecessary to prove apes 'have' human language, it is practically an impossibility. Washoe's tutors, Nevada psychologists R. Allen and Beatrice T. Gardner, defended her use of human language for their own anti-Chomskyan motives (explored later), and to make no mistake, they took the actual utterances of two-year-olds and compared them to Washoe's, reporting that "Transcripts of Washoe's spontaneous signing . . . are strikingly similar to transcripts of the spontaneous speech of children".[6] A generation ago, no one would have doubted that if just one brilliant chimp could match a two-year-old's speech, then it had language; but not so today, because linguists meanwhile had looked long and hard at two-year-olds, only to decide that they too cannot really be said to use human language! Again, this is John Limber, writing in 1977:

> Washoe, like most children during their 2nd year, has achieved a considerable degree of proficiency in using arbitrary symbols to communicate. This is not to say, however, that Washoe *or most 2-year-old children* use a human language.

This infuriating moving target made any consensus on ape language well-nigh impossible; and though linguists were not deliberately shifting it in order to nullify the encroachments of the ape, the results were the same. It is a quagmire we can well do without when discussing the ape's symbolic feats; if we go on chasing the goal of human language, we shall end up following a will-o'-the-wisp: always seeing it, but never catching it. We are getting nowhere fast with the chimp-child comparison because it is not a resolvable issue but an ideological stalemate.

Pongid Expletives

If the apes' possession of human language is not important, their creative manipulation of symbols emphatically is. To call swearing an intensely creative use of words undoubtedly sends shivers down traditionalist spines. To justify such sacrilege, consider this encounter between trainer Roger Fouts and fuming Washoe, demonstrating that she could still raise eyebrows. About to test Washoe's memory of the "monkey" sign (using the sign system of the deaf), Fouts led her to the monkey enclosures at the Institute for Primate Studies in Norman, Oklahoma (where Washoe and Fouts had settled in 1970). One rather testy macaque monkey threatened and obviously took Washoe unawares, driving her into a chimpanzee rage. Fouts intervened and calming her down, carried on with the testing. Pointing towards two placid siamang gibbons, he signed "What are these?" Het-up Washoe was not in the mood after the macaque fracas. Fouts prompted her, signing "monkey" three times, and Washoe grudgingly followed suit. Fouts fingered his foot, asking "What is this?" and Washoe obliged with "Shoe". So he took her over to the little squirrel monkeys to test for the monkey sign once more. Yes, these were "monkeys" too. After a while, Fouts turned to the belligerent macaque, pointed to it and asked Washoe, "What is that?", at which Washoe turned, raised her fingers and signed, *"Dirty monkey, dirty monkey, dirty monkey."*

This sounds so fearfully human. It is so like contemporary slang as to be almost suspicious. Even Fouts admits that such expletives took him by surprise; the thought of actually *training* chimps to swear had never occurred to him. Yet the evidence seems impeccable, even though linguists hasten to denounce anecdote as proof of creativity. "Dirty" is Washoe's sign for feces or soiled fur; spontaneously, she had switched its 'unpleasant' connotations to signal her disgust at a particularly nasty specimen of monkeykind. Anyway, that is how it *looks*, but we are reading a human meaning into Washoe's signs; what she actually imagined herself doing could be another matter. This was far from an isolated incident. Roger Fouts himself received the sharp edge of her tongue (rather, fingers) if he failed to comply with her demands.

> Washoe (caged): *Out, out me, come out me.* (I want to be let out.)
> Fouts: Sorry, but you have to stay put.
> Washoe, furious and stalking away: *Dirty Roger, dirty Roger.*[7]

Nor is this Washoe's particular problem; such proletarian chimp outbursts cut across pongid class and station. An incident reported by Francine "Penny" Patterson seems to strengthen this 'cursing' interpretation. Patterson is currently putting gorillas through their "language" paces at Stanford University. The recipient in 1978 of a £13,000 "Award for Enterprise" given by the Rolex watch company, she intends to plough these welcome funds into her programme for breeding a family of signing gorillas. (Hopes are running high that ape mothers will sign to their newborn offspring. Washoe again showed the way, only under more melancholy circumstances. In 1976 she gave birth, but the tiny infant was born with a heart defect and survived only four hours. Unable to comprehend its listlessness, Washoe gently laid it on the bed and signed "baby" and "hug". It was a tragic situation, yet in another light it holds out so much promise for the future.)

Patterson has intensively schooled a female lowland gorilla, nicknamed Koko, and is making strides with a prospective mate, Michael. Koko's matronly dominance led to an inhuman first encounter – although this is not so strange in light of pongid needs to maintain a hierarchical status quo, against which such 'endearments' ought to be judged. Following formal introductions, Koko took the initiative; she politely informed her future mate, "Me hit you", then promptly delivered the promised blow. Patterson has recently reported some of Koko's more ungracious outpourings. After Michael bit off one leg of a Raggedy Ann doll, Koko finished the demolition job by pulling off the other one; only it was she who took all the blame. "Aware that she is only 50 per cent guilty, the gorilla retaliates with the worst insult in her lexicon", runs the caption to a sequence of stills, so remarkable one might almost imagine it a censored section snipped from a videotape. Koko points to her accuser, Patterson, and signs "You dirty bad toilet."[8]

Somehow this interpretation seems too easy, too obvious; no doubt it fits well with the current crop of slang words, but that alone makes it suspicious. How would Victorians, whose slang was less concerned with bodily functions and more with hell's torments, have interpreted Washoe's or Koko's strange epithets? The apes are too up to date. I wondered whether in fact we were not reading too much into their outbursts. So late in 1978 I visited Columbia University where Dr. Herb Terrace's team had raised and trained another chimp brought in from the Oklahoma Centre specifically to replicate the original findings. I asked Terrace whether his chimp, Nim, swore; Terrace looked a little disconcerted by the question, replied "no" and explained that anyway it was a matter of delicate interpretation. Nim did use "dirty" if he wanted to use the toilet; and of course he quickly learnt that the abrupt way to break off a boring lesson was to sign "dirty" whether or not he wanted the toilet. This appeared to me the seeds of an explanation. Nim was signing "dirty" when he was fed up and wanted to go home; he was not swearing, but manipulating his trainers, since he associated "dirty" with a welcome escape from his lessons.[9] And eventually he signed it in order to remain with a favoured teacher, when another looked like taking over. Of course *now* it could look deceptively like human swearing because it was slowly but perceptively shifting away from its original context. Nim does not discredit the ape swearing interpretation, but he teaches a sharp lesson, to be especially careful about interpreting ape signing.

Fouts, Patterson and Terrace were all using a signing system pioneered for chimpanzees by the Gardners. Washoe was their protégé, before she migrated to Oklahoma with trainer Fouts, and it was the Gardners' seminal paper in *Science* on 15 August 1969, announcing Project Washoe, that ostensibly signalled the ape's onslaught on man's 'impregnable' language fortress. What it really sought to show was that the behaviourists were right and psycholinguists were wrong: language was learnt and not genetically programmed, and hence man's potential was not unique.

Meanwhile, on the Santa Barbara campus of California University, David Premack was training a six-year-old female chimp called Sarah, using a technique (bizarrely shaped and brightly coloured plastic "words" on a magnetic board) that looked like an oblique attack on the same problem. These studies catalysed a chain-reaction through the psychological world, so today two dozen apes are being schooled in

symbolic communication, ranging from the use of finger signs and
plastic "words" to bold new approaches employing typewritten
instructions punched directly into an obedient computer. There is
little doubt about the importance of this work. Indeed, one French
critic admitted in 1976 that the Gardners' and Premack's innovations
"will remain a great moment in 20th-century ethology and animal
psychology".[10] Beautifully conceived and like all great scientific
strides so obvious in hindsight, these experiments would have brought
tears of joy to Darwin's cheeks – which makes it all the more paradoxical that we must sooner or later face the question "Yes, but what are we
really trying to prove?"

Flowers and Fumes

The Gardners hit on the deceptively simple idea of sign language
after watching videotapes of an abortive effort to teach a chimpanzee
to speak, made in the early 1950s by another couple, Keith and Cathy
Hayes. Their 'failure' was Viki, a chimpanzee baby home-raised like
a human child. For six fruitless years, the Hayes lavished time and
attention on Viki, pandering to her every need, desperately hoping
that with painstaking coaxing she would learn to speak. Viki never did;
all she managed were pidgin-English (or rather *Pan*-English) attempts
at *mama, papa, cup* and *up* (as in "lift me up"). Despite her heavy accent,
Viki's words were intelligible, and uttered in the correct context, but
that was an end to the matter, and the six-year-old experiment terminated abruptly in 1954 when Viki died from virus encephalitis. But
throughout the proceedings one important factor was almost taken for
granted, which tended to underplay its critical importance: she *understood* spoken English commands, and often acted on them, even if she
could not speak back. It was a moot point whether cognitive incompetence, lack of a proficient vocal apparatus, or both, held back the ape;
it was equally moot whether a sufficient degree of "humanising" could
supply the necessary cognitive competence.

For some, the soul-destroying failure to elicit anything short of a
few baby words uttered with a thick chimp brogue, even after years of
laboured coaxing, proved nothing but the ape's lack of a human-like
vocal tract. This was certainly a contributing factor. In 1972, a team

led by speech-sound analyst Philip Lieberman of the University of Connecticut (and backed by the Yale anatomist Edmund S. Crelin, and Dennis H. Klatt of M.I.T. and Research Laboratory of Electronics) attacked the problem from multi-disciplinary positions using a computer programme designed specifically to simulate ape and human vocal chords (to gauge the possible range of sounds generated). The root problem is apparently this: unlike man, who stands erect and whose larynx has descended down the neck to produce the extended 'organ pipe' region responsible for the full range of vowel sounds, the stooping ape is handicapped by truncated 'organ pipes'. Even though chimps can generate sounds, they lack the optimum length of modulating air passage in the throat to articulate them into the critical vowels *a*, *i*, and *u*.[11] Hardly a paper has passed the referees since 1972 which did not exploit this as the ultimate explanation and thus an end to the matter. Apes cannot speak because they lack proper vocal mechanics; in junior texts it has entered the biological catechism. But while it is evidently true to some degree, this ignores one absolutely intriguing fact – that according to these self-same computer simulations, the chimpanzee should be able to generate a greater sound range than it actually does, a fact for which no one has yet produced an adequate explanation.

Anyway, Hayes hardly heard a word from Viki. But he did carry out rigorous psychological tests on her conceptual competence, and was pleasantly surprised to find incipient "higher mental functions"; but it was uncertain at this time whether or not these existed simply as a remote potential in the 'uncivilised' ape, being realised only by Hayes' concerted efforts to civilise and "humanise". Admittedly, gone were the days when any reputable scientist could echo Max Müller's notorious dictum *No Reason Without Language: No Language Without Reason* (a motto actually emblazoned across the title page of his monumental book *The Science of Thought* in 1887).[12] More accurately, Müller's thesis was that *thought* was impossible in the absence of language; that words and their logical relations were essential prerequisites to the calculus of thought. (He was not allowed to escape with such mindless murder even in his own day. A whole bevy of Darwinians and non-Darwinians led by the statistician Francis Galton pitched into him, leaving *Nature* ringing with denunciations and counter-denunciations for weeks.) Still, a Müllerian residuum has held powerful sway in some philosophic circles, although rarely as extreme as Müller's own formulation, which is understandable since he was intent on creating an unbridgable chasm between man and ape to halt the evolutionist's advance. Right into the 1950s, consequently, repeated failures to teach apes to articulate left deflated psychologists little choice but to question the ape's mental ability to handle symbolism. Lacking suitable mental equipment, the argument could have been, apes would scarcely have *needed* to refine the vocal chords: they had nothing to say.[13]

But the problem, as ever, was our inability to frame the right question. Watching the film of Viki's tortured attempts to speak, the Gardners noticed that even with the sound track turned down, she was making sense with her hands. A gesture language: the inspirational flash that in retrospect seemed so obvious one wonders why it took a century since *Man's Place* before occurring. The Gardners purchased a bewildered baby chimp from a trader, settled her into her own trailer alongside the family house, and began their programme in June 1966 teaching her American Sign Language (ASL), the native voice of North America's deaf. Christened Washoe (after the Nevada county in which she now lived), the eleven-month-old baby was bathed like any child in a rich linguistic atmosphere. Elaborate 'social' precautions were taken; trainers were forbidden to speak English, having to sign to her *and* to one another in her presence. The Gardners were loath to "make it seem the big chimps talk and only little chimps sign", explaining that this "might give signing an undesirable social status".[14] The object was not merely to have her answer questions, but to 'talk' back. "We wanted to develop behavior that could be described as conversation," they admitted in 1969. And to this end no effort was spared. Washoe was surrounded with games and toys to stimulate her, and companions to sign to her. The stark imprisonment usually awaiting apes was not Washoe's fate; there were no iron bars for her to peer soulfully through. She was a thoroughly spoiled ape, even by human standards, having her own flower garden, being treated to car rides, and making frequent sorties to the university nursery school.

Object names like "toothbrush" and "flower" were learnt by Washoe imitating her teachers, who signed them repeatedly whenever she cleaned her teeth or sniffed a blossom. By two, she asked for her "toothbrush" after each meal, summoning it if it were not present. Some signs, like "funny", were fashioned out of her normal gesticular 'babbling' (in contrast to an infant human's vocal babbling), and this was the first indication that the Gardners were already departing from *human* sign language. Indeed, a few natural ape signs were incorporated into her vocabulary with practically no modification. For example, Washoe spontaneously held out a begging hand, palm uppermost, as in "gimme", and spontaneously signalled "hurry" by excitedly shaking her wrists, using the sign not only to speed up ambling companions but even signing to herself as she rushed hither and thither. In many ways it was the little things Washoe was caught doing which testified so magnificently to her ability. Of course, she could have been ruthlessly conditioned into signing "toothbrush" each time she saw one, a strange ritual performed to please mankind though it had no other meaning for the ape. The fact that she was not blindly signing at the chime of a Pavlovian bell seems certain from the way she exploited signs in unique situations. "We have often seen Washoe moving stealthily to a forbidden part of the yard, signing *quiet* to herself," reported the Gardners.[15] Because the yard was expressly out of bounds, she would hardly have been encouraged to trespass "quietly"! She *knew* she had to be quiet, and even though the sign was first elicited under less surreptitious circumstances, she still thought it appropriate. Many signs were first elicited using classical conditioning, but others were less classical, if not positively devious, as the Gardners confess. An effort to get Washoe signing "no" led to the following trickery:

> Washoe and a companion are inside her house trailer, and he peers out the window and comes back to initiate the following interchange:
> Person: "Washoe, there is a big black dog outside – with big teeth. It is a dog that eats little chimps. You want to go out, now?"
> Washoe: (prolonged and emphatic) "Noooooooo."

The Gardners were soon boasting of Washoe's "linguistic" prowess.

> Washoe seemed to expect everyone to know Ameslan [or ASL], and signed it to every being that she met, including, at first, cats and dogs. Gradually, she came to understand that some people were pretty dense about Ameslan. New research assistants have commented on the singular humiliation of having Washoe sign to them ever so slowly and carefully when they were only beginners at Ameslan.

Since Washoe was rewarded for correctly using a word, one of her earliest acquisitions was "more", usually demanding another bout of tickling (it emerged, in fact, only second to "come-gimme"). Washoe quickly generalised this sign, asking for more food and more play, even requesting encores of her trainer's acrobatics or animal imitations. "Open" was another command stretched from its original context ("open door") to "open" refrigerators, briefcases, jars – even to turn on taps. Children similarly stretch words to cover contingencies, and for both human and ape it can lead to comic repercussions: Washoe extended "hurt" from cuts and grazes to a picture stamped on to the back of a human hand – and even signed it most concernedly at her first sight of a human navel.

On the approach of its second birthday, the child's conceptual categories are stabilising, and it begins to hunt around for words to map on to them. In their book *Language Development and Language Disorders* (1978), Lois Bloom and Margaret Lahey illustrate this with the example of a child who, between sixteen and twenty-three months, stretched the word "fafa" from a bowl of yellow jonquils to other flowers in other bowls, and by the time he was two to sugar flowers decorating biscuits. They add that "one can assume that he had learned a word concept 'fafa' to map on to an already acquired object concept, which at sixteen months included instances of only live flowers".[16] It appears that a parallel process is at work in apes. Washoe learnt "key" for the key to her padlocked trailer, but showed a well defined class-concept by extending it to all keys, even car ignition keys; and Patterson's gorilla learnt "tree" using models of celery and acacia branches, then generalised it to asparagus, green onions and in fact any tall thin vegetation. Her application of "nut" was even more interesting (and not only for being a curse). She learnt it originally for whole nuts, but the word evidently referred to taste as much as shape because she eventually stretched it to peanut butter sandwiches. Proof of this deduction lies in her description of sunflower seeds: on seeing them she signed "candy food", but on tasting she reversed her decision by signing "nut". Psycholinguists have challenged the rigour of these interpretations. They refuse to accept anecdote at face value, and demand that until both Patterson and the Gardners publish full transcripts of ape "discourse" (which would show up error frequency and throw some light on word meanings *for the ape*) judgment must be suspended. Failing full publication, warts and all, ape trainers are open to the savage criticism aimed at parapsychologists – that they are simply picking out the random gems because they happen to make sense to us.

So I began looking at the warts. Not surprisingly, Washoe's more telling slips do show up the way she understood some words. Younger children occasionally mistake an adult's word to mean much more than it actually does. For example, in one classic case an adult consistently said "qua qua" while pointing to a duck; unfortunately, the duck was always floating in water, and the child associated the "qua qua" with both duck *and* water. In other words, we have to be cautious of the way the child or ape originally absorbs the word before we can claim it subsequently generalises its use. After learning "flower", Washoe used it in quite a revealing way. For us, the word conjures up a colourful petal-spray. But for Washoe it signified something else, which became apparent when she caught her first sniff of tobacco smoke and signed incongruously "flower". (Although "smell" was subsequently taught her, she never eradicated "flower" for tobacco and kitchen fumes.) Such are the hazards of cramming too much world into a tiny vocabulary, and it is easy to see how Washoe might have been led on by the ASL action for "flower", which enacts the motion of smelling a bloom. But other intriguing possibilities open up. It could point to one way in which she was trying to classify (or conceptualise) her world, by smell – the common denominator of flowers and fumes. Humans understand "flower" in a highly idiosyncratic way, with the unlikeliest connotations which give it meaning: riotous colour, romance, warm Spring days, funerals. The word is highly charged because we 'read' so much past experience into 'reality'; nature is anything but neutral, every image is value-laden. For Washoe nature might take on quite a different hue, in which case her words would be invested with a peculiarly pongid nuance of meaning. As long as species structure reality according to different conceptual frameworks, words can never have identical meanings for both.

One Man's Vision of Moonlight – Words and Reality

This is the force behind Wittgenstein's cryptic aphorism, "If a lion could speak, we could not understand him."[17] One half of humanity barely understands the other on occasions, let alone comprehends alien minds. Radical feminists spurn well-intentioned male 'sympathy' simply because the female experience must forever remain alien to even the most concerned male. True understanding can *only* grow empathetically; one has to climb inside the skin to feel for a world of alien expectations and values. But if one half of humanity cannot or will not comprehend the other, what hope do we have of ever stretching out a sympathetic hand to the ape?

At last, we are waking to the seriousness of this conceptual divide. As two ape language innovators admitted in 1977, chimpanzees do use *our* vocabulary, though "this is not to conclude that the meanings of words for apes are the same as those for men".[18] But why wouldn't words have the same meaning for apes and us, why indeed don't all lifeforms see the same reality? It is 'out there' for all to see. If ever there were a trick question, that is it. What we *think* we see is the crux: the world may or may not be 'out there', and it may take any form, who is to tell? What counts is our inner thought-world, a mental representation of 'reality', manufactured by the mind's structuring reality. We make the world. We rely on our 'mind's eye', which is far from a polished mirror. After all, a mirror *inside* the cranium does not actually tell us any more than 'reality' outside.[19] That world still has to be interpreted. So the mind's eye has an inbuilt bias; it does not photograph, it symbolises and conceptualises, forging a meaningful symbolic model of 'reality'.

Everything hinges on that word 'meaningful'. A neutral photocopy of 'out there' cannot help us deal with living, and everything, even mind and consciousness, must be an aid to survival. So the mind's eye distorts, it accentuates or suppresses aspects of the world according to their importance to the species. Inner-world images are a sort of covenant between us and reality; but because senses have to enter this covenant before they can extract a jot of information, they naturally forfeit any claim to objectivity – leaving us in the predicament of quantum physics, where the unwitting observer is dragged in as part of the experiment, thus making objective reality forever unknowable. Over untold aeons of evolution, man has been building an idiosyncratic framework to structure reality. But not only man, every creature has an idiosyncratic world view.

Even that precocious mollusc, the octopus, has a ganglionic mind's eye; if we were ever to penetrate it we should find its reality looking for all the world like a piece of incomprehensible abstract art. But to an octopus it makes sense. One can never even dimly appreciate the cleft between molluscan and man's mind. Returning to our own doorstep, perhaps we can imagine a blind world, where sounds stand out as signposts and shapes are 'distorted' by the finger-tips. But are they distorted? That naïvely assumes that our visual images are the norm. The answer of course is that reality changes as one switches senses. With sight suddenly restored, a person is thrust into an alien and shocking world, hopelessly unfamiliar, where noses loom out of faces like mountain peaks and mirrors reflect unrecognisable images. But the issue goes far deeper than considering just *which* sense is doing the sensing. Built into our sensing apparatus is also a species-specific filter: it only lets in what is significant. How often have we seen something in a different light once we realised what it was for? No two humans see quite the same chessboard. Without knowing the functional strategies or rules we do not know the meaning of the positions, hence a chess master can put to shame a novice by recalling every position on the board after only a five- or ten-second exposure.

The point is simply put. Even if apes and men use the same words, they might have different meanings, no matter how subtle. Luckily, the chimp is evolutionarily close to man. Despite our ancestors having parted company some fourteen million years ago, we nonetheless share over ninety-nine per cent of our history since simple cells first evolved. And yet, enough can happen in only fourteen million years to give Victorian moralists grounds for imposing that notorious abyss between the sister apes, one hairy, smaller brained and minimally cultured, the other stretching to the stars. Diverse adaptive strategies must have played differentially on the two minds, colouring their respective images of reality. Had they been pulled too far apart, any attempt at symbolic communication would prove futile. And yet the 1970s surprise is that ape and man at least imagine that they understand one another, talking over common ground, breaking into the stillness of an almost interminable night, some fourteen million years long.

But just how common is that ground? While ape trainers set a disastrous course by naïvely assuming that signs like *please* and *think* used by chimp and gorilla have the meanings assigned to them by humans, they are systematically forfeiting a godsent chance to see the world through an ape's eyes. Guessing how much it might differ from cousin man's is, at the moment, little more than a stab in the dark. Take this trivial example. Chimpanzees apparently lack our human hypersensitivity to pain. Jane Goodall noticed this with her Gombe Stream troop in Tanzania; wild chimps show little sign of pain, remaining quite stoical even after the ravages of polio (to which they are particularly prone) or bodily mutilation. Again, when David Premack's Sarah fell from some height on to a concrete floor, rather than fly into hysterics as might a child, she rushed over to inspect her trainer's sympathetic wince. As a consequence of this, chimps seem coldly insensitive to human suffering, and quite unable to comprehend our emotions. Sarah delighted in squeezing Premack's hand scratch until blood flowed:

> When blood oozed forth in a thin red line along the cut, Sarah looked intently into my eyes, I looked back with equal intentness, nodding to acknowledge her "success" but could never figure out what it was that she was asking me, if indeed it was anything, and therefore I could not settle on the look to give her in return. Howling loudly when blood appears, as I did on several occasions, did not affect her as it might a child. She looked curious but not dismayed and went on staring into my face, asking a question the nature of which I could not divine.[20]

Nim, too, had the same total fascination with blood and cuts; the first thing he would show you were his scabs. And yet, says Nim's trainer and room-mate, Laura Petitto, compared to humans, Nim "just didn't have the same reaction to pain".[21] Someone once slammed the door on his foot, he limped a little but with no visible sign of grief; it was exceedingly rare for him to yelp. Yet one only had to walk away for the petrified little ape to let out screams of anxiety, imagining himself abandoned. Clearly, social comforts were all-important to Nim. Apes, like humans, have an elaborate social organisation, and the juvenile years are extended for the youngster to learn its manners, as well as how to handle the psychological quirks of its elders. This by no means implies that man (who also indulges in a generous childhood) has an identical social scaffolding; ape and human societies do differ in important ways. Even the fact that home-raised apes occasionally act – what can only be described as – perversely by human standards shows their inherent tendency to present peculiarly pongid solutions to some human predicaments. Laura Petitto still bears a scar on her wrist left by Nim. Unfortunately, in inflicting such a deep wound and watching the ensuing emotional stress, the little ape terrified himself; and as Laura began passing out, he resolutely stood guard, barring friends who were desperately trying to reach her.

Only by understanding the physical pain an ape feels can we have any idea what it means by "hurt". And the question then arises of the ape's conscious experience of emotion, and how it differs from man's. What mental anguish swept like a tidal wave through Lucy's consciousness as she signed forlornly "me cry"? Of late, Patterson has announced that she has miraculously managed to disentangle the gorilla's conscious states using words. The psychological furies are set to rage . . .

In 1971, prompted by the spectacular revival of interest in ape intellect, Keith Hayes resurrected an old manuscript on chimp conceptual powers, written in 1956 with Catherine Nissen, but which for lack of academic interest, had never been published. It finally saw light of day in time to add another dimension to the Gardners' findings on Washoe's generalisations.

Concepts are the brain's antidote to chaos, its attempt to classify common attributes, like the metallic element in space-ships and rusty nails, or the yellowness uniting sulphur, sunflowers and bananas. We tease out these themes threaded through nature, relying on all manner of class concepts, from size and shape to race and social standing – categories which speak volumes for the way we see reality. Hayes and Nissen tested Viki to determine if she ordered her world differently, to see if her world was ours.[22] Would she sift and classify an assortment of eating and writing implements according to material or function? Could she pigeon-hole the same object in a number of ways (say, a banana as yellow in one test, a food in another, and soft in a third)? She tested easily, though the results were somewhat crude; she quickly sorted photographs into piles of adults *vs.* children or into animals *vs.* inanimate objects (the animals ranging from people to snakes and ants, among which were hidden clocks and cars, and which she accurately sifted according to an "animal" concept, with the exception of the 'automaton' ant, relegated to the mechanical pile). At other times she showed a natural reluctance to segregate according to human standards, as when presented with a pile of stainless steel cutlery, wooden pencils, brushes and chopsticks. Viki was an inveterate scribbler and free-form painter, she also knew well what chopsticks were for, yet she persistently lumped chopsticks with pencils, employing a wood *vs.* steel distinction while ignoring the functional eating/writing dichotomy. But she was by no means hidebound in her ways of looking at things. She could call up any number of classification schemes according to her mood. Given eighty buttons of every permutation of black, white, round, square, large and small, she segregated them without prompting into colours on some occasions, shapes or sizes on others. Given that Viki took exceptional delight in astounding guests by giving impromptu demonstrations of sorting a mound of mixed nuts, bolts, nails, screws, washers and clips into six neat piles with one hundred per cent accuracy, Washoe's ability to dump all keys into one linguistic category seems obvious. Viki and Washoe spoke elegantly in defence of the ape's conceptual competence. Without it, symbolic communication between man and ape would have remained a pipe-dream. And yet, the really fascinating discoveries are still to come, as a result of finely tuning words to gauge the ape's own individual conceptual comprehension. A perfect relief map of the ape's world is ready waiting, written into its neural circuitry; all we have to do is delimit national boundaries by correctly fitting the geographical place-names to gain a privileged admittance.

"Cry hurt food"

Protagonists demanding that apes "had" human language rallied to one point, what we might call "creative naming". Deaf signers draw up a convention on how to render technical terms and proper names; for example, California is signed "golden playland", and the Gardners translated *psychologist* into "think doctor". The words are reconstituted, and the hybrid transcends the original meanings. After Roger Fouts related how, while out boating with Washoe one day, she spontaneously christened a cantankerous swan a "water bird",[23] it was unanimously accepted that apes likewise invent proper names. This anecdote quickly assumed monumental proportions, being built into the fabric of the fortress around the notion that apes act linguistically.

Even if apes can transmute base words by reconstitution, it says little about their grammatical abilities (the essence of human language), *but* a great deal about their grasp of symbols. Unfortunately the anecdotal nature of this evidence invited its own backlash; already can be felt chill winds of dissension as the critics close ranks. Now Nim's trainers, drawing on their enormous corpus of Nim's utterances, have challenged the Washoe group. Moving with commendable caution, they do not actually impugn Washoe's creativity, but merely insist that other explanatory avenues have been systematically ignored (rigour is fast becoming the name of the game). Theirs boil down to two criticisms, one strong and the other weak. We can, I think, dispense with the latter: namely, on being asked "What's that?" by Fouts, Washoe summarised the scene before her, the main features of which were "water [and] bird". Fair enough. But when, craving a brazil nut on another occasion, and at a loss to know what to call it, Washoe ingeniously invented "rock berry", there were presumably no rocks in sight.

Laura Petitto, writing with Columbia graduate student Mark Seidenberg, and clearly echoing Terrace's thought, falls back on a more searing criticism. Reports of "creative naming" are isolated and anecdotal; and what makes it perilous to build a case for language acquisition from anecdote is that fundamental information is being ignored or suppressed. If on analysis of an entire corpus of utterances ninety-nine per cent of creations were shown to be nonsense, then the remaining one per cent probably are also, even though they accidentally fit the situation.[24] Pulling out the 'meaningful' one per cent would smack of unethical sampling practice, the sort that taints parapsychology. The apes, suggest Petitto and Seidenberg, could be random sign generators. The fact that apes frequently do make mistakes is played down, yet Nim combined one of his favourite talking points, *banana*, with all manner of words – *sorry, drink, tickle, toothbrush, hat* and *handcream*. It seems far-fetched that on each occasion he was trying to say something profound. Yet one cannot dismiss even apparently ludicrous combinations like *banana toothbrush* and *banana toothbrush me* which crop up in Nim's conversation. Not even context could show up their nonsensical nature, because halfway through his banana he *might* have summoned his absent toothbrush; he might even have summoned both banana and a toothbrush to clean his teeth with afterwards. The problems of interpretation are awesome, and I am not convinced that it is simpler to start by assuming that Nim might be a random sign generator or mixer of "word salads". Perhaps it would speak in his favour if Nim used the same combinations frequently and in the correct context. But another ape does just that.

Lucy is an expressive chimpanzee who lives an outwardly human life in Oklahoma as the foster child of Maurice and Jane Temerlin. They raised Lucy from infancy (she is now a teenager, thirteen in fact, but still lives as one of the family), and since they lived near the primate centre where Fouts worked, Lucy received some expert tuition in signing. Lucy's creations seem strikingly apt: on seeing an onion and without knowing its sign she christened it a "cry fruit". But that could – by other canons – be a random potshot that happened to hit the mark. But another of Lucy's combinations, and undeniably her most famous, is for a radish: once having bitten it, she spat out the offending object and signed in utter disgust, "cry hurt food". And now that's what she invariably calls it, the name has stuck.[25] So in any rigorous study of Lucy's utterances, it would show up as a fixed feature that was, by and large, contextually correct. But just to show that there is no end to this linguistic game, Laura Petitto could – and probably would – answer back that the original "cry hurt food" was pot luck, or originally unassociated words that summed up several aspects of the moment, but the humans were so impressed that their praise caused Lucy to retain it, even though it is a meaningless combination to her. Personally, I give apes the benefit of the doubt.

Washoe demonstrated just how much could be accomplished. By the time she and Roger Fouts left Nevada for the Institute for Primate Studies in Oklahoma in October 1970, Washoe was ASL fluent in 132 signs, comprising nouns, verbs, adverbs, prepositions and adjectives.[26] By 1975, her vocabulary had reached 160 words. But Project Washoe hinted at how much more *might* be achieved; after all, as a first tentative attempt at two-way communication, it suffered numerous short-comings. Washoe was almost a year old before training commenced, and no one knew how critical those first twelve months might have been (as they are in human children). The Gardners determined to find out. They were the first to admit that her environment "was still quite impoverished when compared with that of the usual middle-class human child".[27] Foremost among her hardships was the lack of initially fluent ASL speakers to train her. The fact that her human companions were themselves still trying to pick up this foreign language did not lend itself to an ideal learning environment; it was rather like a novice in Russian simultaneously trying to expound on its complexities to a foreigner! How might Washoe have fared brought up by "native" ASL speakers, the deaf?

Both factors – by-passing that crucial first year, then lacking initially competent teachers – drastically retard human language growth. Deaf children fare much better with ASL-signing deaf parents than with hearing parents trying to cope with a foreign language. So the Gardners said goodbye to Washoe and began anew. Into their life came Pili, born on 30 October 1972 at the Yerkes Regional Primate Research Center, Atlanta, Georgia, and arriving in Reno, Nevada on 1 November. Just over two weeks later, Moja was born at the Laboratory of Experimental Medicine and Surgery in Primates, Tuxedo Park, New York, turning up in Nevada on 19 November, one day old. "Native speakers" (deaf persons and children of the deaf) were brought in specially to initiate the tiny apes into their silent world of gesture-words. Precocious Pili and Moja exceeded all expectations.[28] It is not unknown for deaf children to pick up their first sign by five months (at least five months before a hearing child can say his first word). By thirteen weeks Moja already had a repertoire of "come-gimme", "go", "more", and "drink", while Pili regularly used "drink", "come-gimme", "more" and "tickle" by the fifteenth week. At the end of six months (by which time Washoe was using only two words and children might have one) Moja had a thirteen-sign vocabulary, with Pili trailing two behind.

Washoe meanwhile saw herself as good as human, contemptuously dismissing as "black bugs" the chimpanzee inmates on the ape island at the Primate Institute. In the old Reno days she had lived in the lap of (human) luxury, and now she found herself rudely cast among these hairy Oklahoma juveniles, like a cultivated lady surrounded by dreadful ruffians, some little short of delinquents in her imperious eyes. To add insult to injury, she found the island populated by illiterates. But Fouts was scheming. Washoe was an old hand at signing, and he was eager to see if she would initiate the island's younger apes into its mysteries. Cut off from humanity by a moat, she started signalling in earnest to the mainland; her plaintive ASL demands might be freely translated by the unequivocal distress call, "Get me off this bloody island." She slowly warmed to her fellow apes, though it is a moot point whether she raised them to her own human status. From the start she signed to apes spontaneously, but being linguistically naïve they lacked even the rudimentary vocabulary necessary for the acquisition of new words. Frustrated by lack of conversationalists, she even tried talking to dogs, with equal lack of success. One particularly memorable day, a snake spread terror through the castaways on the ape island, and all but one fled in panic. This male sat absorbed, staring intently at the serpent. Then Washoe was seen running over signing to him "come, hurry up."

As part of his plan Fouts began teaching basic ASL to a pair of young chimpanzees before introducing Washoe. Bruno is the Institute's home-grown tearaway. Cocksure (his ASL name means "proud"), he lays pranks on fellow chimps, terrorises the local peacocks, and seems generally to leave his trainers at their wits' end. The outrages serve only to raise his status in the eyes of his companion, Booee. Before arriving at the Institute, Booee's cerebral hemispheres had been surgically split, the corpus callosum severed as part of a laboratory experiment. Apparently this left no detectable mental scars, and Booee was remarkably quick on the uptake, learning new words with the same breakneck speed at which Bruno rushed hither and thither. Booee, the quiet, introvert ape with two brains, picked up new signs with twice Bruno's learning speed, although as Fouts jibed in *Science* by way of explanation, Booee "can best be described as a chimpanzee who was willing to sell his soul for a raisin. This is probably why he did so well in acquisition."[29] These two contrasting personalities, split-brain Booee and boisterous Bruno, soon became the best of friends. By 1975 Fouts had taught them some thirty-eight signs apiece, and had begun detailed recording and analysis of their conversations. These are none too inspiring to date. Fouts related a typical encounter. Bruno, hastily devouring his handful of raisins (knowing Booee's undying passion for such treats) is confronted by Booee, entreating him to "tickle Booee". Obviously a ploy, it struck both Fouts and Bruno as a transparent attempt to divert attention from the raisins in order to secure some for himself. But Bruno was not to be fooled into losing his reward, and signed back summarily, "Booee me food" or *go away, I'm eating*.

Is there a Chimpanzee Grammar?

While the argument hinges on apes having human language, the onus falls not on symbols or words but on grammar. Older children can generate limitless novel sentences by exploiting syntax; they are able, not only to distinguish the diametric meanings of *me hit you* and *you hit me*, but they learn to flesh out the syntactic bones of this abstract structure – subject-verb-object – using it to create an infinity of meanings. Once this technique is acquired, language suddenly explodes – there is no other word for it. The ape's achievement in this respect is hotly disputed, and again partisan positions are clearly demarcated. Washoe's trainers vigorously defend her rudimentary syntactic knowledge; linguists are loath to see it as even rudimentary. But the first point of interest, surely, is that apes should string words together at all. They all do it. Washoe's vocabulary had hardly swollen to eight or ten signs before she spontaneously composed two-word requests, constructing such cryptically quaint phrases as "open flower" (asking to be let through the garden gate) and "listen eat" (after the meal-time bell sounded). Later some of her sequences grew into explicit instructions, asking "Key open please blanket" for the blanket cupboard to be unlocked because she was cold.

The ideological core of the dispute is the question "Does the ape understand syntax?" The evidence again is how you interpret it, although the Gardners are pretty adamant that the answer is an unequivocal "yes". Anecdotes, at least, do suggest that chimpanzees understand the semantics of word order. Play is of the utmost importance to young chimps; to gauge the extent of this, it might be surprising to learn that Nim's most frequent two- and three-sign combinations were not culinary requests but *play me* and *play me Nim*. An integral part of ape play involves tickling, and Nim would sign *tickle me* about as much as he requested food. Under Roger Fouts' training, Lucy was all too familiar with *Roger tickle Lucy*, but one day Fouts was persuaded by the visiting writer, Eugene Linden, to surprise Lucy by switching the word order. Lucy had never heard *Lucy tickle Roger* before, nevertheless Fouts tried it and Linden left an account of the consequences:

Lucy was sitting beside Roger on the living room couch. She sat back for an instant confused. Almost testingly, she said, "No, Roger tickle Lucy." Roger again said, "No, Lucy tickle Roger." This time I could see comprehension brighten Lucy's eyes. Excited she jumped onto his lap and began tickling him while he rocked backwards uttering little grunts in imitation of chimp laughter.[30]

It looks cut-and-dried, so most campaigners have uncritically accepted this anecdote as definitive evidence (though Linden was a model of caution). Yet the subject of syntax is still bristling with contention. Perhaps Lucy inferred that Roger wanted something from his expectant look.

The pace quickened as the Gardners lashed back at doubters, only to discover that their target kept shifting alarmingly; there was not a consensus opposition view, only a loose collective of often mutually inconsistent views. As frustrations mounted, the Washoe-camp – unable to pin down the target – looked set to accuse linguists of double-dealing. They sat in final judgment on the Harvard child-speech expert Roger Brown, who had taken a lively interest in the ape's progress, even conceding that its signing might match a child's earliest telegraphic speech; but that did not go nearly far enough for the Gardners, who saw Washoe competing with more accomplished children. To justify the incipient grammatic structure of a two-year-old's truncated speech, Brown in *A First Language* employed what is called "rich interpretation" – he used context to assign the utterance a meaning. He assumed the child's syntax was rarely a blunder; hence when pre-school Adam said both *Adam sit chair* and *sit Adam chair*, Brown took this to mean either "Adam is sitting in the chair" or "sit in Adam's chair".[31] It deepened the Gardners' worst fears: that there was invariably a way of justifying a *child's* first speech regardless of the variable word order. Yet, as Fouts added bitterly, one glance at Washoe's contradictory statements like *tickle Washoe* and *Washoe tickle* and some linguists "jumped to the conclusion that the essence of language was syntax and that Washoe didn't have it".[32] Dispatches from the Gardners' front line suggested that linguists were having their cake and eating it, while denying ape researchers even a glance at the edibles. A child's variable word order argued its innate mastery of grammar; an ape's condemned it irretrievably. Actually, one can "richly interpret"

Washoe's first signs, and in one sense at least they were like those of a baby. When a child says "bread", the mother reads in the contextual sentence, "I want you to give me another slice", knowing that as its vocabulary increases, the child will flesh out its command. Likewise when Washoe first signed "out", she meant "I want to go out with you". She would scream on being pushed out alone, or if the trainer unfairly sneaked out alone on getting her command. So there was a greater meaning within the message "out" than appeared on the surface. Later Washoe did indeed expand her instruction to "you me go out hurry".

The Gardners hinted in a review of Brown's book that if they were playing the psycholinguist's game, then according to the rules it was precisely "Washoe's variable use of sign order [which] indicates that she could use it as a grammatical device". But the Janus-faced opposition effectively blocked this move with two mutually inconsistent arguments. Some pointed out that since older children undeniably use these syntactic structures, Brown was right to trace them into his infants – but apes never progress to a full syntactic use to justify our reading anything back into these early utterances. Others agreed with Limber that it did not matter, because Brown's youngsters probably were not using language anyway! The Gardners were hamstrung, unable to move either way. Even Terrace at Columbia, who had set out to replicate the Gardners' findings, ended by substantially agreeing with many linguists that apes did not have human language. Piaget has suggested that the true social meaning of words must at first elude young children; the infant only appreciates their value in manipulating parents. First speech is a pragmatic act, little to do with intentional communication and more to satisfy needs; or as Lois Bloom and Margaret Lahey (who have attended closely to the child's utterances to gauge the best means of remedying language disorders) say, infants before their second birthday "perform social gestures and produce social (conventional) sounds as new means or resources for meeting their needs, without awareness of their origin or social significance".[33] Seidenberg and Petitto believe this explanation fits ape signing.

> The apes appear to have learned not the meanings and linguistic functions of their signs, but rather the consequences of particular acts of signing. They know that forming certain signs will have immediate benefits, e.g., someone will give them food or a toy,

take them to the bathroom or perform some other positively-reinforcing act.[34]

It is a moot point whether this holds true for all ape words, though it seems especially appropriate to a word like "please"; I doubt whether the ape understands its human sense (or needs to), though he employs it to speed along a request, since "please" heard by a human is guaranteed to soften the hardest resolve, and the ape has probably unknowingly tapped this vein. So to further confuse the battle lines, a third camp has emerged. Some psycholinguists and Terrace of Project Nim agree that ape actions recall word-use by a child of eighteen months, although in neither case are intentions truly linguistic.

But the Gardners hope to extricate themselves from this mire. They were not playing the psycholinguist's game: "we Gardners", they proudly admit, "are strict behaviorists", implying that this commits them to a degree empirical testing which psycholinguists seem unwilling or unable to match. To demonstrate that apes "have" human language, they have begun a rigorous programme to prove *grammatical* ability by testing ape "word order and other syntactic devices". Their announcement accompanied a snub to psycholinguistics:

> If the standards of experimentation in child psycholinguistics do not improve soon, we will find ourselves in the paradoxical situation of having solid experimental evidence for the syntactic abilities of chimpanzees and a complete lack of acceptable evidence for any syntactic ability in young children.[35]

A marvellous rouser for propagandist purposes, but for maximum impact they might have awaited the results!

To cut through the confusion and test the Gardners' exuberant claims, Terrace's Columbia group set about replicating the Washoe phenomenon. They posed the base-line question "Can an Ape Create a Sentence?", then sought the evidence that a chimpanzee could distinguish "me tickle you" from "you tickle me" and use the underlying format to generate novel sentences: ostensibly a simple goal, yet they spent five years, and exhausted 60 sign-language trainers only to obtain an equivocal answer.

Nim was brought in to arbitrate as best he could. Born on 21 November 1973, at the Oklahoma Center for Primate Studies, the half-brother of Bruno and full brother to Ally (both of whom Fouts is coaching), he arrived at his foster home on New York's West Side twelve days later. Here he lived in a large house with a human family of ten (seven of whom were under sixteen). But he required round the clock attention, which meant a battery of caretakers and trainers; and a total lack of funding for the first nineteen months meant that many of them had to be volunteers, usually students who were willing to sacrifice their free hours. Nim got through an inordinate number of trainers; Laura Petitto trained fifteen herself (and many more were dropped as lacking the tact and stamina to handle a young ape; indeed, he was often so taxing for his trainers that they were forced to lie down after a session). Many adults wandering in and out of his life meant uncertainty and a degree of instability for Nim, a problem accentuated by his having to move midway through the project to a university-owned house in Riverdale, New York, to improve his linguistic environment and give the growing ape romping space. Here he lived with his trainers, including Laura Petitto, commuting daily by car to his classroom at Columbia.

As his training progressed, Nim grew adept at winkling out non-linguistic cues, which could have too easily led to over-estimations of his language ability. Once, when Nim discovered the kitchen cabinet unlocked, he settled down to enjoy a bottle of rug cleaner; frantically, Laura Petitto signed "No stop don't eat" and Nim pulled the bottle from his mouth. But this is far from a test of Nim's understanding of language, since shouting in Russian would undoubtedly have had the same effect; Nim was more likely reading Laura's agonised split-second expression as she glimpsed the full horror of the consequences. The Gardners quickly realised that asking an ape "Whose watch?" or "Where baby?" or "Show me banana" as it thumbed through a picture-book, was an inadequate test of its comprehension of signs. The Gardners appeared merciless in their testing, they even admit to having "over-done" it; speculating that "the continual testing that Washoe endured may have inhibited the free growth of her two-way communication". They instigated a "double-blind" procedure, where one experimenter showed Washoe an object, while another hidden behind a screen and unable to see what she was looking at watched her sign. These precautions established Washoe's comprehension; the Gardners even put deaf signers unfamiliar with Washoe behind the screen, and their testimony not only vindicated Washoe, but showed "that her accent could be learned readily" by native signers.

Nim lacked in spontaneity, in contrast to the too talkative child, and many of his answers simply reiterated what his trainer had signed. Rather than inventing, Nim was cannibalising. Although he might be recorded as saying "eat banana" or "Nim eat banana", which is perfectly respectable, the trainer's prompting question may have been "Want eat banana?" This raises the big question of what the Gardners were signing to elicit Washoe's published responses. About one-third of Nim's utterances were imitative, not that this wholly discredits the little ape, since a twenty-one-month-old child may respond imitatively little less than twenty per cent of the time. In children, however, it is an avowedly creative activity; they echo to get a feeling for those words which are largely unfamiliar, and having learned them, promptly cease imitating. For Nim, in stark contrast, it was familiar objects: the sign *banana* was probably all that was needed to send him into repetitive fits of *banana me banana me*.

Nim learnt his words rapidly. By two he used forty-five signs fluently (understanding twice as many), and at four he had mastery of some 125. Teaching was facilitated by Nim's active participation; trainers deliberately withheld food and toys, telling him to ask for them by name, and since he could not, he would present his hands to be shown how. Like Washoe, Nim spontaneously began stringing his words. But now a peculiar fact emerges, one largely glossed over in the past. To prise out data for their analysis, Terrace's group had to telescope Nim's utterances extensively because of his tireless repetition. *Banana me me me eat*, for example, had to be collapsed to the more economic three-sign combination *banana me eat*. Requesting a banana Nim might even sign *me banana you banana me you give* or more monotonous versions. But in trimming such long repetitive strings the real character of ape "language" is lost. Ape sayings, complain Seidenberg and Petitto, "have been transformed and reduced so extensively as to obscure rather than clarify the character of the apes' behavior".[36] Nim's sign strings, occasionally over twenty words long, sound decidedly less triumphant when the request boils down to wanting to be banana'd. Anything over five signs and Nim was repeating himself; it was nothing for him to throw in three *mes* and a couple of *yous*, as though for emphasis. Adult humans can be equally emphatic, shouting *Damn, Damn, Damn* or coercing a child, "give me, give it to me", and though these are emotional outbursts, the parallel with Nim's signing seems legitimate, since he probably regards a repeated signal tantamount to a stronger claim: he *wants* the banana. So despite the Gardners' defiant claim that on paper Washoe's "language" looks much like a child's, in one crucial respect, Nim's did not. Seidenberg and Petitto are harshly critical of these unrecorded trimming practices which "effectively suppress information concerning the structure of ape sentences" in order to manufacture a human-like end product.

All effort was ploughed into interpreting the massive corpus of Nim's pidgin-sign strings; 2700 combinations were analysed for structural regularities. To those who were expecting confirmation that apes had indeed 'usurped' human language, the results were frankly disappointing. However they did show that Nim was not a mixer of word salads – regularities *did* show up. He placed *more* before nouns (*banana*) or actions (*play*) over eighty per cent of the time; and, in addition, verbs often appeared first (*hug Nim*). But this tells us little, because he might also sign *bite me*, when clearly he was not requesting but warning. So regardless of subject and object, in two-word strings Nim seems to prefer an invariant structure: verb + (subject or object). In answer to the big question: can Nim distinguish *grape eat Nim* (one of his commoner expressions) from *Nim eat grape* – well, if he can, he apparently does not bother to exploit this useful distinction. Terrace and colleagues are as soberly cautious as the Gardners are exuberant: despite certain position preferences, "Nim's sequences do not have the syntactic structure of sentences".

The overriding urge to assist ape in giving man his come-uppance, as if this were a Darwinian imperative, has boomeranged to the detriment of the ape, who is now judged according to an impossible *human* standard which should never have been set. Exaggerated claims boast that apes have finally 'made it', which is more an affrontery to apekind than mankind, since they are robbed blind of their sovereignty by 'evolutionist' do-gooders. The reason that Terrace's conclusion comes as a profound blow is because of this monstrously misplaced standard which has set the tone of the ten-year debate. By any other standard Nim's achievements would appear staggering. Who suffers, but the ape? The cry will now be "They don't have human language after all," but it might as well be "So they aren't human after all," for all the sense it makes.

This obsessive desire to match chimp and child has led to sweeping claims and almost religious conviction; probably little has generated so much heat since Huxley galvanised Victorian London by announcing that "man might have originated . . . by the gradual modification of a man-like ape".[31] Human ancestry is no longer in dispute. Today's ideological divide separates psycholinguists, who see language as innately structured in the human neocortex, and behaviourists who argue that it is learned not inherited: for them there is nothing fanciful in a potential linguistic continuum between ape and man. Fundamentally, the issue is one of uniqueness and to what extent the genes are responsible. Both sides have made out convincing cases. It is not wildly implausible that language structures are written into the human brain's programming, even though apes can name objects, and then manipulate these symbols creatively. Only after Project Nim has begun to clear the air can we tackle the real and momentous achievements of apes which might throw the first real biological light on the evolution of language, and at the same time protect the ape's autonomy by stopping it falling into fourth-class citizenship in an alien and ultimately inhospitable society.

Fireworks Child

. . . Koko grows ever more flexible and sophisticated in communication. Her recent progress is nothing short of astonishing.

She perceives right and wrong, but is touchy about blame. During a videotaping session, when I turn away, she tries to steal grapes from a bowl. I scold her. "Stop stealing. Don't be such a pig. Be polite. Ask me. Stealing is wrong, wrong, like biting and hurting is wrong."

Then I ask, "What does Penny do that's wrong?" Koko says, "Break things, lie, tell me 'polite' [when I'm] hungry pig."

Penny Patterson, October 1978[38]

Koko's ethical and cognitive appreciation is nothing short of astonishing, since it seems also to be man's. Either we now face a traumatic re-evaluation of our psychic peculiarity – or we are the unsuspecting victims of an appalling self-deception. Ape 'language' research is having excruciating difficulty escaping from its flat-earth phase, where man is the explanation of all about him. But the new flat-earth inhabits man's cognitive cosmos. His is the universal cosmic understanding to which other creatures can only aspire, since they have no cosmos of their own. Relativity could still be on the far side of two scientific revolutions. At the moment, we still have an overbearing need to interpret ape actions in terms of human mores, values and customs – of injecting humanity into the ape. Perhaps this is an antidote to the rash of Victorian excesses, perhaps we have to get it out of our system. It is abundantly evident that ape trainers read into their subjects an unwarranted amount of human values; yet mankind's psychosocial realm is probably quite distinct from the gorilla's, so rather than placidly accept an identical understanding of words like *right*, *good*, *please*, and *sorry*, should we not relate them to divergent social and ethical edifices in man and ape, and admit that they might have different meanings to the twin species?

The clash over *meaning* assumes gargantuan proportions as the result of claims by Penny Patterson for the linguistic understanding of her gorilla.

After six weeks of intensively testing a young female mountain gorilla, Yale's fondly remembered primatologist Robert M. Yerkes monographed his verdict in "The Mind of the Gorilla" in 1927. The book-length report painted a depressing picture; the reason gorillas had failed to follow chimpanzees into vaudeville was their "resistance to training", deadened interest and overriding clumsiness. Only with extraordinary difficulty did his unwilling subject learn to manipulate a rake (curiously, her toes were totally fused, although this was apparently no hindrance and cannot explain her stolid refusal to imitate). To be fair, she was ponderously methodical about her tasks, contentedly plodding through some test long after a chimpanzee would have flown into a rage from aggravated boredom. Still, in Yerkes' eyes, this was too little and too late, evolutionarily speaking, to salvage the gorilla's integrity, and he reluctantly concluded that "because the chimpanzee is much fuller of curiosity and more imitative than the gorilla, it has I suspect outstripped its gigantic fellow-ape in the race for anthropoid supremacy".[39]

Fired by the Gardners' successes and riled by history's discouraging verdict on gorilla mentality, Penny Patterson began initiating an infant lowland gorilla into the esoteric world of signs; explicitly, of course, to challenge the child, but Koko could also reprieve the gorilla's down-trodden reputation since that stately old lady of chimpanzee linguistics – Washoe – was now herself a legitimate target for comparison. Koko emerged into the world on Independence Day, 1971: hence her formal name Hanabi-Ko, Japanese for "Fireworks Child". She remained with her mother in San Francisco Zoo, but at six months had to be rescued suffering from chronic malnutrition. Apparently no mental damage was done, so she presented Patterson with a perfect recruit for language grooming. Like Washoe's, her tuition started at twelve months; first in the zoo nursery (in full view of the public), where she received five hours of coaching daily, later stepped up to an exhaustive eight to twelve hours, when the whole entourage shifted into its own house trailer in the summer of 1973. Since the apes' ages, the medium chosen (ASL) and the methods of conditioning (moulding the hands and imitation) exactly matched, Koko's development cried out for com-parison to Washoe's. Both kept pace to a remarkable degree, picking up a sign a month for the first year; by eighteen months Koko scored twenty-two, Washoe twenty-one. And Koko has held on to this skin-of-her-teeth lead up to her present 250 sign vocabulary: evidence enough, Patterson argues with partisan glee, "that gorillas are at least the intellectual equals of chimpanzees".[40]

Like Washoe before her, Hanabi-Ko was prey to the same motiva-tional factors accelerating or retarding her word acquisition. Washoe loved lollipops, so she speedily learnt their sign without any moulding; after all, the word was absolutely indispensable for requesting the desired candy. Koko similarly indicated her preferences, adopting signs for berry, soap and pinch "within minutes"; yet her hatred of eggs and hand lotion meant months of patient drumming to coerce her into calling them by name. Evidently, she was not fool enough to learn words for detestable objects that she was never likely to want, which made hopelessly impractical their use as reinforcers.

Patterson published first in the journal *Brain and Language* early in 1978 a piece entitled "The Gestures of a Gorilla: Language Acquisition in Another Pongid". It caused psycholinguistic palpitations, but she claimed little that had not already been claimed for chimpanzees. Koko was capable of reconstituting words, matching chimpanzee innovations by calling a stale cake a "cookie rock", and for a face-mask she invented "eye hat". Psycholinguists shrugged, for without a statistical break-down of her combinations and error frequencies this stood on the same footing as claims of ESP. But the fireworks sparked off by Hanabi-ko hit the psycholinguistic tinder box when Patterson proclaimed that "language is no longer the exclusive domain of man". Seidenberg and Petitto, speaking at the Chicago Linguistics Society later in the year, flatly rejected this, and in no uncertain terms: ". . . the claims on behalf of ape language abilities are at best unsubstantiated," they conceded charitably, but continuing "and quite probably false". An internecine conflict erupted in the otherwise quiescent pages of *Brain and Language* as Seidenberg and ASL-teacher Petitto, inspired by Terrace stood to slay this sickly theory whose time had come to meet the rigours of scientific selection.

Koko's mastery of seven-word strings (without repetition) resulted in apparently gibbered instructions like: "Come sorry out me please key open." This is a perfectly respectable plea in context: she was locked in her room for misbehaving and was begging to be let out. But is it language? Convinced that it is, Patterson is presently engaged in an analysis of Koko's "conversations", feeding her answers into a compu-ter at Stanford's Institute for Mathematical Studies in the Social Sciences, which is programmed to interpret language emergence in the human child. This commits her to a detailed cross-comparison with child as well as chimp; and although the results are forthcoming, in 1978 she was willing to admit that not only was Koko Washoe's intellectual equal, but that Koko likewise exhibits "close parallels to human children with respect to the development of semantic relations in early language".

These conclusions could not be more at odds with those from Project Nim. Nim had woefully little idea of the syntactic power of sentence structure. Perhaps he was backward, after all, he failed to "swear"; and all agree that the constant procession of teachers pro-duced an emotional strain which *may* have held Nim back. In fact, as an outcome of the stupendous costs and lack of funding, the project had to be scrapped in September 1977, when Nim was flown back to his birthplace, Oklahoma, to join Bruno and his other brothers and sisters. But at the primate centre Roger Fouts assessed him as one of the smartest chimps. And Terrace repudiates the idea that Nim lacked the motivational advantages which gave Koko a Montessori start in life.

I Think, but who Am I?

With apes arrogantly imagined one rung 'below' man any advance
can only be in our direction; any encroachment will only be at the
expense of man's precious uniqueness, by which he has claimed descent
from the gods. Thus the gorilla triumphantly lopes along a path carved
by Washoe through a forest where apes were expressly forbidden to
tread: they have ignored the "No Trespassing" sign. But the arrogant
metaphor of ape as subhuman is positively preDarwinian; twentieth-
century metaphysics have mercifully replaced it with the image of
life's adaptive spread, with no species 'on top'. But this provides a
radical new approach to ape symbolism. In fourteen million years of
independent adaptation gorillas and humans might have developed
markedly different cognitive and social outlooks. Spreading a word
between such species might necessitate spreading its meaning. A word
can only be absorbed if it is relevant; and it can only be made relevant
by mapping it on to one's own psychosocial framework. Meaning is
one area so thoroughly unexplored as to appear sacrosanct. Half the
time, a quaint back-to-front logic is used to prove that child and chimp
have the same understanding - if the ape correctly imitates the sign
and in an "appropriate" situation, it is recorded as having understood its
human meaning. Returning a sign proves nothing of the sort; even
using it "appropriately" may only mean that humans understand both
context and sign differently from the ape (this is almost certainly true
for "sorry").

Consider *cry*, the most blatant misnomer listed in ape vocabularies.
Lucy poignantly signed "cry me, me cry" having rushed to the window
one day as Jane Temerlin drove off. Yet it is a physiological quirk of
mankind that he cries – apes can't weep! Quite why we cry is a mystery.
The parallel between tears in this land-locked primate and the salt-
excreting mechanisms of seals, seabirds and turtles has convinced some
that we passed through a semi-aquatic or sea-shore phase, hence our
other anomaly, a reduced pelt; a pleasant and oddball notion practically
impossible to prove. This tearful distinction between man and chim-

panzee is so blatant as to be shameful; yet *cry* is listed in ape conversation after ape conversation. And the reason is that *we are translating into human terms.* Lucy was sad, or lonely, or grief-stricken; just what she really was nobody has given a second thought. This is the most fundamental yet incomprehensibly ignored aspect of the ape's linguistic predicament.

Matters were brought to a head in October 1978, when Penny Patterson published her "Conversations with a Gorilla" in *National Geographic.* Man might differ from gorilla on three levels, in order of increasing genetic control: cultural, social, and physiological (forgetting the 'cognitive' interface for the moment). Yet on all three counts, Koko is treated as human. In places, her signs become so mangled in translation as to obliterate any ape meaning. First, an outrageous example to emphasise cultural contrasts. Koko is credited with *damn*, though I'm not sure she's considered Hell's torments. Mankind, possibly back past Neanderthal, has had an almost pathological obsession for theologies, and ultimately designed a subterranean abyss for the eternal damnation of his own heretics. Once an awful reality, these fantasies are now locked into our cultural fabric, but the biological function of the bizarre gods and demons which accompanied evolving *Homo sapiens* is still vague. Presumably our death-knowledge was just too traumatic and mind-crippling to assimilate, and necessitated a paradisical afterlife to ease the blow, while threat of roasting flesh served morally to contain social deviation. Presumably, also, heathen gorillas are blessedly free of Judaeo-Christian theology, nor have they need of it (although the gorilla's awareness of impending death is a moot point, evidence for which is discussed later). Hence Koko probably had nothing of sufficiently surreal intensity to map *damn* on to. There is a certain tragic absurdity in assuming that damning a gorilla and having it sign "damn" back proves it understands the grotesque meaning. It doesn't – *damn* is Patterson's evocative rendition of a sign of Koko's dissatisfaction. This is a double-edged sword we are wielding – with it we are liable to sacrifice the greater part of our understanding.

Less trivial is the relationship of certain words to social settings. *Sorry, good,* and *please* are intimately linked to precise human social situations. While refusing to accede to psycholinguist demands that these signs are meaningless to the ape, it seems more ludicrous to assign them human meanings. Any innate departure in social awareness, like the dominance relations and degree of reciprocal altruism distinguishing man and chimp (see the final chapter), renders it suspicious that apes will be humanly sorry, or that we can be pongidly sorry. "Sorry" would be most unlikely to have the same twist in societies of different species. I would even argue that a wild chimp who talked would not dream of saying "sorry" for the same offences for which humans apologise. In fact, it might paradoxically apologise if another ape was in the wrong! (See Ch. 9 on "Intuition".) And if you doubt it, bear in mind that Washoe signs "sorry" when someone is hurt though she is not to blame.

"Existentialists affirm that it is man and man alone who truly 'exists'. This 'existence' is what sets him apart from all other forms of life. The existentialists are perhaps on the right path toward identification of man's basic biopsychological singularity." Thus wrote the geneticist Theodosius Dobzhansky in *The Biology of Ultimate Concern*.[41] He was commenting on man's inturning consciousness, his awareness of self, and he quotes Erich Fromm approvingly: "Man transcends all other life because he is, for the first time, life aware of itself." This is one of the immutable axioms of intellectual history, swept along on the tidal wave of our species-specific theology. Aristotle gave us a "rational" soul and God cut our bonds and gave us "freedom", the two historical identification points of self-consciousness. This was something so tangible it seemed almost disembodied, as though it could float away after death and survive eternity. Sir John Eccles, the eminent neuro-physiologist, still searches for the experimental means to tease out the self-conscious mind from the chemicals of the brain.[42]

But the tide has turned; the ravages of Darwinism are beginning to make dents in our profoundest philosophy. We inhabit an evolutionary world where we can no longer dismiss the apes as sinister and soul-less sports of nature. These are *our* blood relatives; and who but the criminally negligent would not wonder about the existence of their 'selves', their inner beings. To anticipate conclusions drawn later, the ape's cranium is as likely as man's to be a bony dome stretching across an infinite cosmos. In here the ape lives, aware. With this true, might not words provide us with precious tools to tap the ape's consciousness, perhaps even let us peer out at *its* reality? Theoretically they might. But, as I said, Patterson brought the problem of meaning to a head in *National Geographic*. Words can be applied to brain states. But the gorilla's brain is not man's, and it would be perilous to apply words with identical meanings to brain states in brains that differed. Patterson lists the word *think* which she and the gorilla use. *If* Koko genuinely understood that this word even referred to mental processes, then it would prove she was capable of thinking about thinking. The fact that Koko taps her head is far from proving she means "think" or any mental operation. Even if she did understand, "thinking" for her might qualitatively differ from man's parallel mental state, precisely because the two brains diverge anatomically to some degree, and thus probably functionally. We have now hit the core. Koko apparently has a repertoire of abstractions besides "think", including *imagine, understand, curious, idea, stupid* and *boring*. Investing these with human meanings might make the final monkey of Chomsky, and undo attempts by psycholinguists to relate language and cognitive structures. Worse, by flagrantly crediting the gorilla with the entire gamut of *human* mental states – discerned with exquisite distinction: "imagine", "think" and "idea" for example – we effectively enslave the gorilla, robbing it of psychic independence and reducing it to human status. And yes, Koko has been I.Q. tested. She scored about ninety, almost normal in fact for a human, although according to her trainer this belies Koko's real intelligence; asked where it would run in the rain, a child correctly answers "house", but Koko answers "tree" and loses a point.

Oh Darwin, where art thou now?

3

"Humanizing the Ape"

Washoe seemed suddenly to burst upon the world; and many linguists were severely shaken, judging by the backlash. The suddenness, however, belies a century of psychological activity among humans, without which Washoe might still be in Africa with a family, oblivious to the other world of language. To the predictable question, "Why is the breakthrough happening now, and not forty years ago?", the Gardners themselves gave a partial answer: only in the mid-1960s, watching Viki on film, they were struck by the ASL idea. Predecessors had thought chimpanzees might learn sign language – in fact, as far back as the 1880s Max Müller goaded his contemporaries into language-testing the ape (believing it would fail dismally),[1] while in the 1920s Yale primatologist Robert M. Yerkes toyed with the notion of a sign language to achieve this. But no one actually did anything about sign systems until 1966.

Part of the problem was the entrenched belief that apes ought to be able to speak, and all energies were directed into teaching spoken language, but to no avail. But the solution goes deeper than this, down in fact to its methodological roots. To appreciate why mankind waited until the eve of the twenty-first century before penetrating the ape mind, we should understand the Gardners' psychological perspective, viewing them not as individuals striding alone but as the latest and most brilliant experimentalists in a continuing tradition. Only this scientific scaffolding explains mankind's growing desire to humanise chimpanzees, to transmute them into respectable family members of *Homo sapiens* – not merely another species, but another genus. Anyone who has read psychotherapist Maurice Temerlin's astonishing story of *Lucy: Growing up Human* will immediately perceive the strengths and weaknesses of this perspective. Temerlin's narrative illustrates our humanity towards kindred spirits (and not so kindred ones) combined with our difficulty in understanding them as sovereign beings. Lucy is a chimpanzee who lives literally as one of the family. She is analysed according to Freud but not treated according to Darwin, by which I mean that whenever possible she is interpreted as a primal human. But then she can act the perfect lady – reclining on a sofa at cocktail time, sipping a Jack Daniels while perusing *Time* magazine. On occasions she can be devilishly irritating – removing the kitchen door by unscrewing the hinges. Like a human, Lucy presents many faces. At times she is a picture of pathos, mourning the death of her pet kitten; at others, she acts the complete fool, throwing her audience into stitches by lurching blindly round the lounge wearing a crash-helmet back to front, knocking into chairs and collapsing into laughter. Or she might raid the liquor cabinet, pour herself one too many, and stagger drunkenly to the mirror, where she sends herself into hysterics with crazy faces. Without question, these are uncannily human-like antics; and it is frankly impossible not to be captivated by Lucy.

Apes "growing up human" have created an unprecedented moral crisis for mankind, and a lobby is forming for radical changes in the law. One 'environmental' statute of the Boston Law Review already concerns nonhuman rights; Stephen Burr holds responsibility, and he insists that "recognition is needed that animals have a right to live regardless of their usefulness". He continued: "We have recognized in our legal system that individual lives have value. We may not vivisect one mongoloid to save 10 'normal' humans. However, although we may feel emotionally that animals' lives have value to them, we have not granted those lives any real protection in our anthropocentric legal system." Burr focuses his case on the "higher" beasts with an increased hold over their own destinies; and it has particular relevance to Penny Patterson. Whatever the interpretive difference over her scientific results, her stunning announcements have fired the public imagination; then again, her fund-raising tactics and particularly her appearance (with Koko the gorilla) on The Johnny Carson Show have led to murmurs in psychological corridors that she is pulling an academic Barnum & Bailey act. One might even detect a degree of envy in this back-stabbing, since she has managed to raise working capital in a field where funding is precarious at the best of times. Patterson has faced some peculiar legal and moral quandaries over Koko. Acquired as an infant from Stanford Zoo, the sickly gorilla was valued at only $5000; but as she matured, her "property" value – as a female gorilla in breeding condition – rocketed to some $20,000. Koko was only on loan, and the zoo impatiently demanded her return for more "productive" use. In April 1977, the Parks and Recreational Council gave Patterson ninety days to meet the knock-down price of $12,500. But Koko had grown up as a human, her *social* life was amongst humans. To tear her from familiars would be an in-sensitive and cruel act, as it would be for a child; Patterson only has to turn up a few minutes late on her evening visit to Koko's caravan to find an anxious gorilla. The thought of deliberately orphaning her seems diabolical. "To take her away from her family, her environment, to throw her in a zoo cage with a bunch of gorillas – it could kill her," says Patterson. Hence her desperate need to raise the capital, and the undoubted sigh when Rolex recognised her contribution with a cash reward. Few other ape teachers have actually had to buy their pupils.

A Newark attorney and Seton Hall law professor in animal rights, Theodore Sager Meth, investigated Patterson's unique case and told Harold Hayes, then writing a piece for *The New York Times*, that the zoo might have to relinquish all legal claims on the gorilla. The argu-ment is pretty much that against the return of a foster-child, but the reasons Meth gives for equating child and ape in the eyes of the law seem a disappointing return to preDarwinian values which ultimately ends in a derogatory view of nonhuman life and sacrifices the ideal for which Meth himself is striving.

> The gorilla doesn't exist anymore. Under normal circumstances, the only thing this animal doesn't have that we do is language. Now you have changed it. When you give it the conceptual apparatus for conscious reasoning, for mobilizing thought, you have radically altered it. You have given it the pernicious gift of language. If it has never been one before, it is an individual now. It has the apparatus for the beginning of a historical sense, for the contemplation of self.
>
> Her right to remain in a meaningful relationship with the people she has known is greater than the zoo's property rights. This is the whole history of jurisprudence over the past 75 years

– that property rights must give way to individual rights. *In this case you have an ape that has ascended.*[2] (My emphasis.)

The inalienable rights of other beings are a momentous and touchy issue; and the biological philosophy which the law sets store by now might determine the legal course for decades. To prevent it being disastrous, we had best think out our metaphysics very clearly indeed. Hasty judgments based on outdated values will only jeopardise the ape's case. Unfortunately, Meth's conclusions all hang on the assumption that some apes have human language: if *that* falls, their rights simply evaporate. Language has little to do with any newly sought-after status under human law. Nor, I believe, does language provide the "apparatus" for contemplation of the self – an idea fashionable in American sociology early in the century but rejected today by many psychologists, who invert the logic and pin language on a *prior* aptitude for self-conceptualisation (see Ch. 8, "Reflections and Ripples"). Regardless of this, Meth's brief would condemn non-ASL-using apes to a selfless existence stripped of any rights. But most pernicious of all is the underlying metaphysics which measures all life by a vertical yardstick with man at the head, and which assumes that the ape only merits legal or moral consideration once it has progressed to the ultimate human echelon. While a prosecutor might feel smug armed with this philosophy, it is hardly a sympathetic and unbiased brief for the defending attorney to be holding!

The question remains, "What are we really doing to apes when we humanise them?" And why do we *still* imagine that our language elevates them to the human apotheosis?

First Words

In 1909, exactly a century after Lamarck was laughed out of court for his fanciful *Philosophie Zoologique*, William H. Furness, III, a Philadelphian doctor, explorer and chronicler of Borneo's head-hunters, started teaching an orang-utan to speak. It was a memorable effort and a dismal failure, as Furness was the first to admit. And yet it marks the incarnation of the preDarwinian metaphysic, the practical application of what was until then a nebulous understanding of nature.

Now man was to act on that time-honoured understanding. Furness had voyaged to Borneo early in 1909 to study, if not capture, some of its wild men.

> I was possessed with the idea that with constant human companionship and surroundings at an early age, these anthropoid apes – the orang-utan (which of course you know is a Malay name meaning Wild-man or Man of the Jungle) – *were capable of being developed to a grade of human understanding perhaps only a step below the level of the most primitive type of human being* inhabiting the island . . .

After all, he continued:

> If deaf, dumb and blind children have been taught by beings they could not see to use language they could not hear would one not be justified in an earnest endeavor to teach the higher apes with faculties and senses alert and with traditional powers of imitation to do the same to a limited degree? It seems well nigh incredible that in animals so close to us physically that there should not be a rudimentary speech center in the brain which only needed development.[3]

He could not decide whether to treat them as "pupils, or patients", which illustrates our persistent ambivalence towards the ape, part subordinate, part stunted human, retarded in its growth towards 'sapient' perfection, and needing only that final push from sympathetic liberals in the evolutionary camp. Activate the 'latent' speech centre and the miserable wretch could improve a grade or two, nudging ever closer to manhood. Lamarck, it seemed, might still have the last laugh.

Furness leaves only the slenderest clue to his half-conscious motives and prejudices, and none whatever to the back-drop of events in 1909 (he published only in 1916, after years of meagre success swamped by the most infuriating set-backs). Other sources leave little doubt that sometime during the winter of 1908–9, the head of Philadelphia's Psychological Clinic at Pennsylvania University, Lightner Witmer, had actually confronted Furness on the prospects for ape speech, maintaining that any ape who could ride a bike could surely be taught to mouth a few words. The clinic, as its name suggests, was devoted to mentally retarded and backward children, and Witmer's staff were armed with the usual battery of therapeutic techniques to coax from them the rudiments of speech. What worked for a retarded individual, the reasoning went, might equally benefit a retarded race, the apes.

Trying to imagine an 'improvable' ape today calls for a Herculean shift in perspective. Before the turn of the century it was embraced in biological circles as both natural and logical, largely, I suspect, because the metaphysical 'ladder of life' could call up powerful support from that potent, almost evangelical force in America's gilded age, Social Darwinism. 'Improvability' is a curiously loaded term, it carries undisguised class connotations – of the lower orders rising through the ranks by sheer effort (with the social goal, of course, always in clear view).

This aspect explains so much about man's view of nature a century ago, because such an analogy was actually read into self-domesticated man's rise from 'barbarism'. It almost ceased to be analogy. Social Darwinism sanctioned the view that man had progressed explicitly by hacking down less viable human competitors, a sort of self-improvement of the sapient stock. Self-help became the watchword; tycoons were all the rage. 'Improvability' was an intellectual juggernaut carrying on its back the full weight of the biological and social sciences. The movement cannibalised Darwin's works in search of authority and scientific sanction, which were not hard to find in the *Origin*'s thicket of metaphors. But then Darwin himself was born into an age already concerned with civilised man's rise from barbarism, a fact reflected in the *Descent*, and which eased its journey into Victorian acceptance. It was an age, moreover, already witnessing man's genocidal onslaught on nature. Perhaps the most notorious example was the extermination, before the century's half-way mark, of all but a handful of the 4000 native Tasmanians alive in 1800. Truganini, the aboriginal princess, died the last of her kind on 8 May 1876. After the *Origin*, this genocide was explained away as a weeding of the sickly elements to improve the human stock. Competition left 'savages' where they had always been, ranked low on nature's ladder, like some frozen relic from our disreputable past, while Western white man, having done better for himself, sat resplendent at the pinnacle. So to many a mind, Darwin had actually built an impregnable fortress about the 'improvability' ethic; after all, to ram home his evolutionary mechanism, he had cleverly laid great stress on animal breeders' successes in improving their stock by weeding and selective breeding. Natural selection likewise improved life mechanically; it was the means of evolutionary 'betterment', or so it seemed.

Nineteenth-century cartoonists, carrying out guerilla raids against every sombre Victorian endeavour, have given us some valuable insights into popular prejudices. They caricatured the prevailing Lamarckian slant, depicting aborigines progressing towards Piccadilly man in his finery, while apes surreptitiously advance to fill the gap, moving perilously close to those lower human echelons inhabited by institutionlised "idiots". But if man might better himself – and civilised *Homo sapiens* was proof of a long haul out of aboriginal ignorance – might not education improve the ape? At least he should be given a crack at civilisation. The logic was leading this way, a logic depending for its life on the Aristotelian absolutes of "up" and "down", and a corresponding evolutionary scale by which man might measure himself.

Matters were brought to a head by a human-apeing chimpanzee called Peter, who made his début on the Boston stage in September 1909, amid advertising slogans which proclaimed that he had been "born a monkey and made himself a man".[4] No doubt Peter was an especially gifted ape. This first became apparent to his owners on the transatlantic crossing when they brought Peter from England. Rollerskates were fastened to his feet expressly to keep him out of the rigging; within two days he was skating all over the ship. By the time the liner docked, Peter was proficient enough to warrant his first public performance. As an entertainer (and money-maker) he never looked back. Rarely parted from his skates, he delighted in making an exhibition of himself. Witmer was impressed by Peter's Boston show, and met the star himself, smoking filter-tips and clad like some Pickwickian fresh from his club in starched collar, waistcoat and patent leather Oxfords – the whole effect marred only by the roller-skates. Witmer argued that any beast, from seal to flea, can be conditioned into giving a stereotyped performance; Peter's evident joy was precisely in setting himself some death-defying cycling task "with the evident purpose of departing from routine, seeing whether or not he could do it". This convinced Witmer that here was a malleable mind able to create its own contingency – a mind, as his owners insisted, "self educated", and obviously amenable to the full treatment. Witmer called Peter into the Psychologi-

cal Clinic for tests (threading beads, opening locks and the like, designed
to test children for degrees of cretinism) and happily pronounced him
a "middle-grade imbecile". The compliment came as a hefty back-
hander; still, higher praise had never been heaped on a self-educated
ape. Skating about the laboratory, Peter had out-performed many
backward children. It was even said somewhat rashly that his English
comprehension surpassed that of many humans. Asked, "Now aren't
you going to give the Doctor a drink?" he accordingly handed Witmer
a tumbler (the more readily, Witmer joked, because it was now empty).
He understood "Where's Mama?" and "Where's Peter?", pointing
himself out to the assembled by tapping his own shirt-front. It was
only Peter's hairy physiognomy that stopped the doctor promising a
speedy recovery under his care.

> If Peter had a human form and were brought to me as a back-
> ward child and this child responded to my tests as creditably as
> Peter did, I should unhesitatingly say that I could teach him to
> speak, to write, and to read, within a year's time. But Peter has
> not a human form, and what limitations his ape's brain may
> disclose after a persistent effort to educate him, it is impossible
> to foretell. His behavior, however, is sufficiently intelligent to
> make this educational experiment well worth the expenditure
> of time and effort.

Witmer was understandably wary of the public's reaction to an ape's
being tested at the children's clinic. But Peter acquitted himself
admirably, passing the majority of tests with flying colours. Anyway,
answered Witmer disarming the anticipated opposition, without using
a child for comparison, how else is one to test the intelligence of a
beast stationed so uncomfortably close to man? Wrote Witmer of this
talented ape: "his intelligence is not in the class of animal intelligence,
as we psychologists understand the term. The study of this ape's mind
is a subject fit, not for the animal psychologist, but for the child
psychologist." More revealing still, Witmer saw Peter deputising for
the fabled 'missing link' between man and ape, acting Lamarckian-
fashion like some recently discovered penultimate link in the ever-
ascending *living* chain of being. Witmer went so far as to admit that
"Peter's mind practically bridges" that yawning "chasm" which
moralists interposed between reasoning man and brute creation, and

which Neanderthal and the "apelike" *Pithecanthropus* from Java had done precious little to close. Self-help had raised Peter just so much. He had made the imbecile grade by his own largely unaided efforts; there was no telling how much further he might go with intensive education. True, he was unable to speak, except for an excruciatingly painful "Mama" which had to be coaxed out of him. Moreover, in contrast to a normal child, he showed absolutely no inclination to speak, and unlike Furness Witmer was inclined to give convention the benefit of the doubt and assume until proved otherwise that Peter possessed no natural faculty for speech. Even so, he wondered "What might have happened if from his birth [Peter was not civilised until some three or four years of age] he had associated freely with human beings and if he now associated with them as children do." There was always that nagging doubt.

If Peter could be made to associate symbols with the names of objects, and if he could be taught to speak these names, Witmer ventured, "then he will be prepared, as the child is, to use speech as the staff by whose aid he may climb the pathway of intellectual development". For one horrifying moment, there was even talk of moral training; at that, a large part of the Victorian world would not have been amused. But lamentably Victoria had passed away, and with her vanished an intractable view of morality aloof from nature. Anyway Witmer doused the idea with cold water no sooner than he broached it. Peter had in him the "basis" for a moral fibre, although no one held out any hope of his reaching "that stage of development where moral character begins in recognition of the difference between right and wrong. Even though we may grant a fair prospect in the direction of intellectual development, we must assume from our present knowledge of men and apes that Peter is and will remain morally imbecile."

Witmer was caught in an age in transition. 1900 was the watershed between Darwin's feverishly moral age and today's coldly clinical genetic world. Still Witmer saw terrifying prospects. "It would be a nightmare flight of the imagination to suppose that an ape could acquire a will determined consciously by moral motives." For that, in a by-gone age where morality was set against some higher judicial law, meant Peter the ape might earn himself eternal redemption.

Going the whole Orang

In our grand overview, it is impossible to deny that popular aspirations had entered into and actually shaped late Victorian science, leading inevitably to acceptable scientific notions of an 'improvable ape'. This is precisely how Cambridge science historian Robert Young envisages science growing – not as a disdainful parallel to society, not even enmeshed in some social context, but actually absorbing that 'context', which emerges as a constituent in the redistilled theory.[5] Science is moulded as much or more by the metaphysics of scientists than by so-called hard-core evidence (which may be selectively sought *after* the event). The towering example which springs immediately to mind comes from Darwin's highly motivated age, when ideologies were proudly paraded like so many shields. While physicists like the atheist John Tyndall carried on fiery ideological campaigns, reformulating thermodynamic laws of energy conservation as a deterministic bludgeon to batter to death "free will", transcendental biologists like St. George Mivart made "free will" man's specific hallmark, and man the Divine evolutionary goal.[6] These were diametrically opposed evolutionary formulations designed to support mutually exclusive metaphysics. Hence, not *one* evolutionary science but many existed in Darwin's day; each resting on the ideology which motivated its proposer and moulded the product. From Young's perspective, then, science and religion were not openly clashing. Nor was religion operating from within science, but science had actually swallowed up current theology, employing its building bricks for a new world view. Gone are the days when science history is seen as an interminable catalogue of pure 'discoveries'; Young's thesis is helping transform it into a healthy, challenging discipline. A greater degree of sympathy and understanding is now needed to reconstruct the meaning of science at any period.

Psychology is particularly prone to social fads and fancies, and on these soft-core fringes we find many examples to substantiate Young, but none more fascinating than the idea of 'improvement'. By the turn of the century varied aspects of social thought, like the bourgeois 'self-betterment' ethic and Social Darwinism, meshed with nonDarwinian

preconceptions of human 'superiority' and nature's feudal ranking to
shape psychological thinking on the ape question; to the extent that
policy decisions – like the programme for ape 'improvement' by
intensive education – now accurately mirrored the prevailing ethic.
'Improvability' was the key, but that implied human standards and a
predetermined goal. Man was again sitting on the Lamarckian apex
of creation.

Witmer demanded rather harshly that if skating Peter were the genius
among apes that his owners claimed, he "should become the ward of
science and be subjected to proper educational influences". Sooner or
later the ape would be turned over to science for improvement – it was
now only a matter of time. Witmer took a prophetic look into the
future. Peter had been partly educated, "but no effort has been made to
give him what an education really stands for. I venture to predict that
within a few years chimpanzees will be taken early in life and subjected
for purposes of scientific investigation to a course of procedure more
closely resembling that which is accorded the human child."[7]

As it turned out, Peter was spared the trauma of being tugged from
his foster parents. That autumn, Furness returned from Borneo with
an armful of apes, which he and Witmer set about civilising. A year-old
orang-utan had been acquired in South Borneo in February 1909, a
quiet, docile ape, even though a captive for barely a week before
Furness obtained it. In addition, Furness managed to pick up two chimpanzees from a Liverpool dealer on his return to the States, one for
Witmer's clinic, the other for his own purposes. Within five months
Furness' chimp had died of pneumonia, and Witmer's charge barely
escaped the same fate, recuperating under Furness' care. Witmer gave
up trying to teach the ape to speak. Another young orang joined the
menagerie in 1911. Both orang-utans died, probably about 1913–14,
which left the chimp as the sole survivor. But their brief lives had lasted
just long enough to permit Furness' concerted effort to teach the apes
to speak English.

Six hours a day for weeks on end, Furness tricked, cajoled and bad-
gered the young orang into repeating the word "papa", and still,
Furness conceded, this time spent was "not one hundredth part enough".
He even mouthed the word ad nauseam in front of a mirror to a bemused young orang, while forming her lips with his fingers in imi-

tation. "At the end of about six months," he recorded triumphantly, "one day of her own accord, out of lesson time, she said 'Papa' quite distinctly and repeated it on command." Even this was a colossal step for the young orang who, without the human vocal apparatus or a natural breathing-speaking technique, had had to overcome insuperable mechanical problems. Apes do not use their lips like man, nor are their natural cries and hoots made while exhaling. Human speech differs significantly in that we normally speak as we breathe out. Apes try to speak as they breathe in. Witmer soon taught Peter the art.

> I first obtained the proper position of the lips by getting him to blow out a match, which he could do readily enough. I then blew into Peter's face and he blew into mine. I made the puffs shorter and the action of the lips more vigorous until I was saying *pey-pey* with breath but without voice. Peter imitated this exactly, using no voice but a breathed, *i.e.* whispered, *peh-peh* sound. To accomplish this took five minutes.

But it was not to be so simple, and the next step exhausted six months' time and patience. The orang soon associated the sound "Papa" with Furness himself; as he wrote, "When asked 'Where is Papa?' she would at once point to me or pat me on the shoulder." She probably would have done so whether or not she could mouth "papa", since Peter (and numerous other apes subsequently) acquired an extensive vocabulary of understood English. Furness realised this. He admits that eventually "she understood almost everything that it was necessary for me to say [during training procedures] such as 'Open your mouth,' 'Stick out your tongue,' 'Do this,' etc., and was perfectly gentle and occasionally seemed quite interested." This quick comprehension of spoken English inevitably led to semantic confusion, as when she was learning letters of the alphabet in a memory test she would constantly point to her eye when asked to identify "I".

The convoluted training to get her to say "cup" took on the air of a silent comedy. Furness forced her tongue to the back of the throat with a bone spatula. She took a deep breath, and he placed his fingers over her nose to make her breathe out through the mouth. Letting go the spatula, she exhaled to the tune of *ka*. Facing her, Furness would open his own mouth, push his tongue back, and blow *ka* in unison, so she could see the vocal mechanics at work. As the comic routine reached a pitch, the little orang would refuse to say *ka* until Furness' fingers were correctly positioned over her nostrils (placing them there if need be), imagining this to be an integral part of the proceedings. Eventually she learned to manage without support, and Furness was able to complete the act by closing her lips the instant she breathed out to produce the truncated *kap*, which ultimately grew into *kup*. She required no other reinforcement than constant praising and grooming, and all the while she would handle a cup to associate the word with its referent, which she eventually did. Ill one night and dreadfully parched, she leaned out of her hammock and croaked in pathetic voice "cup, cup, cup," which to Furness at least presented a "glimmering" of hope for proper word usage.

But that was pretty much the extent of her vocabulary. By the time she died some months later, she had mastered *th*, preparatory to saying *that*. Still, she put to shame the chimp, who persisted in an illiterate gloom; in five years all it had mastered was a barely intelligible "mama". Furness understandably held out more promise for the orang "as a conversationalist" since it is "more patient, less excitable, and seems to take instruction more kindly". Nonetheless, he was downcast about pongid abilities in general: both chimp and orang remembered a few of the wooden alphabet shapes, although they became hopelessly lost when the words were written, which forced Furness (a little against his will, judging by his tone) to admit that "the ability to recognize the significance of graphic representation is as lacking in the anthropoid mind as is the inclination to speak". Looking back hypercritically (which is all too easy after the "ape breakthrough"), we can lay the blame as much at Furness' feet as those of the put-upon orang. Training procedures left the poor pongid desperately little idea why it was memorising wooden cut-out As, Bs and Cs, or contorting its mouth to stutter *kup*.

"Significance" (Furness' own word) must be radically different for man and ape, and wooden alphabet letters probably have little to recommend them to the latter's mind. Most damaging of all – and Furness himself eventually came to see it – was that the apes were being cued some or all of the time; they would watch his eyes closely, and read from his gestures just what he wanted. Asked to pick up a *red* ribbon, they would watch him unwittingly 'point' to it. Sent to another room to fetch one, however, the baffled apes returned with a random sample.

"I am eager to say truthfully that my anthropoids have showed signs of reasoning," sighed Furness in 1916, "but truthfully I can say that I have seen only the faintest rays of evidence . . ." Unquestionably, chimps can insert keys in locks, turn them, pull back the catch, open the door, go to the tap, turn it on, fill a cup, drink, close the tap – but what was that over and above a "simple succession of ideas", even if it mimicked purposeful or reasonable human actions. Reason, he was forced to conclude, stood outside ape attainments, a conclusion to mollify those pompous divines who seemed forever to be lauding "the superiority of mankind". A few famous lines from moralist Sydney Smith said it all.

> I have such a marked and decided contempt for the understanding of every baboon I have ever seen – I feel so that the blue ape without a tail will never rival us in poetry, painting and music . . . I have sometimes, perhaps, felt a little uneasy at Exeter 'Change from contrasting the monkeys with the 'prentice boys who are teasing them; but a few pages of Locke, or a few lines of Milton, have always restored me to tranquility.

"I regret," added Furness in a paper read to the American Philosophical Society, "that I am forced to admit, after my several years observation of the anthropoid apes, that I can produce no evidence that might disturb the tranquil sleep of the reverend gentleman."[8]

Culture Maketh Man

Nevertheless, 'improvability' was only one side of the coin; dissected and isolated it remains inadequate to explain mankind's desire to educate the ape. Turn over the coin and the face that comes up belongs to the anthropological giant, Alfred Kroeber, whose beliefs unwittingly stimulated the spasmodic ape-speech experiments prior to Washoe and thus lit the slow-burning fuse which culminated in the 1970s explosion.

Kroeber was a University of California ethnographer made famous by monographing American Indian culture, and even non-disciples salute him as the dean of American anthropology. (He died in 1960, at the age of eighty-four.) Kroeber remained aloof, although from his writings emerges an immensely likeable character, who entered anthropology with the ripe Victorian ideal of liberating mankind from "hoary tribal taboos" like religion.[9] His mind – the organ we wish to infiltrate – was an incisive product of its age, or so Kroeber would have insisted, even if he sometimes imagined himself battling full-tilt against anthropological headwinds. Perhaps we should refrain from peering even metaphorically into his mind. Such personal intrusion savours of so much that Kroeber himself vehemently opposed. Kroeber himself had written in 1917:

> The day may come when what took place in the tissue of Darwin's brain when he first thought the concept of natural selection, can be profitably studied, or even approximately ascertained, by the physiologist and chemist. Such an achievement, destructive as it may seem to those [to] whom revelation appeals, would not only be defensible but of enormous interest, and possibly of utility. Only it would not be history; nor a step towards history or social science.[10]

This statement is embedded in an essay, superlative for its age despite a degree of overkill, called "The Superorganic", published in *American Anthropologist*. In 1952, eight years before his death, Kroeber afforded himself the luxury of looking back across a third of a century at his propagandist paper. His chief aim, he admitted, had been to combat Herbert Spencer and his ilk, for whom social evolution and culture flowed from the individual (today we might say that it was dictated by his genes). Deducing social development from the movement of its atomic particles – people – was part of a wider reductionist trend in Victorian days. Its arch exponent and prophet, John Tyndall, was lampooned by tongue-in-cheek Huxley. Tyndall's teaser, laughed Huxley, might be formulated with school-book precision: "Given the molecular forces in a mutton chop, deduce Hamlet or Faust therefrom."[11] What is more, Huxley finished, Tyndall "is confident that the Physics of the Future will solve this easily".

This uncompromising genetic intrusion into cultural 'no go' areas irked Kroeber. It was not the philosophic determinism which galled him – he was enough of a cultural determinist not to let any lack of freedom fluster him as it had so many Victorians. He baulked at hereditarian domination of exclusively social factors. Heredity, the genetic constraints in each of us, has at one time or another been invoked to explain every cultural and racial facet. Indeed, the trend towards genetic determinism has continued unabated, culminating in the 1960s reductionist boom led by Robert Ardrey and Desmond Morris, who lured out the ineradicable beast in us to explain just about everything from office manners to warring instincts. Our cultural destiny was written in a double helix, whose indestructible prophecy could be read like a crystal ball. In 1975 Edward O. Wilson kicked up a storm with his *Sociobiology*. Both sides began rehashing old feuds as the talk once more turned to the alleged genetic basis of class structure (which for the time being Wilson rules out) or homosexuality. He closed with a sociobiological seance which would have delighted Tyndall. High-level sociological theory, Wilson ventured in a sub-section marked "The Future", "must await a full, neuronal explanation of the human brain. Only when the machinery can be torn down on paper at the level of the cell and put together again will the properties of emotion and ethical judgment come clear."[12]

In 1917 Kroeber painstakingly pointed out that there was a less dramatic side to the story, an antidote to the hereditarian rash. And with the prospect of sinister hereditarian implications for racial superiority, Kroeber's campaign was fired by an overriding moral imperative; he was sensitive enough to see that science had a social responsibility decades before the tumultuous 1960s rekindled our interest. While genetic determinists seemed set to prove a sort of god-given racial inequality, Kroeber turned the case inside out like some sociological sea cucumber, suggesting that racial differences could be due to nothing more than unequal opportunity. Today we believe that the delicate balance lies somewhere in between the straining geneticists and culturalists, and that more importantly the two factors are inextricable – the wide *potential* inherent in genes permits diverse environmental coddling to mould the entire gamut of culturally differentiated humans. What Kroeber's environmental overkill did was balance the scores; he was later to admit his excesses and lament his earlier disdain for the human carriers of culture, and he even admitted to trying to "smuggle human nature back into the study of civilizations". But for our purposes it is important to realise that psychologists had already espoused his views, almost uncritically; hence it was an extreme environmentalism that was deeply to inspire the ape educators.

"Civilization," Kroeber had once written, "begins only where the individual ends." Heredity conditions the individual to an arguable extent, although society as a whole transcends its constituent people. Global movements and the emergence of grand philosophies cannot be predicted from the chemistry of the genes. To believe that the destiny of a nation can be deduced from chromosomal material, he laughed, smacks of the ludicrous reductionism that would explain Faust by the molecular rattlings in a mutton chop. Kroeber pleaded for environmental sanity to curb the Victorian excesses, and he persuaded by way of a beguiling analogy from history.

> A hundred Aristotles among our cave-dwelling ancestors would have been Aristotles in their birthright no less [he wrote]; but they would have contributed far less to the advance of the science than a dozen plodding mediocrities in the twentieth century. A super-Archimedes in the ice age would have invented neither firearms nor the telegraph. Bach born in the Congo instead of Saxony could have composed not even a fragment of a choral or sonata . . .

Man, in this extreme environmentalist picture, might be said to do less to mould the age than the age to deliver the man. Only Alexander's Athens permitted an Aristotle to be realised, just as Germany in post Great War years conditioned the rise of a Hitler. Cultural, political and social forces threw up the man of the moment – or men, since the same social forces were operating across a broad front of receptive humanity. Why else, Kroeber wondered, did oxygen have three simultaneous discoverers, Mendel three re-discoverers, and the calculus engender a tooth-and-nail priority struggle between the loftiest geniuses of their day, Newton and Leibniz?

The capricious Olympian gods, teasing earthly mortals by removing their heroes from their proper age and dropping them out of time, would be sorely frustrated by this endeavour to wreak ahistorical havoc. It is doubtful, said Kroeber, if even Darwin's name would be remembered today if he had been born fifty years sooner or later. Dropped on English soil at the time of the French Reign of Terror, Darwin – in his wildest dreams – would never have broached so inflammable a doctrine as "descent with modification". Such nonsense assumes that timeless "Truth" is there for anyone of any age to snatch at

– that even a Darwin in Hellenic times might have hit on the idea. (However laughable, non-historians have unearthed glimmerings of modern Truth 'foreshadowed' by the ancients: indeed, more than once Anaximander has been paraded as the Ionian 'Darwin'.) On the other hand, Darwin born too late would have been pipped to the post by Wallace. Darwin's time was mid-century, Kroeber reasoned, when civilisation was "hungry for the doctrine".

> Can it be imagined, if Wallace had met death among the Malay islands, and Darwin, unspurred by his competitor colleague's activity, had carried his theory in hesitant privacy a few years longer and then suddenly succumbed to mortal illness [a contingency Darwin anticipated, willing his wife £400 with instructions to publish in event of his death: he clung tightly to his theory for so long – 20 years – that one wonders if he would have preferred a posthumous *Origin*], that we of the civilised world of today should have lived all our intellectual lives without a definite mechanism for evolution . . . that our biologists could still be standing where Linnaeus, Cuvier or at most Lamarck stood?

With the age ripe, Kroeber's contention was that another Darwin would have arisen to take his place. This view of history left shockingly little room for personal idiosyncrasy, and altogether denied that creative individuals shaped man's cultural destiny. The upshot was a transcendent civilisation, freed from personal quirks, cut adrift from genetic domination: culture was seen as something *external* to the individual. Gifted scientists only released the potential inherent in the age. Kroeber was quite adamant. The tradition, he maintained, which is "handed along, from one to another, is only a message. It must of course be carried; *but the messenger after all is extrinsic to the news.*" That culture was something over and above individual man (literally *super*-organic) was the vital departure point for ape educators.

Kroeber was certain of another fact: that civilisation was a peculiarly human phenomenon. The old adage that animals were tyrannised by their instincts had grown almost to an article of faith; "subhuman" behaviour was composed of a stereotyped repertoire of performances. The yoke of heredity, he wrote, trapped "subhumans" into an "unalterable pattern" of actions; as such, the "subhuman" mind was not sufficiently malleable to be "inscribed" by tradition – by definition, brutes could have no culture or history. The human distinction, however, was less one of intellectual superiority, as of behavioural flexibility:

> Directly, it is the civilization in which every Eskimo, every Alaskan miner or arctic discoverer is reared, and not any greater inborn faculty, that leads him to build houses, ignite fire, and wear clothing. The distinction between animal and man which counts is not that of the physical and mental, which is one of relative degree, but that of the organic and social which is one of kind.

As an obvious corollary, man stripped of tradition and reared in isolation would emerge in aboriginal innocence; his slate would be wiped clean according to environmentalists. Believing the contrary, inquisitive despots and Christian monarchs, a seemingly interminable procession from the Pharoah Psamtik I through Holy Roman Empero Frederick II to James IV of Scotland, have incarcerated, isolated, and fostered peasant children to goats and deaf nannies, in the interests of releasing man's primordial language or religion. (So persistent has been this dehumanising attempt to prove Phrygian, Hebrew, Turkish or whatever the *lingua humana* that one pundit jokingly proposed that "we perhaps [are] dealing with some form of regal behavioural universal"!)[13] Stripping away the centuries of cultural concretion, replied Kroeber, will not reveal some primal language given Adam to discuss the merit of Eden's fruit.

Kroeber drew out his instinctual *vs.* traditional antithesis by way of an illustration. Pups reared with kittens, he pointed out, failed to miaow – even though heirs to a feline "tradition" – while in utter contrast a baby born to French parents and whisked off to be fostered in Mongolia would grow up speaking fluent Mongolian. Man, and man alone, was the torch-bearer of tradition; Kroeber even tentatively pinned down its first flowering to some ancestral being "more advanced, in general mental faculty, than the gorilla, and much less developed than the first known race that is unanimously accepted as having been human, the man of Neandertal and Le Mousterier." It was a safe bet in 1917 for, ignoring *Pithecanthropus* from Java, which many anthropologists including its embittered discoverer, Eugène Dubois, managed to do, Kroeber had pretty much exhausted his options in Neanderthal and the gorilla.

Kroeber was a man of prodigious learning, whose historical method is still percolating into shadowy scientific corners, even if his environmental enthusiasm has had to be tempered. This makes it the more ironic that he himself should ultimately resort to an almost naïve genetic determinism, a chromosomal explanation which tied culture irrevocably to man. He envisaged culture's emergence as a make-or-break event, a leap to another plane. The seeds were sown in his essay of 1917, when he admitted that "social evolution" started with the "missing link"; although he was quick to check this statement, since a link "implies a continuous chain", whereas he envisaged an all-or-nothing break.

> The dawn of the social is thus not a link in a chain, not a step in a path, but a leap to another plane. It may be likened to the first occurrence of life in a hitherto lifeless universe . . .

From that moment when culture first flowered, he wrote, there were "two worlds in place of one".

One cannot help but read a detheologised Mivart into these assertions. The formal similarity becomes uncanny as Kroeber's position ossifies: the transcendental leaps from inorganic salts to the first cell, and from instinctual life to that cosmic achievement, "reason" (Mivart), the thread on which Kroeber's civilisation hangs. Throughout his life Kroeber developed this theme, underpinning it with a harsh clinical mechanism, a starkly reductionist off/on switch which triggered cultural growth. By 1948, in his monumental 856-page *Anthropology*, he actually speculated on a culture-gene. According to the nineteenth-century transcendental interpretation of man (spelled out, say, in Lyell's clandestine notebooks and Mivart's article "A Limit to Evolution") the instant God implanted "reason" in the ancestral mind, there was no earth-shattering anatomical transformation (which might leave the unendowed feeling neglected), and yet the entire course of human destiny was potential in that microsecond.

In Kroeber's mechanistic interpretation:

> It may have been no more than a change in one chromosome, perhaps no more than in a few genes. The individual organism in which this new constitutional factor first cropped out may

well have been still overwhelmingly like its parents and ancestors in total appearance and behavior, in bodily shape, motivations, and abilities. But on top of this likeness, the innovating or mutant individual manifested a new inclination to communicate, to learn and to teach, to generalize . . .[14]

And thus in one portentous microsecond was culture born, destined to grow in heartless independence of its parents. Such transcendental remnants of nineteenth-century thought have mercifully come under attack since the early 1960s as cultural anthropologists began to take the starch out of Kroeber's system.

We were promoting ourselves up through the ranks again. As a sceptical Clifford Geertz commented in 1964, "Man's humanity, like the flare of a struck match, leaped into existence."[15] The overriding reason for the tenacity of Kroeber's cultural 'flash point' remained the mental chasm between man and ape, almost as gaping as it had been in Lyell's day. Kroeber could still write that man was "an essentially unique animal in that he possesses speech faculty and the faculty of symbolizing, abstracting, or generalizing". Apes said nothing, he once admitted, because they had nothing to say. Of course, he knew from reading Wolfgang Köhler's *Mentality of Apes* that chimps could be remarkably inventive, piling boxes or fitting together canes, fishing-rod fashion, to reach bananas out of arm's reach. Inventive solutions might come instantaneously as insights. They might also "come overnight and without warning. When a human being acts in this manner we say that he has thought the problem out." He even explained the awe with which the chimps treated a stuffed donkey with button eyes as an incipient religious experience. And yet, though inventions might be the fodder of culture, as isolated and enforced incidents they lacked that self-sustaining take-off which defines history and tradition.

Attempts were even made to quantify the 'flash point'. It is notoriously true that slapping a figure on something does more to actualise it than any amount of turgid description. Hence Sir Arthur Keith set the "cerebral Rubicon" at 700–800 c.c.[16] Ravines and rivers, we seem hell-bent on devising obstacle courses; and as a corollary in these days of exponential ape encroachment we seem forever doomed to redefine ourselves. The brain size Keith plumped for was based on his belief that gorillas could not rise above it, nor aborigines fall below, and it was about as meaningless a move to us as Lyell's tortured attempt to decide at what epoch God bestowed a soul on the evolving man-stock. Lyell might have been comforted by Keith's "cerebral Rubicon"; it would certainly have saved his God an agonising decision. But as Darwin said, looking at a fossil series, "It would be impossible to fix on any definite point when the term 'man' ought to be used".[17] But then unlike Lyell, Darwin's primary concern lay not in saving man's "dignity".

Ape Children

Kroeber had said in so many words that fire, clothes and houses were merely products of tradition; unlike the innate nest-building faculty in birds, man's knowledge is carefully passed down by word of mouth, he is schooled in the arts of igloo-making or hearth-building. Strip man of that tradition, isolate him from his culture, or so logic seemed to insist, and he might be returned to primal innocence: an Eskimo ignorant of igloos, an Englishman ignorant of the King's English, no less than of the King. So long as this super-entity called "culture" set man apart, wild boys and wolf children could be reprieved; they might not have been abandoned "idiots" after all, merely lost offspring totally uncivilised. Perhaps Victor, the legendary wild boy of Aveyron found roaming a French forest in 1799, and cared for but never taught fully to speak by Jean Itard, *was* after all 'natural' man stripped of all cultural trappings. Feral children were near speechless, un-house-trained and equally uncivilised. Such were also the circumstances of Kaspar Hauser, found staggering through the Nuremberg streets in 1828 clutching a letter explaining little more than that he was born in 1812. Legend has it that he was a princely German heir; certainly, as he was later able to relate, he had been locked in solitary confinement in a tiny, dark cell, with not even height enough to stand for his first seventeen years of life. On release, he was virtually mute, and quite unable to walk normally or use his hands properly. Kaspar made remarkable progress with tuition, even beginning his memoirs.* In contrast, the "wolf children"

* The only real parallel to Victor or Kaspar Hauser today is the tragic, heart-rending case of "Genie", who was released from her lifelong imprisonment only in 1970, when already an adolescent. Never having known human company, or heard spoken language, Genie is now undergoing intensive therapy and lives in a foster home, while her language acquisition (such as it is long after her left hemisphere has matured) is being closely studied. See Note 18.

allegedly dug out cuddling the cubs in a wolf's den in 1920 were never raised beyond the mental age of two. One managed some hundred words, the other never spoke at all. Tales of real life Mowglis still crop up. The Lucknow Sisters of Charity recently raised a crawling, mewing urchin called Shamdev to partial respectability, curing him of walking on all fours and eating chickens alive (he had an insatiable lust for blood).[19] According to his finder, Shamdev was living with wolf cubs when captured, although the truth behind such *Jungle Book* romance is difficult to winkle out, with counter-rumours flying about of the boy growing caged for exhibition purposes.

The inextricable relationship between language and culture neatly explained why deprived children resembled mute animals. Civilisation moulded the human mind, language gave it a powerful tool to express its thoughts; indeed, civilisation seemed to reach to man's very soul. The psychological mind dimly began to perceive the reverse logic of the situation. If man stripped of culture were left a near naked ape, the naturally benighted chimpanzee with benefit of some civilising influence might ascend the "phyletic scale" to within a few rungs of man. Human society, in fact, had done all it possibly could to *decivilise* the ape: incarcerating it, convicting it to a life-term of imprisonment like some poor pongid Kaspar Hauser. So, perhaps, like Kaspar, a last-minute reprieve followed by intensive education might equally benefit the ape. As long as culture was seen as some *external* appendage of man, something detachable and returnable in Kaspar Hauser's case, then Kroeber with his insistence on cultural uniqueness, yet recognition of pongid inventiveness, seemed to defy psychologists to test the ape's cultural mettle.

In fulfilment of Witmer's prediction, there began an extraordinary experiment, which the Indiana psychologist Winthrop Kellogg actually called "humanizing the ape". To test the environmentalist's reverse logic, Kellogg suggested in *The Ape and the Child*, "Why not give one of the higher primates exactly the environmental advantages which a young child enjoys and then study the development of the resulting organism?"[20] It was wholly rhetorical, because by then Kellogg had actually done it; the exercise performed to discover just how much culture could be inculcated in a chimpanzee.

On 26 June 1931, ten months after the birth of their son Donald, Winthrop and Luella Kellogg took a seven-and-a-half-month-old chimpanzee from her mother caged in the Anthropoid Experiment

Station at Orange Park, Florida, and began raising the two offspring in identical manner, both enjoying the stimulus of a challenging home life. Christened Gua, the infant ape was not to suffer the indignity of being chained, or caged, or indeed fed from a dog's bowl on the floor. She was encouraged to sit in a high-chair alongside Donald, be house-trained and in every way practicable "humanized". Every muscle twitch was to be analysed and contrasted to Donald's; I.Q. tests were to apply equally to both; and word and sentence comprehension were to be compared. In short, the full weight of twentieth-century man's civilising power was brought to bear to give little Gua a fair crack at self-betterment.

From the outset the ape held its own against odds-on favourite Donald, both in word comprehension and "pre-school" tests, although by the end of nine months the human was edging ahead. Since humans have slowed their rate of maturation, one might have predicted better ape scores early on, especially on coordination tests, such as tool use (Gua immediately used a spoon properly, while Donald still inverted his, unloading cereal down his front). However, even in word comprehension and "intelligence" she was one jump ahead from the start. She also showed a surprising degree of initiative. By fourteen months, for example, at which time she understood some forty sentences, she would be ordered to "stay there!" while wriggling to escape her high-chair. On one memorable occasion, she desperately craved attention, and kept slithering to the floor, only to shoot back up at each disparaging glance. Waiting her chance, she slipped to the floor, pushed the entire high-chair a yard to within hugging distance of her human companion and shot back into place as happy as a sand-boy, able both to "stay put" and yet claim a hug. In fact, Gua was so much the irrepressible show-off that she too often held Donald spell-bound; little *Homo sapiens* sat enthralled by his peer's super-human abilities.

After nine months the Kelloggs suddenly terminated the experiment, and began the painful habituation of Gua back to cage life. No reason was forthcoming in *The Ape and the Child*, although reading between the lines one detects an air of unavoidable favouritism. Not only in some ways did Gua outshine Donald at the start, but it seems that the environment created by a strong-willed ape was adversely affecting infant *Homo sapiens*. Nobody had given much thought to the ape's cultural reciprocity: while the Kelloggs were intently "humanizing"

Gua, the little ape it seems was unwittingly "pongising" poor Donald. It was bad enough when he aped Gua by gnawing bark or chiselling board, but when he began giving chimpanzee food-barks at the sight of an orange enough was enough – parental concern overrode any call for impartiality. Matters got worse. Gua naturally never learned to speak, despite intensive efforts to train her to say the obligatory "Pa-Pa" and despite her own excellent word comprehension and ability to convey her meaning by mannerisms. Donald made a normal human start (except that his first word was "Gya"!) but then only managed a couple more proto-words before drying up completely. The silent ape world in which he cohabited was having an inhibiting effect. The disastrous situation was confirmed by standard language tests, which diagnosed Donald as "considerably retarded for his age". The experiment was aborted; Donald returned to normal and Gua to a cage.

From this one gets an excellent feel for the back-drop of the impending "ape breakthrough", especially the philosophic cradle in which psychology was rearing its baby (to mix metaphor and reality). Man's poor relation (a forties book title), the ape, was born in blessed innocence, and stood in a somewhat similarly distressing situation as the ghetto-dweller, caught in a cultural poverty trap. Both were seriously crippled by lack of opportunity, without which any potential stayed embryonic and the individual was doomed to life as a cultural pauper. Exploit the opportunities, stimulate the mind, the remedy was in large part social. The Kelloggs' work, conceived within Kroeber's cultural paradigm, caught the professional imagination. Another couple at the Yerkes Laboratory in Florida, Keith and Catherine Hayes, determined in the mid-1940s to push the Kelloggs' attempt to its limit; in short to test whether genetic hindrance blocked the ape's progress, or, as they evidently assumed, whether some latent potential could be coaxed out by immersing the home-grown chimpanzee in a challenging cultural environment – human, of course.

Viki, their pongid baby adopted a few days after birth, stayed some seven years. Like any human child, she mimicked every adult act, her routine chores took in such household drudgery as dusting, washing dishes, ironing, hammering, painting woodwork and mounting photographs, all of which she evidently loved. At three she would sit patiently at the telephone dialling at random, her targets greeted by an excited silence. But then the Hayes had no better luck than Furness or the

Kelloggs, eliciting only a few cruelly tortured *Pan*-English words. Nor were their attempts greeted with much enthusiasm: an unforgivable lack of interest which led to Keith Hayes' important paper on pongid conceptual powers lying dormant for fifteen years, only being dusted off and printed to underscore Washoe's achievements. Nonetheless, an interim report issued in 1950, while three-year-old Viki was busily engaged in random raids on Bell subscribers, demonstrates just how deeply the Hayes were influenced by the Kelloggs' faith in the ape as a cultureless man.

> We suspect that the importance of this cultural factor in deter-
> mining the abilities of man has been seriously underestimated –
> an understandable error, since men as we know them always
> have culture, giving us no opportunity to observe the effect of
> its absence. If an individual man could grow up in complete
> isolation from culture, and with only such knowledge as he
> could gain directly from his environment, we suspect that his
> behavior would be very different from that of the men we know,
> and would probably be quite apelike. We doubt that such a
> man could survive, in competition with the physically hardier
> anthropoids.
>
> We suspect that the species chimpanzee closely resembles our
> hypothetical, cultureless man, with much the same individual
> capacities – except for language ability, the tool which man uses
> to build and maintain culture.[21]

And not even speech manifests itself in cases of severe deprivation, as in wild or imprisoned children.

Culture makes man; lack of it represses the ape. Genetic constraints were played down, environment came into full focus. Right or wrong, environmentalism as extreme as this was the root driving force behind the humanising and sign language training programmes. Just prior to Viki's death in 1954, Hayes bared his soul in a paper called "The Cultural Capacity of Chimpanzee". He frankly admitted that chimps are probably not neurologically stunted, only culturally so. Otherwise they possess all the mental hardware necessary to perform the "higher mental functions", the thought behaviour characterised as "abstract, symbolic, conceptual, rational, insightful, or foresightful". To be perfectly accurate, he suspected that these may well only exist in man as long as he has had a rigorous learning period, when mental skills are inculcated and libraries of knowledge crammed into the memory banks as ground matter for developing thought. In brief, "We suggest that the 'higher mental functions' observed in man are more nearly results of culture than causes of it."[22] According to this view, without the skills and mental finesse that education inspire, man might well be stumbling about like an ape. Kaspar Hauser and at least the non-"idiotic" wild boys seemed the supreme examples. And, looked at from the other direction, "A primate who has not acquired the same skills and information can hardly be expected to display these functions in the same form as man. If a primate's background of experience is restricted [as in the case of life imprisonment], he may fail to display any 'higher functions' in any form whatever – simply because of his lack of skills and information and regardless of the detailed structure of his brain." He would be only marginally better off than Kaspar Hauser. This then was the uncivilised ape's predicament.

It was also the rationale for giving Viki the benefits of a human childhood to realise her full cultural and mental potential, to "human-ize" her.

Means and Motives

The roots of the "ape breakthrough" are tortuous, tangled, and run deep into a complex past; like an organic growth drawing from mani-fold influences in the social and scientific medium. They encompass Witmer's prediction that apes would take their place in the household, the faith of Kroeber's disciples in the cultural basis of sophisticated thought, and a prophetic passage written by the primatological found-ing father, Robert M. Yerkes, over half a century ago in his book *Almost Human*. If apes can manipulate the world with their fingers like Köhler's stick-wielding and string-pulling chimps, why can't they manipulate it with words? Perhaps such a cross-fertilisation passed through Yerkes' mind; certainly, he hit on the practical solution:

> I am inclined to conclude from the various evidences that the great apes have plenty to talk about, but no gift for the use of sounds to represent individual, as contrasted with racial, feelings

or ideas. Perhaps they can be taught to use their fingers, some-what as does the deaf and dumb person, and thus helped to acquire a simple, nonvocal, "sign language".[23]

But we pick out highlights only at the risk of missing the point. Seeds that appeared to germinate without warning had for a long time been watered and tended. The conditions were ready; all that was needed now was a strong enough motive to catalyse the Gardners into action.

B. F. Skinner's brand of grim behaviourism, which had been gathering momentum towards the middle of the century, was quite hospitable to the Hayes' view of the chimp as a cultureless man. By their reckoning, it was largely the lack of a rich cultural stimulus which retarded the ape; the highest premium was placed on environmental factors. And the environment was all that concerned behaviourists. Manipulating it, Skinner had boasted on innumerable occasions, we can predict and ultimately control an animal's response (hence the ready adoption of his reinforcement techniques in penal and mental institutions, where behaviour deviates from the norm). But the Skinnerian emphasis fell so strongly on the external stimulus that all sight was lost of innate or genetically constrained potential; the organism was treated as a black box – somehow it could be programmed fully from outside, the 'mind' was a *tabula rasa* ready to be inscribed. So pernicious was this view, yet so successful Skinner's conditioning of pigeons and rats, that he imagined the species barrier to conditioning had been broken: any animal could be taught almost any trick, all it required was a rigorous reinforcement programme. Skinner admits as much, conceding that his experimental work on rats and pigeons had "been surprisingly free of species restrictions",[24] and could thus comfortably be extended all the way to human "verbal behaviour". (The ability to achieve the same results regardless of the astonishing diversity of his subject species strikes me as a slamming indictment: a measure of his failure, not his success.) Anyway, Skinner extrapolated to the limit, and in 1957 published *Verbal Behavior*, setting forth his argument that language was merely learnt by means of a complex feedback system operating between parent and baby, with reinforcement guiding the child towards a full appreciation of grammar. If Skinner were correct, grammar took on the distinct guise of a convention.

Not so, insisted an enraged Noam Chomsky, the M.I.T. linguist, and he proceeded to tear the heart out of Skinner's system, writing a taut and caustic review of Skinner's "astonishing claims" for the journal *Language* in 1959. It was a savage attack, born out of a long-germinating frustration over the arch-behaviourist's manifest inability to shed light on the subtleties of language. Since Skinner failed to distinguish species by their responses, and treated each as though it had the same open-ended potential, Chomsky found it therefore "extremely odd that language is limited to man".[25] Looking back, one can almost imagine Chomsky asking why apes had not mastered grammar, if it were acquired by the allegedly simple act of conditioning (in reality, he steered clear of apes, as he still does). For Chomsky, man alone had an innate language potential; the "deep structures" of the universal grammar were embedded somewhere in the neocortical wiring. He wondered how else we could explain the child's fluency, creativity and familiarity with grammatical intricacies which even professional linguists have a devilishly difficult time analysing. Stranger still, the child grasps them in the first years of life, as though he had an innate expectancy of encountering them. No, argued Chomsky: language is not the product of a learned series of reinforced responses.

The cutting tone of Chomsky's piece-by-piece demolition job seemed to invite a behaviourist backlash; and it did come, but from the least expected quarter. Skinner himself refrained from hitting back. Instead the Gardners took up the cudgels. The husband-and-wife team are, as they admit on flag-waving occasions, "strict behaviorists", and they have indeed carried their anti-Chomsky crusade through to the present day. In 1974 they even looked back (*sic*) to the "Chomskian era" and pronounced it a bygone age when "good experimental method was unfashionable".[26] When I talked to Nim's supervisor at Columbia University, H. S. Terrace, it became immediately apparent just how hard Chomsky's assault on Skinner had hit the behaviourists. (Nim, incidentally, is only a nickname; the unwitting chimp was christened Neam Chimpsky – a joke of some delicacy.) Once the Chomskyan cat, with claws unsheathed and sharpened for battle, was unleashed among the behaviourists' pigeons, a quiet, scientific hell broke loose. From that moment on, said Terrace, ape language training programmes were "in the air". The gauntlet had been thrown down, and one (perhaps the only) rejoinder was to demonstrate that apes could acquire language the way man was imagined to – through differential reinforcement. If Chomsky were right, a chimpanzee should never show an aptitude for finer grammatical points; in fact, it was doubted if any amount of conditioning could elicit a truly creative manipulation of symbols by *Pan troglodytes*. On the other hand, those out on Skinner's limb were quite happy to see its feasibility.

Not long after Chomsky's challenge, Washoe's language training began in earnest. The result did not necessarily prove Chomsky wrong, but it did open a startling new window on to the ape mind.

4

A Metalinguistic Leap

"A plague on both their houses!" groaned David Premack at the thought of the Skinner–Chomsky deadlock. Not surprisingly, considering that he had earned his spurs pioneering reinforcement techniques, Premack's own ape research was widely heralded as a triumph for behaviourist beliefs that language sprang from conditioning, not innate endowment. Matters are not so simple. Premack himself admits that "They're both wrong" – psycholinguists and slavishly Skinnerian behaviourists – but he does declare that his "sympathies on many scores are much closer to Chomsky",[1] which tends to illegitimise the behaviourists' claim to his results. Skinner has nothing to say about the cognitive structures underlying language. And this is "the heart of the matter" which fascinates Premack: not language *per se*, but its logical and semantic underpinnings, elements which may very well exist in the ape. Hence Premack's exquisite linguistic probes into the ape mind, probes designed specifically to reach these elusive structures. But mapping language on to the ape brain required a radical and in the early days heretical belief that apes *had* an aptitude for at least a 'weak' language. Without that, any mapping would prove futile.

By 1966, when the Gardners were starting up, Premack at the University of California had long been pondering the language problem. His first fellowship to study the question of "ape language" dates back to 1955, and not long after he teamed up with Arthur Schwartz of the University of Oregon. For them it was axiomatic that life exhibited a "continuum of linguistic competence".[2] It was only slightly embarrassing that nature stubbornly refused to supply anything like a linguistic continuum, and the onus fell heavily on that word "competence". Between the "lowly call system and human grammar", they proposed to synthesise an "intermediate" or "weak" grammar tailored to the chimpanzee's needs – a grammar stripped to bare essentials. Devising the artificial grammar was relatively easy; the real problem lay in teaching it to the ape. The chimpanzee larynx was obviously ineffectual in generating the human spectrum of sounds. Premack's and Schwartz's solution seemed at first simplicity itself: build a mechanical voice-box controlled by a joystick that the ape could operate manually. In other words, give the chimpanzee an artificial voice. With a battery of tone generators at its finger-tips, the chimp could 'talk' in a sequence of discrete tones, each sounding like a spoken phoneme (before being fused into a word). At first, the ape would treat the joystick as a toy. The chimpanzee infant would be raised by a human mother versed in the monotonal ape language; Premack hoped that it would thus pick up its ersatz language 'naturally', as a human infant does – by associating sounds and objects, moving eventually to abstractions and more complex grammatical operations. When the young ape had mastered the system, the joystick was to be miniaturised into an electronic device strapped to its waist or wrist. Scientific instrument-makers at the University of Missouri actually put together a prototype joystick and in 1966 Premack and Schwartz announced its specifications.

But already doubts had crept in. Far from being simplicity itself, the machine looked like demanding impossible feats from the ape. In effect, the chimp would have to 'spell' out words in phonemes, since there would be no means of fusing them (as in normal human speech) – unless the ape simultaneously mastered two voice-boxes (one for vowels, the other consonants), when it could at least generate syllables. And even juggling these two, the result would be little more than the childish effect of spelling out words syllabically. The problem clearly lay in trying to create a speech system based on man's. The grammar and vocabulary might be greatly simplified, so the ape had only to deal with some fourteen phonemes, but that was not the point. A child hears the *word*, which is a gentle fusion of sounds into a discrete unit, while the ape was expected to associate each object or action with a string of unfused tones. The system was fast getting out of hand. Premack scrapped it and began thinking afresh.

All along, Premack had debated the value of mimicking speech, wondering whether a written system might not prove more workable.

After the event, it was apparent that writing was also in some ways preferable to Washoe's signing. It would have proved well-nigh impossible to ask a baffled Washoe what she understood by a word-sign; the very logistics of the situation would have defeated her, since her gestures in question had to be abandoned before she could discuss them. A short memory and still shorter vocabulary might thwart the most determined ape's analysis of language. One can too easily envisage frustration and rage piling on top of the resultant confusion. In these early days, the most practical way of using language to analyse language is by imperishable words; at least, committed to paper, there is less chance the words will vaporise before their merits can be discussed. Talking comes easily, but talking about talking less so. For this, a radically new language form was imperative; Premack's new formula again looked simple, only this time it was. He invented and built a system involving arbitrarily shaped, brightly coloured, plastic word-symbols, each metal-backed for instant fixing to a magnetic 'writing' board.

About the time the Gardners adopted Washoe, Premack started teaching (drilling, less sympathetic critics suggest might better character-ise his method) his chimpanzee Sarah to read and write the bizarre language at his Santa Barbara laboratory. Suddenly we are thrust into an alien environment; after familiarising ourselves with the Gardners' humanising influence, the reassuring home environment, the com-parison between Washoe and children, we emerge disorientated into Premack's psychological laboratory. Sarah is caged, imprisoned by comparison with free-roaming Washoe or Lucy, in such stark sur-roundings as would suggest the crushing of the strongest linguistic spirit. But Premack was not attempting to humanise his ape, in fact he did not arrive at the idea of language experiments via the Gardners' intellectual route. His tradition was more clinical; his approach more rigorous. Hence the longer one compares their respective approaches, the more subtle appears the division between their methodologies and objectives. Premack employed his plastic-word 'language' as a finely honed tool to probe the cognitive recesses of the ape mind, and that to my way of thinking is its legitimate use.

Sarah's metal-backed plastic markers could be converted into 'sentences' by arranging them Chinese-style (vertically) on the mag-netic board. This system took time to evolve. In the early days Sarah snatched her gaudily coloured words and zealously rushed to the middle of her cage to write on the floor, which led to a certain practical incoherence, since no one could see through the huddled furry figure jealously guarding her sentence. Since plastic words were ready-made, they had only to be associated with their worldly referents; the ape's fingers did not have to be moulded, nor gestures practised. Of course, this system had certain drawbacks, as critics were forever pointing out: it crushed any hope of spontaneity on the ape's part, unless she resorted to humping a satchel of plastic words about on her back. But then Premack was not after spontaneity. However, it had its compensations: since plastic words suffer less from the impermanence of manual gestures, words and whole sentences stood for both man and ape to see and discuss, 'externalised' as it were, as much objects of close scrutiny as the world itself. The chimp could sit and ponder this string of geometrical shapes and garish colours, mulling over the appropriate course of action to take in response.

Another incongruity, made still more glaring by the Gardners' success with newborn Moja and Pili, was Sarah's age. She was approaching adolescence, being already five years old when Premack began training in 1966. Yet she soon developed an extensive vocabulary, some 130 words by 1972. The trick was Premack's use of *metalanguage* – using language to talk about language. First Sarah learnt her symbol meanings the hard way, with Premack 'spelling out' social transactions as they were performed, as in "Mary give apple Sarah", whenever trainer Mary Morgan handed over an apple slice. This way she readily identified names of food and transactions ("give" and "wash") and of her trainers who, like the apes, wore plastic name-tags pendant-style round their necks. She soon learned to rectify mistakes, especially when they were to her cost, as Premack recalls:

> Once she wrote "Give apple Gussie," [in error for "Give apple Sarah"] and the trainer promptly gave the apple to another chimpanzee named Gussie. Sarah never repeated the sentence.[3]

With such necessarily harsh conditioning, Sarah mastered the rudiments. She was now introduced to a new symbol, shaped like a geometrical disaster, a word which itself meant "name of": the ultimate Inquisitorial instrument in speeding up the snail's pace process of indoctrination. She would first be shown an apple and its name (known to her), with "name of" interposed between them, the same for banana, and so on until she appreciated the metalinguistic leap involved. From then on, said Premack, "new nouns could be taught explicitly and quickly". A fig, "name of" symbol, and the previously unfamiliar plastic word for fig would be shown her in sequence, and her comprehension assured when she subsequently demanded in her Chinese-style way, "Mary give fig Sarah." Hitches were inevitable, especially when tests involved that ultimate variable, the intransigent ape mind, whose vagaries could cause the most dispassionate experimenter to throw up his hands in despair. Of course, it was highly likely that the unfortunate ape did not *want* to discuss apples, perhaps it had something else on its mind at the time, and with plastic symbols to hand it was likely in mid-experiment to suddenly articulate its new demands and completely throw the results. Hence in tests requiring Sarah to name say, an apple, to see if she had mastered the symbol, she might obstinately write "banana", for which howler she consistently scored a black mark. Only slowly did it dawn on her trainers that she understood the question perfectly, ignored it, and persisted in her demands for a piece of banana. The first and worst hazard in teaching an ape object names must be the grateful recipient's tendency to actually use them.

"Name of" proved the expected boon to increasing an ape's word power. By a similar token, Premack introduced "colour of", "shape of", and "size of" symbols, which allowed him that critical short-cut in increasing Sarah's repertoire of colours and characteristics. There followed an unexpected bonus, since Sarah was now capable of making the same statement a number of ways. Thus Premack could test Sarah's sentence comprehension by fixing two contrasting sentences to her magnetic board, and further asking her if they meant the same. She had already been taught "same" and "different" concepts, when applied to objects, recognising that an apple is "different" from a banana. Now Premack switched "same"/"different" to *sentence* comparisons, moving perceptibly further from concrete reality. Already knowledgeable about interrogatives, Sarah was now faced with the convoluted question, "Is 'Apple is Red' (same/different) from 'Red Colour of Apple'?" She chose by interposing either "same" or "different" between the sentences, and she chose correctly, it was "same". Whereas when asked to judge the content of "Apple is Red" against "Apple is Round", she found their meanings distinctly "different".[4]

Sarah's world is radically different from those of Washoe or Lucy, but then Premack intended it to be; the 'surface' features of the two language-types – plastic words and hand signs – are as divergent as the scientific intentions of the Gardners and Premack. The Gardners set out in old and established tradition to compare chimp and child in their language acquisition during the critical early years. Washoe astounded everybody by her creative and spontaneous use of the medium. She was actively encouraged to venture beyond her linguistic confines – to invent words, to request "rock berries", even to swear. Project Washoe went all out to explore the prime function of language – communication; and the Gardners aptly titled their first major discussion of Washoe's achievements "Two-Way Communication with an Infant Chimpanzee". The whole point was to initiate dialogue, not a repetitious monologue on their part. By stark contrast Premack's unashamedly clinical technique was designed to extort Sarah's knowledge of the logical functions and "information processing capacities" on which a language might be built, not to invite her views on apes, men and life. Hence the inquisitioned Sarah enjoyed all the niceties of what Philip Lieberman judged "solitary confinement or a maximum-security prison".[5] Premack's self-appointed task was to investigate Sarah's aptitude for syntax, operations like the conditional ("if-then") and class concepts (such as "big" and "round"). In quiet contrast to Washoe, there was hardly any flowing communication; Sarah had simply to pick out one symbol in answer to Premack's often diabolically complex questions, one word which said nothing for her linguistic spontaneity, but everything for her ability to understand the question. Thus the whole operation took on the air of an intelligence test, of a one-sided onslaught on the ape mind. By its undoubted brilliance, Premack's approach was pushing into the shadows decades of labour with traditional ape tests. Duane Rumbaugh, himself having taken the innovative step of finally hitching a chimpanzee to a computer console programmed in a special "language", wound up the long-standing debate:

> The language ape projects demonstrate that we have under-estimated not only the linguistic capabilities of nonhuman animals but also their intelligence. We are getting far more impressive behavior out of chimpanzees in language training

situations than we obtained through the more formal kind of
procedures that psychologists have used extensively during the
last thirty years . . .[6]

Whether Sarah actually "has" language is hotly debated, which
rightly astonishes Premack since it puts a totally false slant on his
intentions. The Gardners are the first to deny that Sarah is demonstrating her language aptitude. Since she has only to choose one of two
symbols, they see it as nothing but a forced-choice test, arguing that
this requires no linguistic competence whatsoever – even though her
"meaningless responses were scored by means of artificial codes and
interpreted by elaborate linguistic theories".[7] How Sarah actually
understood the rigmarole surrounding these plastic "words" might
best be glimpsed by simulating the procedure in humans. Eric Lenneberg of the Massachusetts Institute of Technology actually tried this;
he trained two school pupils in Premack's system, following to the
letter Premack's role with Sarah. Given Sarah's tests, the students
scored brilliantly (better than the chimpanzee), but they were quite
unable to translate the bizarre "sentences" into English. "In fact,"
admitted Lenneberg, "they did not understand that there was any
correspondence between the plastic symbols and language; instead,
they were under the impression that their task was to solve puzzles."[8]
But in solving those "puzzles", the two humans revealed their comprehension of concepts like "same"/"different", which is precisely what
Premack was searching for in the chimpanzee mind. Those embroiled
in the debate over language simply miss the point of his work.

Premack meanwhile tried an experimental approach to discover how
Sarah understood her "words". Do plastic words, he wondered, carry
the same charge for chimpanzees as spoken words do for us? He assumed
our words were powerful triggers for information retrieval, and began
to investigate the 'recall power' of the plastic symbol for Sarah. She
was given tantalising snippets of fruit, often only a seed or stem, at
other times a more helpful slice or section of skin, then asked to conjure
up the whole fruit. The method was to present Sarah with, say, an
apple seed, then ask her to choose between an apple and pear stem. If
she matched it correctly, it seemed safe to conclude that she pictured
the intact fruit. Clues varied in strength; some chimps readily recalled

the fruit shown a slice, but sometimes struggled to identify a seed, though Sarah performed well with all clues. Next, she was asked to match the seed or stem with the *word* for that fruit. Scores shot up. "The results of these tests were unusually clear-cut," revealed Premack, writing for *American Scientist* in 1976. Indeed, the "words were more informative than parts of the actual fruit".[9] The apes scored higher if matching seeds to a symbol than to another portion of the same fruit, an intriguing result which strongly suggests that symbols evoked the fruit with all its attributes, and with an overwhelming intensity. Concluded Premack, "Since, in the ape, the word substitutes vigorously for its referent, it seems proper to speak of the 'power of the word' for the chimpanzee and not only for man."

Still more provocative, Premack wondered "Was Sarah able to think in the plastic-word language?" Had those gaudy plastic symbols become 'internalised' to engender gaudy plastic thoughts? Perhaps an analogous case is to ask someone learning French whether they yet *think* in French as a test of their competence. It is a deceptive question. One probably does not think in any set language at all, but in some symbolic or representational form underscoring all languages; nonetheless symbols, from plastic words to Egyptian hieroglyphs, must enter into a strict relationship with our mental constructs, and Premack's tentative answer to the question was "yes". To back his contention, he related a critical experiment which, perhaps above all others, has softened the cynics.

I doubt whether it proves that Sarah actually thought in plastic word images, but Premack's demonstration certainly established Sarah's powers of symbolism. What, he wondered, passes through her mind on being shown a blue plastic triangle. The short way to find out was to ask her, which he did: describe, he wrote Chinese-style on her magnetic board, the following – and he held up the blue plastic triangle. Yes, she responded; it was red and round with a stalk on top.

The blue plastic triangle was her "word" for apple – so designed because it bore no earthly resemblance to the fruit. The plastic disc was a symbol or, if you like, a code, enabling her to neatly package away the 'real' world inside her mind. In characteristic unsensational tones, Premack outlined the real import of Sarah's power to abstract.

The ability to achieve such mental representation is of major importance because it frees language from simple dependence on the outside world. It involves displacement: the ability to talk about things that are not actually there.[10]

It commended itself to others: comparative psychologist William Mason wrote in *American Psychologist* for 1976 that Premack's apple test was "One of the most convincing demonstrations of the ape's ability to adopt an abstract attitude . . ."[11]

Apes and Computers

> Several things strike me as odd about Sarah's achievements; odd simply in the sense of not fitting easily into my framework of ideas. She seems to do about as well on one problem as on another (generally correct about 70–80 percent of the time) in spite of what I, at least, think of as great differences of complexity among the problems . . .
>
> Roger Brown, *A First Language*
> (1973)[12]

Suspicions grew that Sarah owed her unvarying level of success to being tipped off by 'social cues' from her trainer (who, of course, knew the answer and might unwittingly have given the game away by his or her mannerisms). Premack earnestly began to allay such fears; he instigated a "dumb trainer" procedure, by using a new investigator illiterate in plastic-word language. With the word-backs numbered, the dumb trainer could be informed (from outside) of the required sequence of numbers, without ever knowing the meaning of the sentence manufactured. Likewise, Sarah's answer was relayed, translated and judged to be right or wrong. Not surprisingly, perhaps, her performance dropped marginally from eighty-five per cent correct (her norm) to seventy-five per cent; this was probably due, Premack reasoned, "to emotional factors induced by peculiarities of the test", the emotionally susceptible ape put off by an unfamiliar trainer wearing earphones and persistently whispering into a microphone. Harvard linguist Roger Brown still had qualms and apologetically stuck to his guns in what was fast becoming a delicate situation.

Total automation seemed the logical answer; by eliminating the human factor the ape would be thrown back on its own 'linguistic' resources. Spurred into action by the impressive successes of Washoe and Sarah, Georgia State University psychologist Duane Rumbaugh began checking the feasibility of what he termed a "computer controlled language training system for investigating the language skills of young apes".[13] To initiate the "LANguage Analogue" or LANA project at the Yerkes Regional Primate Research Center in Atlanta, Rumbaugh harnessed the diverse skills of a computer specialist, electronics consultant, psycholinguist, infancy consultant, biomedical engineer, and ape-trainer Timothy Gill (who was to become a behaviour expert in his own right, co-authoring many of Rumbaugh's papers and doubling as ape teacher and Georgia State doctoral candidate). Vetted and meticulously planned, the LANA project was eventually launched on 1 February 1972: the goal to design and construct a computer-run language trainer which would speed up the process, respond automatically to the ape's request (as long as it was formulated correctly) – which meant that even with no trainers on call the little ape Lana could still watch her favourite film in the dead of night – and generally record and analyse all exchanges and their outcomes.

A novel 'language', stylishly titled "Yerkish", was assembled to talk to Lana, and each of the keys on her console was embossed with an arbitrarily shaped lexigram. As Lana depressed a key it lit up, while a short pulse of light indicated that another word had been added to her sentence recorded on a screen above the key bank. This incorporated the best of Premack's system: Lana could watch her sentence grow and then examine it, while a similar screen outside her cage permitted her trainer to check for blunders of Yerkish grammar, and a teleprinter recorded her utterances for posterity. The language form, too, was similar to Premack's, being lexigrammatic; but Rumbaugh's object above all was to stimulate conversation, which by definition involved the generation of novelty. In this, he parted company with Premack, and indeed remained deeply critical of Premack's procedure which, he and Gill suggested in *The Journal of Human Evolution* for 1974, "severely limited the ability of Sarah to respond in a creative manner",[14] as though Premack almost intended to stifle Sarah's spontaneity. (A valid, though unfair, criticism, since Premack sacrificed innovation implicitly to affect a deeper probe into the ape's cognitive structures.)

Lana was anything but straitjacketed by the machine, in fact she proved herself a speed-reader. She first sat down at the console (or rather swung from the 'go bar' which activates the computer) at the age of two, and within a fortnight had mastered her stock phrases (to request life's necessities), rendered into English as *Please machine give* such delicacies as *fruit, juice* or *piece of banana*, and *Please machine make . . . movie* or *music*. To force her hand, she was limited to infuriatingly brief glimpses of film (*A Gorilla's First Year*), thirty-seconds' worth, or just enough to whet her appetite. Lana soon got the hang of the machine, and began making her own modifications. She was expected to pay strict attention to both the lexigram meanings and their place in the sentence, erasing the sentence to start afresh if she made a syntactical error. For this she had an eraser key, but the "period" key also wiped her screen clean, so she took this short cut midway through what was promising to be a piece of Yerkish gibberish.

The immature ape had become totally dependent on her Yerkish ability for supplying all her food and entertainment. The computer was now lifeblood and lifeline to her. Just as we talk to ourselves, Lana moves to her console in the middle of the night and talks to herself out loud, as it were, punching in such instructions as "Please Lana groom", replying with "Yes" before getting down to this all-important task. With ninety per cent accuracy she would construct sentences such as *Please machine give piece of chow* (commercial monkey food), although in her first two months she often attempted to short-circuit this laborious procedure, and to extract more than one item per sentence by punching in such abortive requests as *Please machine give water chow*. She erased grammatical mistakes, and could correctly complete any sentence begun by her trainer. Rumbaugh and his team were understandably jubilant. "Lana could read and she could write! After only six months of formal training, she was further ahead in the acquisition of language-relevant skills than we had originally thought she might ever be."[15]

But could she *really* "read" and "write" in any meaningful way? True, she could accurately punch out an invariant sequence which her *trainers* translated as "Please machine give . . .", but that said nothing for her comprehension. Her sentence *Please machine give fruit period* looks grander than it is. Lana was not demonstrating her genteel qualities with "please", nor a keen eye for punctuation with "period". These were initiators and terminators required by the programming: "start" and "stop" buttons which controlled the message analyser. Translating them as "blip" or * might be less misleading, since there is no hint of pleasantry or punctuation in them. This leaves * *machine give fruit* *.

But how do we know that the second lexigram corresponded in her mind with the machine she was operating?

Lana's achievement could still be written off as a magnificent piece of conditioning, the like of which no self-respecting pigeon was incapable. Columbia psychologists actually tried indoctrinating pigeons in a Yerkish equivalent, to get some idea of the profundity of Lana's "language-relevant skills". They simulated her early rote learning, training the birds to peck four colours in a specific sequence, regardless of the order in which they were presented. If the last colour could be associated with food or drink (this has yet to be done, but it presents little problem), then the pigeons might peck Red-Green-Blue-Corn or Red-Green-Blue-Water, although there is no question of translating this as "please give pigeon" corn or water! It is simply an invariant sequence indoctrinated into the bird. The implication is that one is no more justified in translating Lana's first three fixed signs as "Please machine give". To vindicate the ape and prove that she put some specific meaning into the symbols (irrespective of whether they tally with *our* meanings), Lana would have to manipulate her "words" creatively. Psychologists were not going to let her off that lightly.

Meanwhile Premack was again being hauled over the coals, but this time, unbeknown to anyone bar her intimates, Lana had charitably rushed to his rescue. Georges Mounin, Professor of General Linguistics at the University of Provence, published a major review in *Current Anthropology* for March 1976 in which he admitted with barbed caution "that the chief limitation of the Premack experiment lies, to begin with, in the *poor social relations* set up by the type of experimentation chosen. Life in captivity and experimental behaviourist conditioning do not stimulate relations that allow true communication, which in turn would initiate the use of and enrich the system of communication taught." Which is long-hand for demanding that there exists as much difference between Washoe's stimulating human environment and stifled Sarah's incarceration

> as there is between learning a foreign language in a foreign country, under the conditions of true communication, and learning that language by doing structural exercises in a language laboratory, under the most fictitious and abstract conditions of communication.[16]

Language is pre-eminently a social activity, its prime function is both communication of information and a sort of linguistic social grooming (as in everyday pleasantries, which form a large part of our language output): indeed, word meanings can only be truly evaluated by setting them firmly in the social context in which they were uttered. I stand by this solemnly, yet it in no way invalidates Premack's exemplary research – provided, of course, it is viewed correctly: not as an exercise in man-ape communication but a means of launching a singularly effective probe into the little-explored ape mind.

Mounin's arrows were aimed squarely at Sarah, but it was Lana who effectively deflected them. The kernel of Moulin's critique might best be left in his original words:

> In October 1972, Sarah did not yet ask questions. If she had it would have been an astounding fact, not because interrogative transformation is a universal, but because it would have shown that communication with Sarah could really function in both ways, with the ape acting as the initial transmitter (without the influence of an experimenter). Premack did not realize the crucial importance of this fact.

Lana too was caged, surviving under somewhat similar "sterile" conditions as Sarah, worse perhaps, since she often had only a computer with which to converse. Yet on Monday, 6 May 1974, Lana startled Tim Gill by turning the tables.

Without warning she asked *him* a question. In fact, Tim was goading her, holding out a box baited with sugar-coated candies. Lana did not know the word "box", so she scurried through her repertoire, twice requesting "this can", followed equally ineffectually by "this bowl". Frustrated in her efforts, she cut Tim short before he could again palm her off with an empty bows, finally demanding *Tim give Lana name-of this*. From then on conversation took a predictable turn.

Tim: *Box name-of this.*
Lana: *Yes* (adopting Tim's tactic when *she* got something right – proving that role reversal was pretty much complete).
　　　Tim give Lana this box (which he did).
Tim: *Yes* (she tore it open to extract the candies).[17]

It happened again that afternoon. Tim baited a cup, and she immediately asked for the receptacle's name specifically so she could request it to be given her. Without being trained, Lana had spontaneously assumed the human role of question master. Commenting in 1977, Rumbaugh and Gill admitted, "Although we had asked her hundreds of times to name things she already knew, we had not taught her to ask us for the names of things. She had apparently abstracted from the former experience", donning her inquisitor's cap to prove that once again chimpanzees could confound the cynics.

"One of our initial goals was to engage a chimpanzee in conversation," confided Rumbaugh and Gill. Lana had been groomed for just this, of course; by 1974 she seemed ready, and her teachers began laying aside schemes for luring her into conversation. As it transpired "these all proved unnecessary. It was Lana, on her own initiative, who instituted conversation with us, composing an appropriate request through use of components of stock sentences. She did so on 6 March 1974, in the late afternoon." The dramatic flair might be excused. They had reason to be well pleased with their prodigy, as she hammered out her first novel utterance from cannibalised phrases and familiar words. Tim was standing outside her cage, leisurely sipping a Coke, with Lana watching enviously and, as always, desperate to share whatever was going. Her own machine's obstinate refusal to deliver a Coke naturally accentuated her craving. "Lana looked at Tim," recalled Rumbaugh and Gill, straining to be fair, "and either by a highly improbable sequence or with comprehension asked *Lana drink this out-of room period*."[18] Looking uncomfortably like a tortured scrap in English, her linguistic conglomeration deserves considerable respect – if, that is, it was not a lucky pot-shot. Grammatically, it was perfect. She seemed to be saying "Please let me out to share your Coke," and in the event Tim was only too happy to comply. He hurried to fetch the others, invested another 15 cents in the Coke dispenser, and repeated the episode. Nonchalantly, he stood sipping his Coke; once more Lana tried her empty vendor, then came back with her stunner: "Could she come out to drink this?" *Drink what period*, teased Tim, provoking her urgent rejoinder *Lana drink COKE out-of room period*.

Lana had welded this sentence from components of three stock expressions, giving to each a novel twist. *This* she had picked up almost incidentally, by way of her teacher's constant cross-questioning "What is the name of this?", a sentence she now gladly cannibalised for useful parts. *Out-of room* was one of her staples, usually in the form of *Tim carry Lana out-of room*, and now switched to a novel context. She had long been familiar with the noun *drink* – or, at least, what everybody took to be a noun. But *Lana drink Coke*, a string of three nouns, was Yerkish nonsense, so her trainers charitably assumed that she had manufactured a new verb. But isn't that a case of bending over backwards to make Lana's creation respectable? She might have understood it as a noun. Then again, she might always have seen *drink* as an action – or we might be quibbling about grammatical niceties that simply have no fine distinction in her mind. Grammar is not important. What is crucial is whether her statement was *intentionally* appropriate. Was this a lucky concoction that just happened to make sense to humans (after a bit of readjustment)? Or did she really intend this message? – and was she *aware* of what she was writing?

Between the summer of 1974 and the following winter Lana began manipulating her trainers. Her food vendor was filled from behind, so she sought to guide the technician by demanding *move milk* [or chow] *behind room* (meaning "take it round the back and fill the vending machine"). But this left far too much leeway for human error, and by January she was explicitly ordering *Tim put milk in machine*, to leave no excuse for his faltering in such urgent matters. Tricks to elicit Lana's linguistic novelties were indeed rife, and they left a frustrated ape groping for an explicit order that even the most incompetent human could carry out. In an attempt to outwit her, Tim often carried out her order to the letter: asked to put "chow" in the vendor, he did just that – one pellet at a time. Laboriously punching in her request for "chow" and being rewarded with a solitary piece pushed Lana into a novel move to beat Tim's stinginess. "What is the name of that you're holding?" she inquired. Tim told her a bowl. Right, she said triumphantly, "take the entire bowlful round the back and put it in". Or, as she expressed it in Yerkish *You move bowl of chow* [*behind room*].

She refused to be rattled by human lies. Consider this eight-minute clash with Tim, who was intent upon perpetrating a grand deception. The snippet was recorded by the teletype on 11 June 1975. Lana needed chow, and Tim deliberately filled the vendor with cabbage. Five times in two minutes she asked for chow, each time Tim insisted that it was in the machine. Realising this could have gone on all night, Lana changed tactics.

Lana: *Chow in machine?*
Tim: (lying) *Yes.*
Lana: (exasperated) *No chow in machine.*
Tim: *What in machine?*
Lana: *Cabbage in machine.*
Tim: *Yes cabbage in machine.*
Lana: (not settling for any monkey business) *You move cabbage out of machine.*[19]

Straw Parrots

Exactly a century before the Gardners' opening shot in *Science*, elderly Charles Lyell (who egged Darwin on to publish the *Origin* even though he himself was never able, as he put it, "to go the whole orang": to accept human reason as the evolutionary outcome of the ape's irrationalism) reminded Darwin in a letter "that a parrot endowed with the powers of Shakespeare might dictate the 'Midsummer Night's Dream', and that Michael Angelo, if he had had no better hand than belongs to some of the higher apes, might have executed the statue of Lorenzo de' Medici".[20] That was in 1869. His point was this: the parrot's chatter is meaningless, only by mating that talkative beak to a rational brain would it miraculously transform into a creative language. In Darwin's day, the ape shared the parrot's predicament. In fact, papers on ape anatomy were strewn with a word not much used by psychologists today – the ape was "irrational". It is a peculiar word, giving us a feeling for the preDarwinian image of nature split asunder. Rationalism was the spark of divinity which brought us the promise of symbolism and culture. Early Victorians, armed with a set of prior expectations, found the ape a shamefully benighted brute, incapable equally of rational or moral action. Every age sees the ape in its own distorting mirror, judged by contemporary prejudices (as Harvard biologist Stephen Jay Gould recently wrote, " 'truth' as preached by scientists often turns out to be no more than prejudice inspired by prevailing social and political beliefs"[21].) We see the ape as we expect to see it: it was "irrational", dumb and devoid of thought before Darwin's day; pleasantly revamped, even logical and conceptual in powers today. Assuming the ape itself has not transmuted into a rational being during this last century, that leaves a profound shift in our own horizons. Testing ape minds, we can never excise the human factor in the results. History *must* have taught us this much. Of course, ideologies are as evident today as they were yesterday; it would be stupid to assume that they ceased with Darwin's feverishly Godly age. The Gardners are out to prove a point, an anti-Chomskian and anti-uniqueness point. This is made the more blatantly obvious by their contrary assertions that they *never* let prior theory colour their fact finding.

Armed with new ideologies, mankind incessantly manoeuvres round the ape, determined to expose it in its "true" light. Lyell's theological imperative has long since vanished, taking with it the rigid distinction between "rational" and "irrational". Lyell's parrot, however, lives on, and this worries the Gardners. They see Lyell's spectre in Chomsky's chauvinism, especially when the father of psycholinguistics declares that human language "is based on entirely different principles" from animal communication.[22] The Gardners satirise this as the "Straw Parrot Problem": for decades, indeed centuries, the issue of language uniqueness was settled by interminable proofs that parrots, the Earth's only other talkers, were mimicking. The straw parrots blew over in the constant wind, leaving man unique. At last behaviourists grasped the nettle and gave Washoe half a chance to prove her language potential. Now, insist the Gardners, the question is no longer *whether* apes can use human language, but "how much human language, how soon, or how far can they go?"

To better understand their apes' needs, the Gardners flew to Tanzania, to study the wild chimpanzees in Jane Goodall's Gombe Stream Reserve. They returned convinced that the one-chimpanzee learning environment was too artificial. The Gombe apes live in collective matriarchies, with offspring able to watch and learn from a succession of elder brothers and sisters. To simulate these conditions, the Gardners now planned to introduce a newborn chimpanzee into the 'family' every year or two, allowing it to grow surrounded by experienced ape elders. Pili had died of leukemia late in October 1975, and infant Tatu was brought in from the Oklahoma Institute for Primate Studies to take his place. On 6 August 1976 four-day-old Dar joined the family. If communication is the primary objective, as Mounin states, then the Gardners had created an ideal environment for eliciting signs. And, as expected, the infants learned their "language" quickly, outstripping Washoe in vocabulary count at each age. Yet far and away the most intriguing observation was made in 1976, and it promises to take the furore over "language" on to a wholly new plane. Chimpanzees are inveterate doodlers. Their paintings have even been exhibited, and although art critics noted pongid preferences for certain shapes or colours ape art never achieved more than novelty value. No one dreamt of suggesting that these abstracts might represent the apes' world. The issue suddenly came alive when three-year-old Moja one day executed four flowing lines in chalk – then stopped. Usually her scrawls were a disaster, but not this one. The trainer urged her to continue, but she threw down the chalk and signed *finish*. Routinely he asked her what it was. She replied *bird*. It was too good to leave there. The Gardners asked her to draw a berry. She picked up an orange pen and deftly executed a few paraboic strokes that would defy mathematical description. Later she was asked to name it, and she reminded them that it was a *berry*.

The Fates have suffered cruelly from the Gardners' provocations. Perhaps that is why one cannot help but admire this husband-and-wife team. Yet academic sympathy for them seems to be at its lowest ebb. By 1978 the linguistic air had thickened rather than cleared. Once the three schools – based round Washoe, Sarah and Lana – drew at least a semblance of moral support from one another. Now they appear wider apart and more antagonistic then ever before. The Gardners dismiss almost out of hand the claims of the lexigram schools that have "sprung up" in Washoe's wake. Despite all the "paraphernalia", the electronic gadgetry and the "elaborate software", argued the Gardners in 1978, Premack and the Rumbaughs have fallen headlong "into some of the worst of the classical pitfalls". This was not guaranteed to strengthen the cause of unity. But then where was the unity? All three schools were by now arguing different propositions – which left the Gardners (by their own estimation) holding the real linguistic baby.

In their eyes, Premack's position was totally invalidated by that unwarranted English gloss he put on the outcome of forced-choice tests. (It was little use Premack counting on the Rumbaughs for support. Even Sarah's apple test fails to unduly impress them, since she was presented with a choice of two possible answers, and had only to choose one.) Sarah's ability boiled down to little more than rote learning, and there was nothing fantastic (or linguistic) in that. In fact, a well-drilled rhesus monkey "could have passed all of Premack's transfer tests at an average level he required".[23] Premack might agree with the Gardners, only he is less likely to see this as an indictment of Sarah than a vindacation of his belief in a linguistic continuum stretching through the primates. According to the Gardners, Lana had achieved no more than Sarah. They wondered if she had the faintest idea of her lexigram meanings.

In retaliation, the Rumbaughs began pouring out their own doubts about the Gardners' claims. Was Washoe doing anything qualitatively different from Viki, whose iconic pointing and gesturing (she would often act out demands) got the message across? Iconic gestures, like patting the head (*hat*) or begging (*gimme*), might simply be a context-bound imitation of an object or action. Was Washoe just going through the motions, or had she really comprehended "the nature, function, and symbolic power of the ASL signs . . ."?[24] The Rumbaughs answered their own question. Premack's and the Gardners' results were "interesting", even "suggestive", but presented little by way of evidence to suggest that "Washoe or Sarah are employing symbolically-mediated, abstract communication similar to that involved in human language".

Teaching four new conscripts the rudiments of Lana's "language", the Rumbaughs and Sally Boysen, who was working with them, began to realise that the apes were progressing through levels of understanding of each word. Hence at a primitive stage of comprehension, the chimpanzee might correctly type (or sign) a "word", while being totally unaware of its symbolic nature. Raw recruits Austin and Sherman were being trained specifically to test whether chimpanzees really could communicate symbolically *with one another*, via Lana's keyboard. This could finally settle some hotly disputed issues, proving that apes can understand the context-free symbolic nature of lexigrams and can use them to transmit specific information. The planned procedure was to teach Austin and Sherman tool names (*key*, *straw* and *coin*) and then give one a tool-kit and another access to food in a locked box, covered cup or vending machine. The Rumbaughs' course of action seemed deceptively easy. In fact, teaching the tool's name proved to be the major stumbling block – causing them to look afresh at the process of "word" acquisition.

The Gardners had written off Lana as a none-too-magnificent rote learner, but matters were not so simple. The new apes found it excruciatingly difficult to associate the lexigram *key* with a key, even though the Rumbaughs tried to drum it in rote fashion. However, show the apes a box being unlocked to extract food, then make them punch *key* when they demanded a key to follow suit, and they quickly got the hang. Paradoxically, Austin and Sherman could now correctly request a key, *but they still could not name it.* At this "primitive level" of understanding, the lexigram *key* conjured up no Platonic Ideal of keyness for the apes. They understood it not as a symbol, but an initiator of events; punching *key* on the computer console was a ritual act which began the process leading to the opening of the food box. As such, the word *key* was still linked to one highly specific context. Of course, when the apes needed to open a locked door to reach more food, they knew what they wanted – a key – but they did not know what to ask for. The door key, after all, wasn't their *key*, a lexigram which set in motion a different train of events.

At this stage, the lexigram still could not substitute in context-free communication for the absent key. Tied to the food box ritual, it had minimal symbolic potential. But Rumbaugh's team now taught Austin and Sherman that the door key was also a *key*. The apes began stripping away the superfluous attributes of *key*, like food boxes, locks and the act of unlocking, and the word slowly assumed its recognisable guise of "keyness". This vastly increased its symbolic potential, permitting it to deputise for the absent key in communication.

The simple act of naming is a momentously complex event, one which chimpanzees using Lana's keyboard or Washoe's signs seem to have mastered. The Rumbaugh's returned to their original experiment, and shortly Austin and Sherman were answering one another's requests with appropriate tools. Rectifying mistakes showed how keenly aware they were of the situation:

> on one trial Sherman requested *key* erroneously when he needed a wrench. He then watched carefully as Austin searched the tool kit. When Austin started to pick up the key, Sherman looked over his shoulder toward his keyboard, and when he noticed the word *key*, which he had left displayed on the projectors, he rushed back to the keyboard, depressed *wrench*, and tapped the projectors to draw Austin's attention to the new symbol he had just transmitted. Austin looked up, dropped the key, picked up the wrench, and handed it to Sherman.[25]

The Rumbaughs had already set up their idols, knowing them destined to fall. If chimpanzees could switch roles as tool-requester and tool-provider, the Rumbaughs wrote, "if they could comprehend the function and *intentionality* of their communication . . . then, by all definitions of human culture, they would surely have taken a large step".

5

Stretching Between Worlds

A pe symbolism is the visible tip of the iceberg. To be able creatively to exploit object names requires an immense cognitive substructure; a rearrangement of the mechanics of the mind to throw open a profoundly new window on the world. No longer can we reassuringly imagine dumb brutes tied to the immediate present, tyrannised by nature, at her instant beck and call. It is even hazardous to deny the ape an imaginary world, where reason can run through its strategies, devising the right course of action before committing itself to the real world. That was once our prerogative; it was also the basis of a 'transcendental' morality. Hence reason could neither be relinquished nor shared by those wanting to keep the afterlife a species-specific haven, even though comparative anatomy cries out against man's aristocratic gall. The ape can distance itself from the concrete world, as Sarah elegantly demonstrated by her analysis of the mouth-watering blue plastic triangle. Such abstraction is simply the geometrical space in which we reason.

Faces of Reality

With remarkable timing, to coincide with the announcement of Washoe's first words, experimental results published in *Science* for 1970 suggested that apes were capable of *cross-modal matching*. A few years before, monkeys had failed this trial, and though apes had never been tested, hopes were not high for their succeeding. Yet they survived this baptism by fire, unexpectedly opening up a second front, thus making sense of Washoe's achievement and shedding important light on the ape mind. Cross-modal matching might best be explained by way of illustration. Each sense feeds raw data into a specific area of the cerebral cortex concerned with its interpretation; here a unique representation of reality *as scanned by that one sense* can be fashioned. An orange can be felt, seen, smelled, tasted and so on; each of these sense organs then relays the information to its own cortical association area where respective sense-dimensions of the orange are analysed. 'Reality' as interpreted by individual senses thus emerges in remarkably diverse guises. Indeed, a sensuous infinity separates the feel and sight of apparently the same object.

In man (and, it was assumed until 1970, in man exclusively) the neocortex collates these disparate representations of reality. It pools the stimuli from the separate sensory channels, each clinging to its own reality. Some psychologists even envisage it coalescing them into a single, supramodal or unified representation, metaphorically disembodied in that it is divorced from the limitations of any one sense. One is Richard Davenport, a psychologist concerned with the Lana project in Atlanta, Georgia, who also leads the investigation into the possibility of chimpanzee cross-modal matching. This he defined in 1977. It requires, he explained:

> the derivation of a modality-independent "representation," cognition, or concept of a stimulus or event. Animals that can have the same or similar "representations," regardless of the means of peripheral reception, possess a great advantage in coping with the complex demands of living . . .[1]

The advantage of a disembodied 'whole' representation lies in recall being total, regardless of the sense doing the detecting; merely smelling an orange conjures up the taste in our mouths. It is as though stimuli channelled from one sense call up ghosts from all the others, a process mediated by some neocortical crossroads in the brain's parietal lobe.

Norman Geschwind, the James Jackson Putnam Professor of Neurology at Harvard Medical School, writing a lengthy report on neurological problems for the journal *Brain* in 1965 – long before apes again became a fighting issue – suggested a location for the neocortical crossroads. In man, the cortical association areas of the brain, each responsible for interpreting the senses of vision, touch and hearing, are clustered round and plugged into a structure known as the angular gyrus. Geschwind dubs this the "association area of association areas". It was also the likely neuroanatomical location for human cross-modal association. Seemingly, here was an explanation of man's unique ability in this respect, as Geschwind realised: "The situation in man is not simply a slightly more complex version of the situation present in the higher primates but depends on the introduction of a new anatomical structure, the human inferior parietal lobule, which includes the angular and supramarginal gyri . . ."[2] A search of the literature suggested that it certainly was not present in macaque monkeys, and even in "the higher apes these areas are present only in rudimentary form". Pinpointing this neuroanatomical site in the human cortex, the picture could be completed. Information from any sensory association area was relayed to the neighbouring angular gyrus, there to be collated with sensory information from the other centres, in order I suspect to build a supramodal composite.

Before Geschwind's study, the world stood on its head; sure enough, object names were thought to be related to cross-modal association, but there was never so blatant a neuropsychological chicken and egg situation. In fact, it had been taken for granted that object names themselves mediated between the senses. The word was a rallying point for individual senses; a verbal hat-rack on which to hang all manner of toppers, only to discover that they fitted the same head. It boiled down to the claim that the evolution of speech was an essential prerequisite for sense association. Since man could speak, or so the reasoning went, only he could cross-modally associate. It all smacked rather disconcertingly of Max Müller's dogged insistence on the foundation of thought in language – which made animals so many mindless automatons, and human consciousness a shining light on an otherwise barren planet.

Geschwind put the world to rights; he too accepted cross-modal association as being implicated in object-naming (though not without being criticised for it), but cleared up the confusion by insisting that naming depended on an ability to associate the senses, not vice versa. Man, he points out, learns to associate an object, say, a banana, with the word "banana"; he can in effect link a visual to an auditory stimulus, a sight to a sound. But the association *is* learned, because the name is quite arbitrary, simply a collection of sounds, and only convention

links the sounds *ba-na-na* to the yellow tropical fruit. Thus man or
ape must be able to link its senses before symbolism is possible. Geschwind was quite adamant on the point, italicising for good measure:
*"it cannot be argued that the ability to form cross-modal associations depends
on already having speech*; rather we must say that *the ability to acquire
speech has as a prerequisite the ability to form cross-modal associations"*.[3]
The emphasis could not be stronger.

Thus it appears that symbol-wielding apes should be able to associate
their sense impressions; certainly, Lana and Sarah learn to identify
lexigrams with worldly referents, Washoe and Koko link gestures with
objects, and many apes reared in the home understand speech (even if
they cannot produce it): Ally, for example, can switch freely between
spoken English, ASL and real objects. So Geschwind gave logical
reasons why cross-modal association preceded symbolism, but he
said nothing of cross-modal *matching*, which is something different.
This is not a matter of associating diverse objects – words and their
referents – but diverse perceptions of the *same* object (which need not
be learnt, since there is no arbitrariness). An ape shown a cube, say,
must be able to match it to a cube as it is felt hidden behind a screen. In
the mid-1960s, Geschwind was less concerned with this; nonetheless, as
he admitted recently, he "did not believe that cross-modal *matching*
need have anything to do with language at all. It is difficult to see why
the ability to recognize a cube tactilely after having seen it has any
relationship to language."[4] Here I take my leave of Geschwind, since
I believe that cross-modal matching may be important, if not crucial,
in symbol acquisition. Any ape which can recognise the *same* object
regardless of the detecting sense probably has the power to build a disembodied mental representation. This strikes me as essential for symbolism; one needs some sort of free-floating supramodal 'image', divorced
from any one sense, before a name tag can be hung on it. The linguistic
upshot, with an economy guaranteed to please Ockham, is that only
one name is needed per object. The alternative is too chaotic to contemplate, a world where an everyday item is buried beneath a plethora of
symbols, each oblivious to the other's existence, and where dictionaries
are five times too long.

With the first signs of Washoe came the expectation that sooner or
later chimpanzee cross-modal matching would be detected, despite
disbelief that apes could usurp this human faculty, and in face of that
apparent absence of the angular gyrus.

Prior to 1970 the odds were stacked impossibly against apes, taking the form of three mutually reinforcing facts, looking as cast-iron as Newtonian physics and as reassuring as aristocratic privilege. Transfer of stimuli across modes had never been demonstrated in apes, nor of course in monkeys (which bolstered prevailing notions that nonhuman primates were tied very much to the moment, and to each separate sense; unable to distance themselves from reality, they missed the world as a whole). Further, ape brains seemed to lack a crucial structure; admittedly not so grand as that notorious convolution of the posterior lobe – the hippocampus – by which Richard Owen tried to separate humanity from the rest of creation over a century ago. (T. H. Huxley located the offending hippocampus in the ape's brain, then gleefully demolished Owen with a ferocity which set all London agog.[5]) Latter-day debates lack that moral earnestness, and the angular gyrus was passed uncritically as a peculiarly human structure without thereby implying man's transcendental uniqueness (the burning issue, of course, at heart of the tooth-and-claw antagonism between Owen and young Huxley). Lastly, no one doubted that language was uniquely human, which in light of man's cross-modal abilities seemed only too obvious. Whatever strange one-dimensional thoughts apes might summon up, they could never have approached the lofty heights of human logic and reason.

In April 1970, walls began crumbling. Richard Davenport and Charles M. Rogers, his co-worker at the Atlanta primate centre, published preliminary findings in *Science* on chimp and orang-utan abilities to integrate across sensory modalities. Their apparatus required the compliant ape to view one object and feel (but not see) two others, one of which matched the visible object. To earn his reward the ape had simply to cross-match, and so as in no way to trick the ape, such obviously different items as coil springs, paper clamps and door handles were employed. "Compliant" was the operative word. Davenport and Rogers started with eleven two- to four-year-old apes, but four chimpanzees and both gorillas simply failed to see any merit in the exercise whatever, and repeatedly threw temper tantrums when not joyously smashing up the apparatus. They were excused. The remaining five (two orangs and three chimps) initially performed at 'chance' levels until it dawned on them just what was wanted. (Since only those random choices that accidentally cross-matched were rewarded, the apes quickly developed the knack.) Now performances shot up to over ninety per cent accuracy. It seemed unequivocal, although results are rarely so in science. For every scientist alive there are ten critics; to play the game to win, one has to anticipate the harshest criticism, thus deftly pulling the rug from under potential detractors. Since the tests numbered thousands, some well worn door handles, drill points and coil springs were incessantly shuffled and reused, which left Davenport and Rogers wide open to the criticism that the apes were now well-conditioned into matching the same recurring objects. Sticklers for precaution, Davenport and Rogers sprang a set of unfamiliar items on the three remaining apes (one orang was gainfully employed elsewhere, one chimp had died in "experimental surgery", a sour reminder of the social role of the ape in human society). Presented once and only once with each of forty unique combinations, the primate survivors were tested to see if they "had grasped the essential nature of the problem . . ."[6] Evidently, they had, because scores stabilised well above chance at some seventy-five per cent accuracy.

The following year Davenport and Rogers made matters harder, switching photographs for three-dimensional objects in the viewer. Not that that rattled the participating orang and two chimps one jot: a glimpse was enough for the correct match to be made, regardless of whether photographs were colour or black & white, and scores rising to ninety per cent accuracy were chalked up. Impressive evidence that apes, like man, form "modality independent" representations of worldly items, and without the mediation of words: it was a triumphant vindication.

Moreover, by way of an unexpected spin-off, the Atlanta psychologists had demonstrated "that apes can perceive a photograph of an object *at first sight*".[7] Nor were these primates confusing photographs with reality; they interpreted them as pictorial representations, just as we do. Viki, the Hayes' humanised ape, for example, once held up a photograph of a glass of iced tea to inform a visitor that she was thirsty, while dragging him towards the kitchen. She clearly was not confused: the photograph was an undrinkable likeness of the real thing in the refrigerator. This is not to say that chimps cannot become as emotional over photographs as we do. (In fact, considering human behaviour towards iconic pictures, which are not only adored, but actually *kissed*, one might be excused for wondering whether we sometimes lose sight of the distinction ourselves.) Lucy positively ogles the naked men in *Playgirl*, and during oestrus evidently enjoys sexual fantasies about them. And Premack currently tells this engaging story of Sarah:

> Recently, when shown a videotape of a TV program on wild orangutans, Sarah . . . watched with uninterrupted attention for almost 30 minutes. When a young male was captured in a net, Sarah hooted and threw pieces of paper at the screen, seemingly aimed at the animal's captors. The trainer, watching with Sarah, reached up and touched the image of the captured animal on the screen; Sarah shuddered and turned a wildly startled face to the trainer.[8]

But we cry at such historical nonsense as *Gone with the Wind*, and may even take more violent action akin to Sarah's. One incensed anarchist, to draw a remarkable parallel with Sarah's antics, launched a rather appropriate beef curry at the screen during the London première of John Wayne's flag-waving *Green Berets*. Such blows for freedom might have met Sarah's wholehearted approval. Probably, the perpetrator was no more nor less confused than Sarah by what is real and what celluloid. This is not to deny our uncanny ability to submerge in fantasy worlds: celluloid analogues of our mental creations, equally horrific and sublime. In fact the mental wanderings made possible by abstract thought are our proudest possessions, the end product of sophisticated displacement. Our reasoning strategy for survival depends on the very unreality of the situation; in our imagination we can play the world, and if we lose, as philosopher Karl Popper once said, our thoughts and theories will die in our stead. Sarah enjoys a rousing movie; Lana spends lonely evenings absorbed in her gorilla epic, even though she must by now know every line by heart. Rather than suggesting a befuddled ape irrevocably confused by this trick two-dimensional reality, movie buffs among the apes are exhibiting a remarkable capacity for human-style displacement.

A stream of papers since 1970 have consolidated ape cross-modal integration, and opposition to the wily pongid interloper has withered away. But before we concur too hastily with psychologist William Mason that "apes and man have entered a cognitive domain that sets them apart from all other primates" ' we would do well to note that in 1975 experimental psychologists at Oxford University detected the first signs of cross-modal matching in a rhesus monkey. By 1977, capuchins – the organ grinder's monkey – at London's Institute of Psychiatry had joined the fold,[10] proving it ultimately unwise, if not downright hazardous, to draw hard and fast lines across nature: we are probably dealing with variable thresholds, not gaping chasms. If anything is gaping, it is the hole through that shabby argument over cross-modal ability which insists, as Davenport related, "that only humans are neurologically equipped for the process". Clearly, apes are too, lest we be dealing with a neuromiracle more marvellous than Victorian explanations of free will.

Usually, human cerebral hemispheres are lateralised in respect of function, with language abilities coordinated by a region in the left temporal lobe. Functional asymmetry (such as this) *without* some tangible anatomical correlate has always proved depressingly irritating; indeed, it often drove preDarwinian scientists into taking transcendental escape routes to explain nature's mismatch. For example, shocked that man and orang looked so alike, and equally baffled that only one could, or would, speak (it was sometimes suspected that orangs deliberately remained dumb to escape servitude), Buffon in the late eighteenth century naturally concluded that man's "body is not the most essential part of his nature".[11] So it came as some relief in 1968 to hear that Norman Geschwind and Walter Levitsky had detected a visible, structural dichotomy between the human hemispheres within this language region – which turns out to be expanded on the left (language) side.[12] Using the latest "noninvasive computerized tomographic techniques", in the terms of the trade, the architectural disparity is becoming clearer: in post-mortem examination of brain sections it can now be detected right down to the thirty-one-week foetus stage.[13]

That the neuroanatomical basis for the ape's cross-modal competence has escaped detection comes as no surprise, considering that even a cerebral asymmetry of the ape brain remained unnoticed until 1975. Having detected a structural rearrangement of one hemisphere in the human brain's language region, Geschwind took up Marjorie LeMay's suggestion and turned to apes. LeMay was a radiologist at Massachusetts General Hospital, fresh from her studies of the 'speech' areas on the endocast of the Neanderthal fossil. In 1975 she and Geschwind took the brains of sixty-nine primates, including twelve orangs, nine chimps and seven gorillas, to plot the course of the diagnostic Sylvian fissure, which cuts like some familiar gorge through the featureless badlands of the temporal lobe. In man, the longer Sylvian fissure stretching almost horizontally across the face of the left temporal lobe marks out (among other structures) the expanded Wernicke's language area. Ape brain topography in this region compares favourably. The hemispheres are likewise asymmetrical, though to a lesser degree than in man. Moreover, the asymmetry seems to vary among species; surprisingly, it is most marked, not in the chimpanzee, but in the orang-utan, to the extent that Geschwind and LeMay suggest that we best look to the orang to "cast important light on the evolution of handedness [the dominant right hand being controlled by the left hemisphere in man and perhaps ape] or language".[14]

The surface sulci of the temporal region follow the same patterns in man and ape, the latter sharing that longer horizontal convolution on the left side, marking out an expanded "language" cortex. Still, however, no internal structural differences between the orang's left and right temporal lobe have been located, although this may only be a matter of time. Mapping is pretty much in infancy, our charts of the ape brain are far from the subtlety of even Ptolemy's *Mappi Mundi*. But definite patterns are emerging, and certain expectations are leading us along a dimly lit path. Early in 1978 Geschwind speculated on the neuro-anatomy lying at root of the ape's cross-modal ability. He admitted "that we have not done studies specifically in the brains of the great apes," but continued, "my guess is that one will find that the area which eventually becomes the angular gyrus in humans is already beginning to expand in the great apes as compared with the monkeys". This was shown, of course, by that Sylvian fissure, subtly deflected and stretched across the left lobe, "almost certainly" pushed out of place, in Gesch-wind's opinion, by "the expansion of the angular gyrus region". He concluded, "My guess would therefore be that one would find, for example in the chimpanzee, an area of some size which was similar in its cellular architecture to the angular gyrus region in humans."[15]

It opens up intensely exciting possibilities, foremost being the prospect for language-training the Socratically-sad orang. But it comes down like a mallet atop the sensitive scientific cranium, bringing on that nagging headache, the sort welcomed with masochistic delight by scientists: Why, in a wild orang-utan which apparently uses no symbolism, has the "language" area of the left cerebrum expanded?

Thoughtful Mutes

In 1972 the McGill linguist John Macnamara put forward a refreshing thesis of language learning by children. He believes that for an infant to extract the same meaning from two such syntactically clashing commands as *Give me a kiss* and *Kiss me* it must necessarily ignore sentence structure. Since they mean the same while being couched quite differently, the meaning must be got across additionally, for example, by the mother holding her cheek to the baby's mouth. The infant shuns confusing and sometimes conflicting sentence structures and homes in on the mother's meaning from social cues. Macnamara might argue that the infant only 'hears' meaning, which explains why preschool children are so quick on the uptake, despite the syntactic pandemonium confronting them.

Unlike psycholinguists who insist that early words are means to an end, or pragmatic devices to manipulate parents, Macnamara's case "rests on the assumption that in the period when infants begin to learn language, their thought is more developed than their language". If children grasp meaning before syntax, they must already possess some interpretive frame of reference. A one-year-old, in fact, has begun classifying his world, exploring his relationship to anything within clutching distance; and once his conceptual apparatus is stabilised, he is equipped to interpret words. Of course, the ape is too; but with its different social and psychological background, it has a peculiarly pongid frame of reference. Hence it 'hears' an ape meaning. It absorbs a word only if it is relevant to the ape conceptual world.

Macnamara assumed that words and sentences were not giving children new concepts, these were simply being 'mapped on'; which is precisely the position taken by Premack. Writing for *Scientific American* in 1972, Ann and David Premack adopted this Piagetian line, arguing that the form of the word, whether plastic disc or manual sign, was not important.

> The important thing is to shape the language to fit the infor-
> mation-processing capacities of the chimpanzee. *To a large extent*
> *teaching language to an animal is simply mapping out the conceptual*

structures the animal already possesses. By using a system of naming that suits the chimpanzee we hope to find out more about its conceptual world.[17]

This is the *raison d'être* of ape 'language'; by teaching chimpanzees symbol-usage, we can gauge the type of pre-existent concepts and logical relations embedded deep within the pongid mind. In this, Premack has met with unprecedented success.

Coming down to specifics, Macnamara felt that the spontaneous use of *and*, as well as *or*, *all* and *more*, which humans may acquire as early as twenty-four months, reflects the equivalent logical operations emerging in the child's mind. Hearing *and* did not suddenly suggest to the child a radical new way of ordering its thoughts. "Indeed the only possibility of his learning such a word would seem to be if he experienced the need for it in his own thinking . . ." So perhaps we can map these words on to ape minds to uncover equivalent logical operations. After little more than an introduction to *more* and *to*, employed in their correct context by her trainer Tim, Lana was spontaneously demanding *Tim give ball to Lana* and *You put more bread in machine.* "More", of course, meant extra rations and was immediately extended in range to meet every culinary contingency. By stretching words in difficult situations, Lana could subtly bend their meaning. *No* was taught her as one possible answer to the question "Is the window open?". Having learned that response, she demonstrated her comprehension in a dramatic manner. When technicians 'stole' a favourite food from her vending machine, the enraged ape, hair bristling, thumped *No!* into her computer console. Then again, on being misinformed that her vendor was well-stocked with monkey food she pulled up Tim smartly with *No chow in machine.* Apparently she recognises the common negative element to "The window is not open" and "Do not take that", even though they are embedded in radically distinct contexts.

And yet, through all this and despite the marvellous word-bending ability, Lana's conversations rarely rise above the gastronomic, except perhaps when she requests a movie or a tickle. As Rumbaugh and Gill conclude on a downbeat note, "Lana's persistence in conversation has been strictly pragmatic – once the desired incentive has been achieved, the conversation *ends*!!" Rumbaugh and Gill extrapolate from Lana's insights to the limits of ape abilities, suggesting that they might stop well short of the potent human 'will to know'.

. . . Lana has never initiated conversations to "broaden her horizons," if you will. She has never asked for the names of things unless they held some food or drink that she apparently wanted; she has never "discussed" spontaneously the attributes of things in her world nor really ever capitalized upon conversation to extend her access to information about things. It might be that these limitations are artefacts of her training to date; perhaps she will do so someday, but at this time we are doubtful if chimpanzees will ever be noted for their exploiting linguistic-type skills to request additional information that might enhance their broad understanding of their world and how things in it work. We believe that this is an important point that might reliably differentiate language utilization by the child from the ape – perhaps the ape will use its language-type skills to the most pragmatic ends (as to obtain things), whereas the child readily goes beyond that use of language to learn about the nature of things, how they work; in short, the nature of its everyday world.[18]

There may never be an Ape Physics, based on pongid perspectives of reality, which is a shame. Of course, it is true that Lana, like Sarah, was not conditioned to air her thoughts on life. Still, it could be argued, neither are children, and that does not stop them growing into Darwins and Einsteins. Yet latent potential and social conditions favour only one child in a million; it is largely his or her word that is passed down like some cultural gem, simply polished and admired by the rest of us.

One ape in a million, the genius, might yet work wonders with words, exploiting this godsent gift for more than just filling his stomach; but a stimulating social environment is a must to coax out any latent potential. And in this respect the chimpanzees seconded to rival teaching schools fare better. Rumbaugh's programme was not designed specifically to encourage Lana to "broaden her horizons", since her horizon was invariably four walls and a computer.

Ally, apparently, delights in commenting on the world; but then his is a free-wheeling ASL environment, not a prison predicament. A boisterous male, he is now about seven, and still at Oklahoma under Roger Fouts' care. Not being caged or computer-bound, he is less pre-occupied with food demands, and quite able to floor everybody with his disarming comments. On smelling tobacco smoke one day as Fouts lit a pipe, Ally beckoned another trainer, George, and signed "George smell Roger". Ally's utterances have been assessed by Lyn Miles of the University of Connecticut, with a view to comparing them to those of a three-year-old child; but in the process, her analysis has shown up a quite underrated component of Ally's conversation. He is perfectly able to appraise physical events without any gustatory overtones. In fact, in free-ranging conversation outside the rigid question-answer test sessions, one quarter of Ally's language topics revolve round the environment, his health (complaining about his shoe pinching) and the peculiarity of humans ("George smell Roger"). Even at three a child's talk has an air of rationality about it. "Ally's discourse was similarly striking," commented Miles, "and contained long conversational exchanges about various objects including environmental referents such as birds flying overhead, and a cat stalking a frog."[19]

Causal Inference

The overriding advantage of the Lana-Sarah system was that it allows a deeper penetration of cognitive powers. Under Premack's tutelage, Sarah revealed unexpected abilities; the sort, we pride ourselves, which stand as the backbone of Western science. Since Greek cosmologists departed from Egyptian tradition and looked behind heavenly effects to their planetary causes, cause-and-effect has been a potent means of material explanation of the universe. If abstraction is the geometrical space in which we reason, causal relations are our logical means of traversing that space to unseen regions.

If language does map pre-existent concepts and thought-operations, then Sarah's use of the conditional "if . . . then" implies that she can handle causal inference. An example of a conditional appropriate to Sarah might be "If you cut the apple, then you will have two halves", or "If you shriek, then someone will come running." As Premack explained in 1976, "Only a species that made a causal analysis of its experience would use sentences of this form productively."[20] This is the root of causal thinking, and if a chimpanzee *can* comprehend the "if . . . then" type of relation, it might safely be described as engaging in one crucial aspect of the reasoning process.

Put to the test, Premack's chimpanzees left little doubt that ape minds could causally structure the world. Presented with a whole apple and two halves, a dry and wet sponge, and a clean and scribbled-on scratch pad, each ape was asked how the change came about, being given a knife, bowl of water, and pen as alternatives. It seems like child's play, placing the knife between the apple and its parts, or the water between the dry and wet sponges. But how was the chimpanzee to know that what was needed between the apple and its slices was not another red object, to complete the trio red-red-red. The sequence did not have to be interpreted causally, yet that is how the apes saw it. Moreover, a knife can be classed in all manner of ways: as silver, metallic, long and thin, or as a cutting instrument. Chimps invariably picked that attribute which completes the causal equation. "Because the subjects read the sequences in a specific and consistent way – finding the same question in each of the sequences," said Premack, "I infer that they have a [causal] schema, a structure that assigns an interpretation to an otherwise infinitely ambiguous sequence."

If apples and knives fail to leave an indelible impression of ape causality, conditionals couched in Sarah's plastic-word language ram home the point with a vengeance. The sheer structural complexity of such sentences understood by Sarah leaves the human mind dazed. After being taught the *if-then* symbol, Sarah was presented by her trainer Mary Morgan with the most cruelly tortuous conditional, which read:

If Sarah take apple – then Mary give chocolate Sarah;
if Sarah take banana – then Mary no give chocolate Sarah

Sarah was presented with pieces of apple and banana while reading this condition. She preferred banana to apple, so her natural inclination would be to seize the banana. But if she liked banana, she *loved* chocolate; and the instructions clearly stated that if she did choose the banana, chocolate would not be forthcoming. However, if she picked apple, even though she wasn't crazy about it, she could thereby gain her favourite reward. To take that tortuous route to the coveted chocolate, Sarah had to scrutinise the sentence intently: she also had to grasp the essential nature of a condition – that if she took one step, another would surely follow. The upshot was that she had to think two jumps ahead. Bargaining with chimpanzees, like talking them into completing their day's schooling in exchange for a tickle, wrote Philip Lieberman, "is a complicated logical operation", of a sort not mastered by children until they are four or five.[21]

Premack, desperate as ever to keep one jump ahead of his apes, began casting his net wider, passing from the physical to the social domain. Could chimpanzees connect social actions into a cause-and-effect sequence? he asked in *American Scientist* late in 1976. Obviously they can in life – begging would be pointless if it didn't touch the heart-strings and result in a shared meal – but could they make the connection in a picture-book world? Premack began throwing out suggestions for testing ape social awareness. He considered showing Elizabeth and Peony (Sarah's successors, equally adept with plastic words) two pictures, the start and finish of a story, with the middle, connecting, frame left blank. "For example, in one such test, the three pictures would consist of Elizabeth begging food from Peony, a blank frame, and Elizabeth and Peony playing, hugging, and engaging in mutual grooming. The alternatives [for the missing frame] would include: (1) Peony ignoring Elizabeth's request, (2) Peony sharing with Eliza-beth, (3) Elizabeth stealing Peony's food, etc." Of course, such options assume a naïvely human sense of fair play, since (2) is the choice *we* would make, and Elizabeth is here expected to follow suit. But pongid ethics aside, one gets Premack's drift. By spotting the hugging/grooming "thank you" in frame three (where food is conspicuously absent, so the ape has to infer from the *social* outcome that it was shared), Elizabeth would have to identify the cause in the missing frame two.

> Assume for the sake of discussion that the apes can pass the social tests as they have passed the physical ones, which may not be too risky an assumption given the evident social intelligence of the chimpanzee. If the ape can recognize representations of both physical and social actions, perhaps it can take the next step and recognize higher-order structures that are composed of physical and social actions. Physical and social acts are the building blocks of stories, novels, tales, and the like. Indeed, all narrative prose is formed by appropriately combining physical and social acts. If a species can recognize the basic elements of which stories are formed, perhaps it can also recognize stories them-selves.[22]

One suddenly recalls old Charles Lyell, busying himself with man's bruised moral status under Darwinism, and jotting feverishly in a clandestine diary that no professor could ever know the future and expect to remain tenured. Premack mentions in passing that he has already begun Sarah and Peony on story picture-books and scarcely a murmur rises (still less does the threat of dismissal dangle over his head!). Perhaps, as a sign of the changing ethos, we should look to philosopher Alfred North Whitehead's claim that the future's business *is* to be dangerous. Or to the more familiar Popperian call to arms, that not even our most entrusted dogmas are sacrosanct: nothing can escape criticism, not even the reassuring notion of man as the sole causal reasoner among apes. Lyell would be horrified.

Like other humanised chimps, Washoe is an inveterate skimmer of glossy magazines, singling out the Cadillac and vermouth advertisements that strike her fancy. Koko too: the young gorilla's reaction to magazine pictures she recognises is to name them, without reinforcement – the reinforcing kick seems to be nothing less than the sheer enjoyment of having identified something. In fact, Koko has invented a sign (which for some while remained indecipherable) consisting of running her index finger across her lips. She did it on recognising an advertisement, and followed it with the name; the nearest equivalent in translation might be "Aha! I have it", accompanied in Anglo-Saxons by raising the index finger heavenward. But all this tends to be coffee-table pulp for the pongid with time on its hands. Premack's story books raise the perplexing problem of exactly *how* one could tell that an ape was following some story line, tracing a 'narrative' thread through the picture sequence. Premack has set out to test just how much (or little) a literate ape can read into a picture-book; whether it can, in fact, add the necessary mental component to thread still-frames together. Premack reasoned that scrambling the pictures might cause a perplexed chimp to throw down the book in disgust. (Then again, it might struggle on heroically, fruitlessly trying to make head and tail of the mishmash.) Sarah and Peony are currently tackling sensible and sabotaged stories, with Premack analysing their preferences for the faintest hint that the apes have an inkling of the plot (the book's, not Premack's).

Merest mention of apes picture 'reading' for pleasure is greeted by rank incredulity followed by flirtatious excitement, the kind of confused response Lyell felt for Darwin. Yet all the ingredients are housed in the ape cranium: symbolic representation is second nature to fluent chimps, their mind's eye "imagery" like ours is probably propositional in structure, allowing them mentally to operate on the world and play out their strategies for success (reason by any other name); they can sufficiently displace themselves, so why not cast them adrift in a fantasy world of a Chimpanzee Brothers Grimm? It could have redeeming social consequences, keeping hundreds of idle minds innocently amused as they while away those interminable prison sentences.

Lyell is turning restlessly in his tomb at Westminster Abbey, but Premack has barely warmed up. He begins a little further teasing, the sort to surpass the most dreaded heresy imagined by the already traumatised Victorian mind. A grey London day in 1860 somehow seems appropriate to Premack's wilder dreams. Staunch Victorian moralists stood shocked and delighted by Darwin's probing, petrified of burning their fingers with inflammable issues of man's brute origin and the ape's status, yet determined to strike at the "Truth" whatever the cost. Surely Premack is reaching out mischievously to tease *them*? The "burning" issue is, what else? – God and the ape, the perennial Victorian anxieties.

Huxley was much abused for his *Man's Place in Nature*. But then the man of his disquisition was mindless: it was anatomical man that concerned Darwin's disciple, and *that* concerned his merciless critics. To amputate the mind was immoral if not criminal in their eyes; it was, after all, language, morality and knowledge of God which made him (man, not necessarily Professor Huxley) so immeasurably superior to the ape. Darwin carried the entire Victorian world with him when he admitted (for tactical reasons) in the *Descent of Man* that the benighted ape could never "reflect on God".[23] Through a stroke of master surgery, modern psychology has returned the minds to man and ape. But intoxicated by its dizzy successes in storming every bastion of supposed uniqueness, it has begun laying siege to enemy forts long since abandoned.

> We are, I believe, the only organism that salutes flags [Premack writes], though that should not be difficult to teach the chimpanzee. In addition, man has a mystical literature (e.g., Cabala) and at one time many men prayed to God. The mystical literature is too formidable a challenge, though prayer and a sense of God may not be; they should be operationalized as soon as possible and an attempt made to inculcate them . . .[24]

Huxley could have seen the point to such irreverent needling. Bishops bristling with indignation would once have fired off angry letters to *The Times*, but those days are long gone. As a criterion of human uniqueness (and a pretty powerful one only a century ago), "knowledge of God" today has a hollow ring to it. The best that might be said for risking Sarah's conversion to the ranks of the God-fearing (heaven forbid), is that it might halt Fundamentalism in its tracks. Still, Premack is serious. Indeed, his track record leaves little doubt that he could overcome the almost insuperable odds. Operationalising God, he explains, "is something I have had in mind for years though only recently as a research project". Where he could be defeated is in actually getting funded for such delightful perversity. As he admits, "this is not the sort of thing for which you should request a grant until after you have succeeded".

Levels of Explanation

On a more sober note, where exactly has the 1970s psychological leap forward left us? It has taught us to treat human and ape minds with less of that characteristic Victorian dogmatism that grew out of theological certainty, but instead with a modicum of respect. To those dismayed by the insidious implications of Max Müller's notorious battle cry 'No Thought Without Words' – which effectively reduces 'subhumans' to automaton status, and acts like a moral sanction to treat them as such – the outcome is as responsible as it is pleasing. It is as true today as yesterday that men speak and apes do not; but that is of little importance in the long run. And we are still bickering over whether apes "have" language, which somehow seems to miss the issue. As Philip Lieberman says in exasperation:

> Asking whether chimpanzees have language is pointless and silly when you've already restricted the scope of the word 'language' to linguistic ability equivalent to that of present-day *Homo sapiens*.[25]

The crucial point is that apes take readily to words, gestures or type: symbols which may take on idiosyncratic ape meanings and may even be manipulated according to a unique syntax – we still do not know. These symbols form a surface topography, allowing us to map out the subterranean representational processes of the mind. All we have concentrated on till now is the surface gloss, the ape revelations teach us to tunnel deeper to the cognitive foundations. Gordon Gallup commented in a review of Lana's progress that, "Although it will no doubt remain an issue of concern, the question of whether language is uniquely human is no longer an issue of much consequence."

> A more substantive issue is whether animals share cognitive, conceptual, and representational processes in common with man (e.g., cross-modal perception, self-awareness, intention, attribution, etc.). Language represents one but certainly not the only means of mapping these underlying capacities.[26]

In the same spirit, William Mason recently admitted that the hoary old question of whether man and ape differed in degree or kind "may well prove to be beside the point". It all depends where you look for an answer.

> For example, at the level of speech – in the sense of vocalized language – the contrasts between man and ape are manifestly qualitative. On a different level, let's say the ability to form concepts, or to combine various acts or subroutines into larger functional units, the differences appear to be matters of degree.[27]

Whitehead felt that the difference was one of degree, but that degree made all the difference. The same is true of any two molluscs. Fortunately for molluscs, there is none of that ideological commitment which gives Whitehead's man-ape comparison its chauvinistic sting.

6

Cries and Whispers

"Does *Washoe* evince language-like behavior because she is employing neural/cognitive systems similar to those underlying human language . . .?"

Berkeley anthropologist William Malmi at the 1975 Language Symposium in New York.[1]

With England in the 1860s frenzied over gorilla brains and "higgledy piggledy" selection, Paul Broca, the Parisian surgeon and anthropologist, was quietly putting anthropology on a fresh footing. In the year of *The Origin* he founded the Société d'Anthropologie, whose reputation rapidly stretched across the Channel, and Huxley – who was quick to adopt Broca's craniometric techniques – advised those interested in man to correspond with Broca rather than humour the anthropological "quacks" in London.[2] Almost incidental to his programme of skull measurement and race characterisation (which Darwin's age considered the obligatory first step for its anthropological foundling), Broca resolved with one momentously casual stroke a conflict over speech localisation that had raged for decades. The phrenologist Franz Gall had long before broken the old 'holistic' stranglehold on cerebral function, where speech and consciousness were thought to be diffuse products of the integrated, intact brain. In contrast, Gall imagined the mind capable of being anatomically dissected. It was far from an inviolable whole (hence his phrenology). Indeed, in 1825 J. B. Bouillaud tracked speech function to the forebrain, and anxious debates raged over this while Broca was still in medical school. At times they almost assumed political overtones – conservatives clinging to a holistic stand with radicals in opposition. Broca was seemingly oblivious, and far more concerned with his craniometry. Then during an early session of Broca's anthropological society, Bouillaud's son-in-law (another fervent localisationist) again raised the issue. Were it not for the death of his speech-disabled patient, Broca might never have looked into the matter. As it was, the autopsy revealed a lesion in a left frontal convolution, and the radicals gained a powerful recruit. Broca systematically studied aphasics (*aphasia* is a general term covering speech loss from a variety of causes), collecting a mass of evidence. By 1863 he had localised the speech area, and presented to the Société "eight cases where the lesion is situated in the posterior portion of the third frontal convolution", adding that the "most remarkable thing in all these patients, the lesion is on the left side".[3] This pinpointing, achieved with such unheard-of precision, effectively coalesced the forces of the medical left. Speech, at least, stemmed from a small locus on one side of the brain: "we speak," Broca suggested in 1865, "with the left hemisphere."

But the age was one of evolutionary continuity. Darwinians at this time were emphasising the gradual transmutation of brute into man by barely perceptible steps – hence the down-grading of savages and up-grading of apes. Continuity became the order of the day, for which reason evolutionists accepted that animal cries, despite their highly emotive context, had turned by insensible degrees into articulate speech. Darwin, replying graciously and almost apologetically to Max Müller for his gift of a less than sympathetic paper, admitted in 1873 that he would gladly have avoided the whole subject (he tried his best – the *Descent* skims over language, *The Expression of the Emotions in Man and Animals* skirts the intractable subject completely). On specifics, Darwin pleaded ignorance and stuck to what seemed the obvious general deduction. "He who is fully convinced, as I am, that man is descended from some lower animal, is almost forced to believe *a priori* that articulate language has been developed from inarticulate cries."[4]

Nineteenth-century evolutionary logic seemed to demand that animal cries had been stripped of emotion and refined by stepping up the information content, so man could discuss holocausts or his sublimest pleasures quite dispassionately. This model retained the continuity, although exactly *how* the transition occurred remained baffling. Darwin himself variously suggested that protohumans might

have duetted like gibbons (the rhapsodies evolving into articulate
sentiments of the heart) or else he imitated the growls of beasts, where
each growl signified a particular predator or prey (here Darwin does
not emphasise cries evolving *into* speech: imitation is totally different).
Still, the continuity theory exerted an immense pressure to deduce
speech from cries. Hence the eccentric Victorian explorer R. L. Garner
in the 1890s actually read explicit and semi-articulate meanings from
"love" to "death" into chimpanzee hoots and barks. The upshot was
obviously that the neuroanatomy mediating animal cries was thought
to have evolved into the lateralised speech centre, or Broca's area, as it
is now known.

In 1874 Carl Wernicke investigated another form of aphasia from
which he concluded that a comprehension area in the left temporal
lobe was additionally linked to language. Norman Geschwind has
summarised the language impediments when Broca's and Wernicke's
areas are severed. Lesion of Broca's area results in aphasia which
"characteristically produces little speech, which is emitted slowly, with
great effort", whereas in contrast Wernicke's aphasic speaks rapidly
and effortlessly, "and in many cases the rate of production of words
exceeds the normal. The output has the rhythm and melody of normal
speech, but it is remarkably empty and conveys little or no information."[5] One clue to the solution of these contrasting symptoms is
given by the respective locations of Broca's and Wernicke's areas.
Broca's lies adjacent to cortical regions coordinating the tongue, lips,
palate and vocal chords; it thus probably controls the rules and means
of articulation and language coding. Wernicke's area, however, is
sited near the auditory regions of the cortex and thus, thought Wernicke, "was somehow involved in the recognition of the patterns of
spoken language" – in short, it deals with comprehension. Destruction
of this region leaves the patient free to speak because Broca's area
remains intact, although what issues forth is largely empty babble.

Thus the reorganisation of the human neocortex for language is at
least partially understood. But work on the monkey limbic system by
Bryan Robinson of the Tallahassee Neurological Clinic and others has
shaken the older evolutionary faith that cries anteceded speech. As he
summed up older notions: "most workers assumed that the neural
apparatus supporting animal vocalization was related to the human
speech areas, that the latter developed or evolved out of the former,
and that human speech was itself a highly developed form of animal

vocalization". But as Robinson told the 1975 New York Academy of Sciences Symposium on the "Origins and Evolution of Language and Speech", the limbic system was largely undefined in the last century "and techniques for studying the subcortical and basal parts of the brain were a number of years away".

> However, evidence gathered in the past fifteen years has suggested *that animal vocal communication is limbic in origin*, and that human speech arose from new* tissue [Broca's and Wernicke's regions in the neocortex].[6]

According to Robinson, the continuity is irrevocably severed, as effectively as by a neocortical lesion. If he is right, animal cries could not have evolved into intricate speech with its high information and low emotion content because they are controlled by different areas of the brain.

The limbic system itself explains some of the characters of animal communication. (The system, by the way, comprises a wide array of structures, the limbic lobe and subcortical regions, hypothalamus and brain stem – regions shrouded by the mushrooming hemispheres.) Being phylogenetically older, they regulate basic autonomic functions – respiration, blood pressure, temperature and so forth. Stimulating specific limbic regions can fill a monkey with fear, rage or even sexual obsession. Indeed, limbic stimulation can so alter the temperament that a submissive male can quickly rise to dominance (and stay there). The limbic, then, is in charge of overall emotional tone, the feeling of well-being. But it also triggers alarm cries or mating calls, each related to a specific emotional state which the monkey wishes to communicate. In fact, artificial stimulation of limbic sites in squirrel and rhesus monkeys has exhausted the entire repertoire of natural calls, as often as not echoed by a chilling chorus from free-ranging peers, who received and understood each vocal 'message'. Robinson called attention to two critical factors stemming from this work.

---

* The word *new* is misleading: these are probably not new areas at all, but enormously expanded homologues of regions similarly existing in monkeys and apes. Geschwind remarks, "I think that the forerunners of Wernicke's area are clearly present in the monkey and I suspect that the forerunner of Broca's area is also present." (See Note 15.) If these are not new areas, they *are* retuned to a new use in man – language and all it entails.

First, loci producing vocalization were distributed equally on both the right and the left side of the brain. There is, thus, no dominant side of the limbic system as regards vocalization. Second, there was no evidence that the neocortex participates in limbic vocalization [as demonstrated by stimulating electrically the rhesus monkey neocortex].

Particular calls are elicited from specific limbic areas. For example, Raimund Apfelbach stimulated over 2000 sites in the lar gibbon's limbic system by means of deeply implanted electrodes, and although he was unable to elicit duet singing, he did generate hoots, barking, calls to synchronise a mate's behaviour, alarm, play and contact calls, each from its distinctive site.[7] These calls sounded natural to the experimenters (and spectroscopic analysis proved them acoustically identical to the real thing). More pertinent, nearby gibbons accurately read the 'message' and either began calling, became restless or attempted to escape, depending on the signal. These are exactly the results Robinson achieved earlier with rhesus monkeys. What the situation is in great apes (the gibbon is a lesser ape) is conjecture. To my knowledge, limbic stimulation has never been tried, and Malmi's explanation why is revealing: "it requires chronic deep electrode implantation, and, usually, ultimate sacrifice of the subject. Despite the scientific benefits, it becomes increasingly difficult to justify such techniques for chimpanzees due to financial, conservational, and ethical considerations. [Note the order of priorities.]"[8] It is generally assumed that pant-hoots, barks, and so forth stem from limbic activity, since they are of the same emotive and communicative nature as gibbon and monkey calls.

Both the behaviours (speech *vs.* animal vocalisation) and their neuroanatomical substrates (frontal neocortex *vs.* limbic) testify in Robinson's opinion to a radical break in the type of communication. The fact that language did not materialise out of gibbon duets does not preclude the limbic system playing some emotive, reinforcing role in human communication. Robinson has been instrumental in hooking up a limbic 'reinforcer' to neocortical speech. The obvious test to determine the limbic's role in man is to stimulate it electrically. Even more obviously, it is an experiment scarcely tried. The massive electrode implantation could result in permanent damage. But there *is* some evidence from limbic stimulation during surgery that – even if Broca's area is damaged – the patient will cry out; "the sounds," reports Robinson, "are crude and contain a strong emotional valence".[9] Because Broca's area is severed, Robinson assumes "that limbic vocalization follows a different neural pathway to the speech mechanism than does neocortical speech". If this is true, it highlights still more dramatically the split between the types of communication and their underlying neural networks. But we are already moving into contentious areas. Robinson speculates that the human limbic (as far as communication is concerned) acts as an emotional bracer. He cites as evidence that cortical patches surrounding Broca's region are wired to limbic sites. Moreover, one of his recent patients suffered a benign tumour which, after removal, left the speech region *partially* damaged.

> Postoperative speech in this patient was limited to occasional profanity and vulgarity or to simple exclamatory phrases during periods of excitement, such as "Look out," "Hungry," "Hurt," and so on. This type of vocalization I postulate as arising from his intact limbic system . . .

Perhaps, but another school of thought sees these profanities as the work of the right hemisphere. Robinson's patient was peculiar, however, in that at times of mania he actually became quite fluent and prosodic, hinting that the neocortical circuitry was partially intact. It was almost as though the weakened language area was at times swamped by strong 'gut' signals, leading to the highly charged outbursts. Whatever the truth as to the right hemisphere's profane thoughts, Robinson at least believes that the limbic can still pack an emotional punch. His overall conclusions are worth repeating.

> These considerations suggest that human speech normally depends on two systems rather than one. The first and phylogenetically older system is located in the limbic system, is bilaterally represented without hemispheric dominance, antedates primate development, is closely related to emotional, motivational, and autonomic factors, and is capable of transmitting only signals of low information content. The second system is supplementary to the first, was developed in man, is neocortical, lateralized, and usually dominant in the left hemisphere. As is so often true in the central nervous system, it did not arise "from" or "out of" the old system but from new tissue, namely, the neocortical association areas. This new tissue

permitted speech greater independence from emotional factors
and provided it thereby the means and circuitry to carry com-
pact, dense, and precise informational loads. This system arose
in parallel with the old, surpassed it, and relegated the old system
to a subordinate role.[10]

Preadaptation

The most provocative question was posed by Malmi: Are the symbol-
wielding apes employing *neocortical* pathways homologous to the
language areas in man? When Washoe, Sarah and Lana grapple with
the intracacies of signs, words and lexigrams, are they forcing an
entirely novel function on to grey matter otherwise gainfully employed?
One can immediately see the critical importance of this question. If
Washoe's signalling and Lana's writing are mediated by some neocortical forerunner of Wernicke's region, the issue suddenly becomes
relevant to the evolution of language proper. And if we can *switch* its
function, that means it probably existed originally to serve a different
purpose.

How are we ever to know if an electrical storm sweeps across
Sarah's neocortex when she faces the tantalising *If Sarah take apple, then
Mary give chocolate Sarah; If Sarah take banana, then Mary no give
chocolate Sarah*? Where exactly is the site of mental activity when a
frustrated Lana demands *You move bowl of chow behind room?* or Lucy
signs to herself while reading her favourite magazines? One harmless,
non-intrusive test seems the obvious opening move, especially since it
has now been applied to human speech – electroencephalographic
(EEG) monitoring: the use of scalp electrodes to pinpoint the sites of
electrical activity in the brain.

Its successful application for human speech was something of a
triumph (though it is an extremely tricky procedure to interpret, and
no one is unaware of the danger of misreading the often chaotic
results). Broca's theory had never looked healthier, and experimental
confirmation of speech coding in the third frontal convolution stems
from a century-long study of the dire effects of occluded blood vessels,
as well as tumours, lesions caused by missiles passing through the
cranium, surgical stimulation, haemorrhages and excision of cortical

tissue during treatment of epilepsy. This is Geschwind's list (I wrote "gory list", but as he reminded me, occluded blood vessels are bloodless!). As a rule, we do not tamper with intact humans; indeed, a splendid corpus of laws has been designed specifically to keep us intact – to which end, of course, we justify the often wholesale sacrifice of even our closest hominoid relatives in what is, undoubtedly, a magnificent form of tribalism. But nature knows no taboos about tampering with our delicate soft circuitry. Yearly, literally millions of humans suffer thromboses and occlusions, often leading to clean and precise cortical lesions; and from this depressing circumstance has grown our intimate knowledge of that most inscrutable organ, currently mushrooming to cover the planet with a fungal grey matter. But corroboration from a new and promising technique (albeit in its infancy) is always welcome. It has been known for a decade or more that electrical potentials can be detected in both hemispheres up to one second before body movement. Attempts to monitor negative potentials across the neocortex when a subject speaks, however, proved fruitless until 1971, and only succeeded when Dale McAdam and Harry Whitaker of Rochester University developed a suitably rigorous technique. Their subjects were trained to speak a string of polysyllabic words beginning with "p" or "k", with a minimum of irregular swallowing, tongue or breathing movement (all of which send the recording pen soaring). For controls, the subjects coughed, reproducing the "k" sound without the attendant speech, and spat with a non-symbolic "p". Sets of electrodes across the scalp picked up negative potentials with a maximum intensity over Broca's area in the left hemisphere when subjects spoke. Again, neocortical activity started one second before speech began. "The data," McAdam and Whitaker wrote jubilantly to *Science*, "provide the first direct physiological evidence for localization of language production functions in the intact, normal human brain."[11]

EEG monitoring while a chimpanzee or gorilla is busily engaged in symbolic communication could similarly provide the strongest evidence of neocortical activity. Of course, arm waving (or even typing) and speaking are vastly different motor activities, so Broca's area might not be the most productive region to search first. Also the actively signing chimp's body movements could make the results doubly difficult to interpret, so it might be best to start on Sarah or one of her successors, who sit quietly meditating on Premack's symbolic teasers. Then the area roughly approximating to Wernicke's comprehension region in man might profitably be scanned. The implications, if this were achieved and showed positive (or rather negative) activity, even if it is not lateralised, are tremendously exciting. Nor need the symbol-using ape be unduly disturbed, since all that is involved is the placing of surface electrodes at strategic positions on the scalp.

The Wada test to determine the side of speech dominance has been known for thirty years, and Malmi suggests that this could provide an alternate attack on the ape 'language' problem. When in 1948 Juhn Wada was working on epilepsy he accidentally discovered that an injection of sodium amytal into the carotid artery induced temporary aphasia *if the dominant hemisphere was injected* – injections into the other carotid left speech unimpaired. This proved, subsequently, an invaluable test of hemispheric speech dominance for brain surgeons.[12] Accurate knowledge of the speech side is absolutely critical for surgeons about to operate in neocortical zones. (The mental damage resulting if the Sylvian cortex were cut out of the dominant hemisphere is too dire to contemplate.) The carotid injection is quick and the ability to count and speak returns within two or three minutes. Incidentally, Wada's patients had no recollection of *not* being able to speak, which seemed quite unaccountable to him at the time. In fact, they fully believed they had carried out various counting commands satisfactorily (even though they actually stopped seconds after the injection). They remained alert and cooperative in wiggling their toes, yet they were ›pparently suffering amnesia.*

---

* What happened was that self-conscious functioning on the left (speech) hemisphere had also been knocked out. So why didn't the minor hemisphere remember? The eminent neurobiologist John Eccles interprets Roger Sperry's famous work on split-brain epileptics to mean that self-consciousness is solely a function of nervous integration in the dominant (speech) hemisphere – uncharitably designating the minor hemisphere an "automaton" under the same roof. Hence, there was no self-aware being after the injection of the drug to know about the loss of counting! Sperry, however, challenges Eccles, and perhaps carries more conviction. Probably, the minor hemisphere is not so much unaware as mute, and though unable to express articulately its introspective feelings because the semi-autonomous left has a monopoly on speech and refuses the right access, it *can* comprehend instructions and make its answers known by "thumbs up" or "thumbs down" signs. Says Sperry, the mute hemisphere is "alert and consciously cognizant" of all that its bullying twin does. In split-brain patients this shows up in "disgusted shaking of the head or irked facial expressions triggered from the minor hemisphere after it has heard its speaking partner making what it knows to be an incorrect answer".[13] In split-brain patients there thus seem to be two parallel worlds within one cranium; two flowing streams of consciousness; two humans who at times can violently disagree.

Excited by the prospect for understanding a mite more about ape powers of symbolism, Malmi fired off another string of questions at the 1975 conference on the "Origins and Evolution of Language and Speech":

> Would it [sodium amytal] affect chimpanzee production or comprehension of "language"? If so, is there a lateralized effect? If the behavior is in some sense lateralized, is it consistently dominant on a particular side of the brain for all chimps? Does the Wada test also interfere with other kinds of activities?

Yes, it does, but not quite the way Malmi meant. The unavoidable consequence of sodium amytal is technically *contralateral hemiplegia* – paralysis down the opposite side of the body (injection into the left carotid results in slumping of the right arm and leg). The effect only lasts a few minutes and patients suffer amnesia during this time. But Washoe, Sarah and Lana would be doubly handicapped by this, since they need their arms specifically to indicate comprehension or issue requests.

We can see what Malmi really had in mind: crudely, that if the drug inhibits symbolism *and* some other behaviour, we might discover what is preadapting the ape for handling symbols. Paradoxically, it is extremely fortunate that wild apes fail to speak or sign, otherwise we would be no better off in explaining the origin of language. If, as seems evident, illiterate wild apes possess powers that can be *switched* to "language" function, the big question is obviously: switched from what? What else might the ape be doing naturally that unintentionally enables it to decode symbols?

Preadaptation is the key – the evolutionarily sudden switching of a structure evolved for one purpose to a new and quite unintended one. I regard this as evolution's greatest asset; many of the seemingly momentous but otherwise inexplicable strides – fish first crawling out of water as the first amphibians, or dinosaurs taking to the air as birds – make sense under 'preadaptive' explanations. In amphibians and birds the nineteenth century saw unimpeachable evidence of Design, the work of Providence guiding life towards some foreseen end. Invoking the more mundane principle of preadaptation, we can see that fish and dinosaurs were not 'aiming' to take over land or air – on the contrary, selection equipped them with lungs and wings to serve wholly distinct functions. Impossible? Well, one theory of the amphibian assault of the land, for example, suggests that legs and lungs were originally intended to keep lobe-fish *in* water. As the Devonian ponds stagnated 400 million years ago, only fish with lungs could gulp air to stay alive, and that required legs to push the expanding throat off the bottom. Lobe-fins were preadapted to land lubbering, and thus were amphibians born. Again, feathers need not have evolved specifically for flight, but instead for warmth in tiny, predatory dinosaurs.* The principle is simple and effective: preadaptation by-passes nineteenth-century objections, for example that every state must be functional in the same way as the finished product. Clearly, a partial wing is an aerodynamic absurdity, as Mivart argued, and natural selection would have scrapped it. Darwin's critics saw the wing preordained and natural selection scrapped. In fact, foresight did not enter into it. Arms could have been fully feathered for warmth before flight became an option. The point, of course, was that wings *were* functioning during their formation – but not as wings. The dinosaur, becoming increasingly specialised to capture the 'warm blooded' niche, unintentionally sported a feathered form ready for take-off.[14] Lobe-fin fish and the tiny dinosaurs were happily headed elsewhere when they found themselves standing on the threshold of new worlds.

Language is a peculiar social adaptation to a nebulous niche. With it we conquered our new world, and the momentous consequences of this event match the amphibian assault of the land and the bird's conquest of the skies. If, as seems distinctly likely, this is another and remarkable case of preadaptation, then our Socratic digging has unearthed one real teaser: What behaviour preadapts the ape for symbolic communication?

Norman Geschwind has sought to answer this and at the same time solve the riddle of the ape's expanded Sylvian cortex in the "language" region. He points out that our naming ability depends on the angular gyrus hooking up auditory and visual signals: words and objects. But

---

* In the summer of 1977 James Jenson disinterred in Colorado a potential bird fossil which threatens to push the celebrated *Archaeopteryx* off its prestigious perch as the "first bird", shunting it ignominiously into a sterile side branch of feathered dinosaurs. Whether or not Jensen's new fossil was also a dinosaur descendant remains to be seen. In any case, it makes no difference to the tone of our argument.

the ability to jump from one sense to another would be of tremendous advantage to wild apes. As he says, if an ape hears a scream, it would be better if it did not immediately panic, but first pictured the predator, which would allow it to adapt its response – either flight or group defence.[15] Cross-modal association would permit greater flexibility; and has probably developed to the extent that the neocortex has asymmetrically burgeoned in the ape brain. This could be preadapting captive chimpanzees for object naming. Ally, like most apes, can associate the spoken word with an object, but he has gone one stage further and translates human speech into his own signs. So clearly apes can link two arbitrary signals, both in the visual mode.

The existence of the self-concept may also hinge on cross-modal abilities. The ego may be considered a multi-modal "image" whose umbilical cord has snapped. The self has withdrawn inwards, displaced from the world; the "I" has split from "me", so consciousness becomes both subject and object to itself. This is probably an essential prerequisite for any linguistic-type communication, which relates "me" to the world in a symbolic equation.[16]

Whatever the status of Robinson's radical man-animal split in respect of speech and calls, when it comes to comprehension nothing is so neat. Natural calls, wherever they are elicited, are subsequently interpreted by the left hemisphere, even in rhesus monkeys. This surprising find was only announced in *Science* on 20 October 1978 by a team from the Kresge Hearing Research Institute and Rockefeller University. They had played tapes of Japanese rhesus monkey calls to captives wearing headsets, channelling the sounds through one earphone at a time. Other monkeys evidently found the calls irrelevant and listened indifferently whichever ear was subjected. So did the rhesus monkeys when the calls were played in their left-ear speakers. But when the channels were switched, they suddenly paid attention, and tests showed that only when listening on the right side could they differentiate the calls' components. Evidently, the left hemisphere alone was receptive, demonstrating its functional lateralisation. Whatever "specialized mechanisms" were at work, guessed the team, they "may be analogous to those used by humans in the analysis of speech".[17]

Looking at this new work, it is not wildly irresponsible to assume that comprehension and cross-modal functions were established in the left hemisphere long before man spoke; language was less a gift of the gods than an exploitation of primate potential.

The Grammar of Tool-Making

Geschwind concentrated solely on what he called the "rather un-
glamorous activity" of object naming. Human language consists of so
much besides, but nothing presents a more intractable problem than
explaining the evolution of grammar. The glibbest explanation has
been sitting on the tip of the anthropological tongue for decades. Few
have not, at some time or other, suspected that tool-making was
intimately though mysteriously connected with human language. If I
sound disparaging, it is because solutions involving tools are infuriatingly vague; there has never to this day been a really rigorous tie-up
between the two, nothing to make anyone sit up and say "Of course!"

Columbia's Ralph Holloway made a valiant effort in 1969, in a paper
written before the Washoe Project was announced. Holloway is a
physical anthropologist, indeed some of his best work has been on the
endocranial casts of early man, but this led him to an unnecessarily
hard-core, almost intractable, attack on culture, the 'other' anthropology. The tone of his paper, "Culture: A *Human* Domain", was so off-
putting to fellow anthropologists – especially the gradualists, who
wanted an easing of the precipitous divide between man and ape – that
his efforts were slated before they got off the ground. The clue to the
ruckus stands in those offending italics in the title. Holloway hit a
sensitive nerve by insisting dogmatically that, with his radical reinter-
pretation, we "might give culture back to man, regardless of what the
clever baboons, vultures, ants, macaques, or chimpanzees have done
thus far".[18] That was it, of course; the spectre of 'uniqueness'. One
critic was so incensed that the whole science fell under his axe to atone
for Holloway's sins: "Anthropology is a pseudoscience with a pseudo-
language, and is bristling with pseudoproblems", of which Holloway's
was a prize example.[19] Moderates simply deplored such a violent
snapping of man's umbilical cord to nature, sensing a Mivartian ghost
at work in Holloway's mental machinery.

The debate was needlessly aggravated by Holloway's insistence on
analysing only fashioned stone tools, whereas none of his critics
doubted that these must have been preceded by countless millions of
years of perishable wood workings. Fashioned flints were the net

result of an apprenticeship that probably stretched back past australo-pithecine days (the late Louis Leakey imagined the twelve-million-year-old Miocene *Ramapithecus* an adept stone wielder, shattering antelope bones to extract the brain and marrow). Would Holloway's reasoning stretch to cover early human, or even chimp wood-users? He answers an emphatic "No". Others are not so sure. The reason Holloway found flint-making and language "similar, if not identical, cognitive processes" was that both structured the world *in a certain way*. In Holloway's own italicised words, culture was "the *imposition of arbitrary form upon the environment*". That "arbitrary" is the key; for example, "arbitrary" in language means that symbols bear no morpho-logical relation to their worldly referents, just as *cat* the word looks nothing like the furry fireside pet. Another "arbitrary" form imposed on the world was the stone tool – "arbitrary", according to Holloway, because the shape of the initial pebble does not suggest the shape of the axehead inside. *Man* imposes this form; more importantly, the flints were fashioned to meticulous specifications, that is, all axes, cutters and scrapers were turned out to a standardised pattern. Hence Holloway imagined specific rules (a "grammar") governing tool-working as well as speaking. This explains his reluctance to give apes even half a chance. But then this was still the preWashoe era, and Holloway could legitimately admit that "There is no way of knowing what a chimpan-zee is thinking, but it does seem fairly clear that its thought processes differ from man's in the absence of arbitrary form." (To be fair, he conceded that apes probably possessed a covert symbolism, "*organic*" he called it, meaning it was not coded into arbitrary words by "social convention". Washoe and her compatriots have established that apes are *capable* of acquiring this arbitrary form, which undermines Holloway's neat partition of nature.)

Holloway thought the "explicit rules" generating words and tools were rooted in man's symbolic cognitive processes, supported by crucial concepts like the Ego and the Self (both unique). The point, easy to make out of Washoe's earshot, was that man (as Mivart never doubted) had entered a new psychological realm, and Holloway was adamant that this new "psychological dimension" thwarted the etho-logist's perennial attempt to model man's early evolution on, say, baboon society (baboons being presumed to lack Egos, Selves and symbolic potential – to which we might shout "not proven"). Hol-loway's tactic, of course, was to knock the vagueness out of "Culture" by rigorously deducing man's cultural attributes, especially speech and tools, from the same cognitive process – hence finally unifying culture under one banner. And he was unabashed if it did smack of chauvinism.

If it sounds unconvincing today, Holloway cannot really be called to account. Ape symbolic potential suggests that, if the tool tie-up is valid, it might extend deeper into hominoid nature. Gordon Hewes, who incidentally coined the term "pongid breakthrough", also finds Holloway too pernickety in sticking to speech and flints. Hewes, from Colorado University, is the premier exponent of the gestural theory of language origins, and he is equally convinced of the link between language and tool-working. (There the comparison with Holloway abruptly ends, for Hewes is concerned with tools and gestures, not speech – nor is he hidebound by eolithic blinkers, but it quite open to the ape's tool-use.)

Hewes' scenario for man is a piece of informed and intriguing speculation, an overt attempt to step gingerly round the hoary problem of how speech ever started if not from animal cries. Basically, he believes that protohumans first devised a *gestural* language; this was elaborated over untold thousands of generations, although it always remained less refined than today's language of the deaf (which is partially a back-development from speech). Hewes is happy pushing these early gestures into the distant australopithecine past, correlating them with *Australopithecus'* use of "crude stone tools".[20] He speculates that the action performed in making or using a tool became increasingly stylised, eventually doubling for the tool's name. Whether or not he used stone, Raymond Dart's "Southern ape man" was undoubtedly more comfortable working wood or bone. Dart imagined *Australopithecus* a truncheon-wielder, and argued ceaselessly that he effectively brandished an antelope humerus, smashing open baboon skulls with it to extract the tasty brain; and Dart had both the proposed humerus truncheons and baboon skulls with matching 'double-headed' fractures to prove his point.[21] The coding and decoding of gestures would have been greatly facilitated if not actually permitted by the prior lateralisation of the neocortex in the "language" region, which had burgeoned to cope with its cross-modal duties. The final switchover from sign to speech might have occurred only recently, perhaps 40,000 years ago with the phenomenal spread of *Homo sapiens* at that time. By then Hewes believes that the gestural potential was exhausted, and the system was fast becoming ill-adapted to the specialist needs of modern man.

Apes Making Tools

Whatever logic is invoked to link tools and language (and logic is little more than a smoke-screen to cover ignorance), it is undeniable that academia has about-faced on the issue of ape tool manufacture. The occasional wild ape brandishing a stick had been noticed as far back as the 1840s, but such sporadic reports seemed to emphasise the 'freak' nature of this aggressive act. It was an anomaly, and an exceedingly rare one at that. In point of fact, the literature is littered with numerous, clear and unequivocal descriptions of tool-wielding apes. In 1887 Alfred Carpenter even went so far as to paint a vivid picture of the macaque monkeys on the South Burma islands wandering the beaches clasping small stones to smash open oysters. The stones were fetched distances of up to eighty yards, and the technique, to quote Carpenter, was "to dislocate the valves by a blow on the base of the upper one, and to break the shell over the attaching muscle".[22] One could hardly hope for a clearer description of standardised tool-using. Still, it remains true that the importance of tools went completely unrealised – whatever feats captive chimpanzees might achieve – until the 1960s and the first systematic and thorough studies of wild apes. From this, a well documented catalogue of tools has been amassed, and amassed is putting it mildly. Benjamin Beck of Chicago Zoo (himself a specialist on baboon tool-use) recently listed *fifteen* categories of tool-using by wild apes, including clubbing baboons and hurling stones at them (the baboons fail to reciprocate), prodding frightening objects, like a dead python, raking in food, hammering open nuts, prying arborial ant nests off a branch and digging out the entrances to bee hives.[23] Even for apes, necessity is usually the mother of tool invention, as is evident from this list. Jane Goodall cites the delightful example of Flint, a young male in her Gombe study group, who was systematically refused permission to touch and investigate his tiny sister Flame. Frustrated, he picked up a straw and poked her, drawing it back to sniff the end.

All credit goes to Jane Goodall, of course, for her eighteen-year observational marathon in the Gombe National Park (Tanzania). "Thorough" sounds decidedly like an understatement when describing her research on a single group of chimpanzees. One finds it difficult to appreciate how little was known about wild apes before her pioneering study. In fact, until 1960, Adriaan Kortlandt admitted, "no observer ever singled out and followed up an individual chimpanzee for more than about one day",[24] and Jane Goodall is watching the passing generations. Some of her sightings have been extraordinary. She has seen Fifi (sister to Flint and Flame) gently dabbing a bleeding wound with a handful of leaves. Elsewhere the Gombe chimps have been spotted using leaf wads to wipe clean their faces and fur, they have even been seen wiping one another. As anecdote turns into observation, one is left with the uneasy feeling that chimp psychology has been sorely underrated.

> Evered, as he climbed through a tree [Goodall relates in *In the Shadow of Man*], suddenly stopped and, with his face close to the bark, peered into what looked like a small hollow. He picked a handful of leaves, chewed them for a moment, took them out of his mouth, and pushed them down into the hollow. As he withdrew them we saw the gleam of water. Quickly Evered sucked the liquid from his homemade sponge and poked it down into the hollow once more. At that moment Gilka came up and watched him closely. When he moved away she made a tiny sponge and pushed it into the hollow, but it seemed that all the water had gone. She dropped her sponge and wandered off.[25]

Many chimpanzee actions are technically accomplished. Consider this final example of tool-use, the insertion of probes into ant and termite hills to fish out the soldiers, which make good eating. It *sounds* simple, but another Gombe observer, Geza Teleki, after months of studying the technique, actually tried it and failed. By his own estimate, he scored on par with a four-year-old chimp novice (juveniles learn the trade by studiously watching skilled adults, then perfect it with practice – it is, in a very real sense, a chimp tradition). Termite 'fishing' is now well known. Nonetheless, breaking it down into components reveals an unsuspected technical and cognitive complexity. Jane Goodall's first encounter with fishing chimps occurred within months of her arrival at Gombe. Unbelievable as it now sounds, tool-use by wild chimps had only been observed a couple of times prior to this, fishing never. After spotting the old male David Graybeard poking grass stems into a termite hill, she erected a hide nearby.

On the eighth day of my watch David Graybeard arrived again, together with Goliath, and the pair worked there for two hours. I could see much better: I observed how they scratched open the sealed-over passage entrances with a thumb or forefinger. I watched how they bit the ends off their tools when they became bent, or used the other end, or discarded them in favor of new ones. Goliath once moved at least fifteen yards from the heap to select a firm-looking piece of vine, and both males often picked three or four stems while they were collecting tools, and put the spares beside them on the ground until they wanted them.

Most exciting of all, on several occasions they picked small leafy twigs and prepared them for use by stripping off the leaves. This was the first recorded example of a wild animal not merely *using* an object as a tool, but actually modifying an object and thus showing the crude beginnings of tool*making*.[26]

"Crude" is not a word much used by Teleki; not, at least, after his year of study and dismal attempts at apeing. He concluded in 1974 (and many of the new breed of field observers might agree), "that anthropologists tend to underestimate pongid technical skills when defining the 'uniqueness' of man".[27] Consider the deceptively simple fishing routine. First, the ape accurately locates the sealed tunnel openings (invisible until the surface is scratched away). Teleki (who could not locate them) suspected that apes *memorise* the hundred or so tunnel positions per mound. That alone, he admitted, revealed "knowledge far beyond my expectations". Since there are only two good fishing months (October and November), the chimps had to know the termite season. They arrive early to examine mounds, aware of the season's onset. Almost the entire population will then spend anything up to five hours daily fishing, sometimes two or three to a mound – up to five have been recorded, sitting like haunched, hairy fishermen, concentrating intently, with their stem-rods bowed down in anticipation of a catch. It is critical that probes are selected to a high specification. Good ones may be brought in from elsewhere; chimps have been seen carrying them for over an hour across half a mile of terrain (often in batches, anticipating a good haul). Probe selection, Teleki admits, appears "deceptively simple"; the vine must bend with the twisting termite tunnel. Teleki failed this test too. Where an efficient chimp judged the correct pliancy, Teleki's trial-and-error method consistently let him down. Next, the probe is modified, stripped of leaves, and the end bitten off for the optimum length, then inserted into the tunnel with a fluid, twisting motion to just the right depth to bait the soldiers. Having failed the preliminaries, Teleki expected this to be child's play. After weeks "of nearly total failure" he "began to grasp the problems involved". His ham-fisted approach ruined any chance of a catch. The experienced chimp employs a remarkable subtlety: the probe is vibrated gently to actively bait the termites, then retracted with a "graceful" motion so as not to tear the jaws of soldiers clinging tenaciously to the stem. By this time, Teleki has lapsed forgivably into eulogistic prose, punctuated by such leading descriptions like "finesse", "graceful" motions and "technical skill".

> Incompetent as they were, my attempts to acquire the skills of locating tunnels, selecting materials, inserting probes and extracting termites left me with a healthy measure of respect for chimpanzee technical ability, as well as with a nagging suspicion that the physical and psychological capabilities needed to develop, apply and transmit such skills may differ in degree but not in kind from those needed by humans [hunter-gatherers] to locate, expose and gather insects and subsurface flora.[28]

The baboon's incompetence at mimicking the termiting procedure, even when shown the ropes by fishing apes, strikes at the heart of the difference among tool-users. Only very occasionally will wild baboons hammer open a leathery fruit or dab blood with plant fibre, even though (as Beck has shown) they can become proficient in captivity, raking in food and the like. They love termites, spending hours on termite mounds picking up soldiers, or jumping to catch them in flight. Periodically they are ousted by chimpanzees, who swagger in armed with probes, and the baboons retire to sit patiently and watch as the invaders fish out the juicy soldiers. When the apes depart, leaving their probes in the tunnels, the baboons resume their antics, without a thought of re-using the discarded fishing stems. Since individual baboons do occasionally master the art of tool-wielding, their reluctance now to follow the apes demonstrates their poor capacity to learn the trade through imitation. As Beck explains, tool-use hit on accidentally and reinforced by a food haul might be retained and refined *by the individual* baboon, but those watching fail to profit unless they too follow the same accidental route.[29] Chimpanzees are irrepressible copyists, and novel acts spread infectiously (particularly via the susceptible young, who enthusiastically mimic fishing or wound dabbing, sometimes in the most ludicrously inappropriate contexts; perfection takes many years, at least six for fishing). The baboon's very inability to learn by observation scuppers any chances of a tool-using tradition arising, hence they have never been observed *making* tools or importing raw material.

No one has yet tackled the question of what mental prerequisites are necessary for tool-making. No one has really *had* to. Until apes in the 1960s caught us on the hop, we had only to account for tool-use in man, hence our laxity, since we assumed rather sloppily that it was a practical manifestation of our "reasoning" powers. Apes have taught us to peer more closely, to question again the bases of our own actions rather than take them for granted (too much has hidden behind the skirts of "reason" for too long). I suspect there is no single answer to the question of the prerequisites to tool-making in man and apes, since a mosaic of cognitive, learning and behavioural skills is employed, although crucial, I imagine, are conceptual and cross-modal abilities.

Since Kenneth P. Oakley made regular tool manufacture dependent on conceptual thought, we might expect little resistance to the ape as a conceptual thinker. (To put it this bluntly is almost tempting Providence.) In defining man, an almost perennial occupation, Oakley in 1962 adopted Dr. Johnson's venerable definition ("a tool-making animal"). Since these were effectively pre-Goodall days, he could argue that "The *manufacture* of tools requires mental activity of a different order" from the ape's.[30] One craves some idea of *how* different. The only clue Oakley throws out is this: "The power of abstraction or conceptual thought is basic to the regular manufacture of tools. In apes it is no more than nascent." The emphasis was dogmatically placed on the first deliberately manufactured stone tools (which Mary Leakey has now traced back 2·6 million years). These, for Oakley, signified that "the complexity of organization for conceptual thought" had been reached. Fact and theory fell so beautifully together. Man made tools and tools made man. First fact, and now theory, have been violently shaken.

It is enlightening to watch anthropologists manoeuvring as the first

reports of regular chimp tool-making trickled in. In *Nature* early in
1964, Jane Goodall reported chimpanzees termite-fishing, stone-
throwing (once with a 15 lb stone) and manufacturing leaf-sponges
and leaf-wads. Scanning the literature for the ensuing couple of years,
one finds a veritable spate of *ad hoc* amendments to Dr. Johnson's
definition, designed in effect to readjust the wording, while leaving its
intent unchanged. Paradoxical statements like the following abounded.

> Despite this rather impressive demonstration of a kind of tool-
> using, it is unlikely that we must change our definition of man,
> the genus *Homo*, and remove the criterion of toolmaking
> simply because chimpanzees use tools.[31]

Chimps merely "stumbled into making tools". One gets the feeling
that it was little more than a lucky accident and scarcely worth bother-
ing about. In *Origin of Man* (1966), John Buettner-Janush argued that
"man makes and uses tools in a distinctly different way than chimpanzees". Expansion of the human cortex in those areas "concerned with
conscious control over complex behavior" gave man the neuro-
mechanics necessary for proper tool-making. It was "the consequence
of the capacity to use symbols", implying that because chimps were
apparently incapable of using symbols, they could not have been
making real tools. Oakley, in *Man the Tool-Maker*, resorted to arguing
that systematic tool manufacture in man was guided by conceptual
thought "in contrast to the mainly perceptual thinking in apes".[32]

Ages struggling with transition should be shown the greatest toler-
ance. Times were intellectually hard; they tend to be when the status
quo is threatened. It is all too easy with the benefit of hindsight and the
impressive 1970s platform to be hypercritical. After all, the mid-1960s
were not to know that apes *did* have a potential for symbolic communication, or conceptual thought, or cross-modal association, or even
self-consciousness. We should beware feeling smug with this knowledge. Subsequent psychological findings have placed ape tool manufacture into a reasonable cognitive context, making it no longer the
freak act of a perceptual thinker.

Goodall's termiting chimps rocked the boat with some strange
repercussions. Early in 1971 R. V. S. Wright was contemplating the
problem when a delicious thought crossed his mind. What would have
happened if "Jane Goodall had seen a group of apes striking flakes from

a core and using these flakes as cutting tools? How would the news have been received by anthropologists?"[33] Rather than banning such heresies from his mind, Wright humoured himself. He guessed the answer. Nobody wants apes labelled 'human' just because they act like us, so the discovery would have been played down, as it actually was with chimp termiting ("rare", "opportunistic", *etc.*). In the event, humanity would have seen its beginnings at a more advanced stage, say, the trimmed flint stage. Wright's heresy began to assume mammoth proportions. But apes do not fashion flints, besides, nobody would credit an orang-utan with either the manual dexterity or mental competence for such a momentously human action. Doubts had even been openly expressed about *Australopithecus'* ability to manufacture tools, despite Dart's discovery of humerus bludgeons. Swept along by his heresy, Wright hit on a devilish experiment, designed to cast a storm-cloud of doubt over the prevailing belief that *Australopithecus* had neither brains nor skill. Wright reasoned that, even if the stone tools were originally made by *Australopithecus'* contemporary, the bigger brained *Homo habilis* (by 1970 it was becoming apparent that two or more human types lived alongside one another in the East African Rift Valley), still the smaller-brained *Australopithecus* could have watched attentively and imitated the procedure.

Wright wondered whether an even more handicapped ape could learn "to use a hammerstone to strike a flake from a flint core, and to use this flake as a tool to open a box". The odds were against his succeeding in teaching an ape, and lengthened alarmingly when he found that only orang-utans were at his disposal. With orangs hampered by crooked fingers and stumpy thumbs even shorter than those of the chimp, the test was as much for anatomical as psychological inabilities to work stone. (Another point prejudicing its case was the orang's genetic distance from man. They are also arborial in the wild, which was thought to militate against chimp-style systematic tool-making: necessarily a terrestrial, free-hand activity.) So with the odds stacked heavily against him, Wright set out to teach the tool trade to Abang, Bristol Zoo's five-and-a-half-year-old orang. Sitting inside the orang's cage, Wright found himself as much the focus of public attention as Abang. The spectacle proceeded: first, he repeatedly showed Abang how to cut a nylon rope with a flint in order to open the food box. Then he passed the flint saw to a bemused Abang. After little more than an hour's exposure (during two sessions, a week apart) a hungry Abang set about sawing the cord each time his food box appeared. To achieve this, he had mastered the pongid 'precision' grip, grasping the flake between the thumb and side of the index finger, with the fist held clenched.

Wright moved on to phase two. With a pebble hammerstone, he actually struck a flake from the flint core. Abang watched attentively; he evidently enjoyed the cacophony but repeatedly failed to make the connection, banging this curious hammerstone on the cage walls as much as the core. After continually wrenching the core off its support (mechanical failure bedevils any ape experiment), Abang struck a flake, only to pick it up in his teeth and begin cutting the cord (it did not work, but the technique was sound). By the eighth session, Abang was detaching flakes, by the tenth he was severing the cord (total experiment time was now about three hours). Presented with a fruit box, hammerstone and flint nodule, he now ran through the sequence of striking a flake and sawing the cord. There was, of course, a subtle technique involved, human Palaeolithic flint-makers were well aware of this, and Abang too apparently realised that for his best chance of success, the core should be struck on its rim. And being frustrated by Wright's bungling in steadying the core, Abang took the initiative and grasped it in his toes.

Light relief aside, Wright had defied the odds and shown, contrary to all expectations, that even an ape with the orang's physical and psychological 'disabilities' could work stone. Wright concluded that Abang's achievement made "it improbable that Australopithecines were prevented from imitating stone flaking by deficiencies in their intelligence and manipulative skills". However true this might be, Abang is not an *Australopithecus*, but a heavy red ape who prefers brachiating through tree-tops; so, if anything, this excursion into tool-making should tell us more about apes than 'ape-men'. Wright was quick with a disclaimer: he was not, he insisted, out to prove insight. It was, however, a clear case of learning by imitation and trial-and-error practice – but that is how technology is transmitted once the initial insight occurs (the process is enhanced, but not superseded, by language in man – many skilled trades are still learnt by imitation). And even talk of Abang's "mimicry" essentially ignores his constructive innovations, like grasping the core with his long toes to steady it, holding the flake in his teeth, and learning where exactly to strike. But we must beware of claiming too much for Abang, of placing this ape hero in our pongid pantheon alongside Washoe, Sarah and Lana. Abang, like so many apes before him, simply demonstrated an ability to learn. The experiment gives no indication of how that potential is actually realised in some adaptive situation (which was not Wright's intent). For that, we are better off observing the Gombe apes' less ambitious attack on the ant problem.

7

Is Romance Really Dead? - An Historical Interregnum

".... language is no longer the exclusive domain of man".
Penny Patterson (1978)[1]

"Chimps do not have any significant degree of human language and when, in two to five years, this fact becomes properly disseminated, it will be of interest to ask, Why were we so easily duped by the claim that they do?"
David Premack (1978)[2]

The air of bravado in behaviourist circles was guaranteed to raise psycholinguist hackles. The Gardners hinted that it was now those, defiant in their stand on what a chimp can never do, "who must proceed with caution".[3] The psycholinguist riposte has been variously interpreted as anything from tempered scientific caution to a paranoid desire to exclude the ape interloper at any cost. Some saw it as a last ditch defence of human language, comparable almost to Lyell's moral imperative to retain human "dignity" in the face of encroaching evolution. To this end Lyell had willingly stripped geological history of any vestige of progress which might emphasise man's bestial origins (just as linguists were imagined robbing Washoe of her achievements). Even when, in the 1860s Lyell conceded that man might, as the *Athenaeum* said, have 100,000 apes for ancestors, he still clung to an 'ordained' evolution and Divine implantation of human reason. Darwin trod heavily on Lyell's feelings. He admitted not giving two straws for "dignity"; indeed, Darwin cared little "whether we are looked at as mere savages in the remotely distant future".[4] Behaviourists now took up what they imagined to be Darwinian cudgels to slay the slain, seeing the spectre of Lyell's "nobility" in the language bastion.

Jacob Bronowski and Ursula Bellugi were harangued for answering the Gardners with what many felt was a traditionalist reaffirmation of faith. Bronowski, of course, was shortly to reach millions with his *Ascent of Man*, Bellugi was an ASL analyst, and both at this time were attached to the Salk Institute in California. Their rejoinder in *Science* appeared in May 1970, hot on the Gardners' heels; entitled "Language, Name, and Concept", it attempted to show that Washoe differed from a child in her "failure so far to develop any form of sentence structure", in "the reconstitution of language, in which we believe the human capacity is unique", and her failure to ask questions.[5] I pick out these salient points because it shows how premature was the rejoinder. There *is* some kind of, perhaps idiosyncratic, structure to ape strings; chimpanzees and gorillas *do* reconstitute; and Lana *does* turn the tables by asking questions.

But if the point of their paper was to eke out some uniqueness criterion in human language, I would utter a word in defence. Each lifeform is preciously unique, the whole gist of Darwin's *Origin* was to derive the teeming multitudes of peculiar lifeforms from a common ancestor. Darwin was the first man in history to see novelty as the great gift of evolution. His embarassingly simple explanation was that each animal or plant specialises into its own ecological cranny – thus slowly but irrevocably growing apart from its cousins. Winkling out man's real point of evolutionary departure aids us immeasurably in explaining man – naturally. But apes are unique too; and where the uniqueness argument becomes so terrifyingly chauvinistic is when *that* is conveniently forgotten. Too often chimpanzees are seen as fallen by the wayside on our human road: they never made it.

Today's disheartening situation might be parodied as follows. The 'establishment' denies apes language almost on a point of honour, and is confronted by ape sympathisers, arguing indignantly that the last bastion has fallen. Human language is the shimmering prize awaiting the winner of this scientific scrap. Eugene Linden in *Apes, Men, and Language* (1975) leaves the impression that apes have overturned the final language barrier; it was no longer the vaunted distinction of mankind.[6] I applaud well-meaning attempts to demolish arrogance (and there is enough to go round in psychology and anthropology). But it is suicidal to demand a fair hearing for apes and then break all the commandments by measuring them with a *human* yardstick, when they can only come off second best. I stand on the same reformist platform as ape sympathisers, although I see only Pyrrhic victories being gained as long as the argument rests on a spurious philosophic footing.

The whole issue again recalls that Huxley–Owen fiasco a century ago – right down to its ignominious conclusion. Owen categorically denied apes that cortical convolution, the hippocampus. In this, man was unique, and deservedly sat alone in a separate subclass. As a brash contender, Huxley had been spoiling for a fight, his private letters in the later 1850s just ooze antagonism and the desire to go for Owen's throat. Huxley as good as called Owen a liar, dissected out the missing hippocampus, and took his case to the people. The people, of course, loved nothing more than to watch the mighty fall; children could even follow a cleaned-up version of the fight in Charles Kingsley's parody *The Water Babies*. The *Athenaeum* rattled for two years to blasphemous charges and counter-charges. Each side accused the other of intellectual dishonesty, deceit and worse. Surgeons and anatomists joined in the pelting, and ape brain papers flooded anatomical journals. In 1861 it quickly became *the* evolutionary issue, almost surpassing the *Origin of Species*. It looked for all the world as though man's descent from a gorilla hinged on the outcome (indeed, the debate partly ran under the explicit title "Ape-Origin of Man as Tested by the Brain"[7]). Owen was wrong and he suffered appallingly for it. Caught in a cruel fix, he was roasted by Huxley (the Huxley archives in Imperial College, London, house wads of letters from supporters, egging on Huxley to "challenge" Owen and topple the "dictator"). But throughout the controversy, nobody stopped to ask "So what?" Only later did a scoffing *Edinburgh Review* point up its "extreme absurdity", laughing that if top scientists will lay their lives on the line, "it is at least desirable that the subject in dispute should have some real meaning".[8] Nothing whatever was known of hippocampus function and it was "a matter of perfect indifference to the real progress of science" whether apes are endowed or not. Somehow the whole issue got side-tracked.

Opposing ideologies have an infuriating habit of settling for irrelevant factual battlegrounds. If man's gorilla ancestry hung on the ape's hippocampus, the matter would have been sealed in 1863. The interminable debate over the ape's possession of human language is an equally bogus issue. Not because language lacks an adequate definition, but because the case rests on a dead metaphysics, which sees man the measure of Creation. Just as the *Edinburgh Review* denounced the Huxley-Owen fracas as a "silly dispute" so today Lieberman finds it "pointless and silly" to haggle over whether or not apes have human language.

The point surely is this: If the chimpanzee is imagined squatting one rung below man, then to destroy man's claim to uniqueness the ape has to be hoisted up *in man's direction*. This seems to be what 'pongists' are fervently doing; and with the greatest success, judging by the fact that in the eyes, not of the law, but her defending attorney, Koko has "ascended" out of the ape grade. Indeed, I was drawn from an analysis of Darwinian *vs.* nonDarwinian evolution to study the ape's artificial "language" precisely because my excitement over Washoe and Sarah turned to confusion as I looked to experimental objectives. Goals seemed confused, or so I thought, because the problem had been formulated in nonDarwinian terms.

NonDarwinian Evolution – The Meaning of "Ascent"

"[Orthodoxy accepts] that the rise from the sponge to the cuttlefish, and thence through fish, reptile, and bird to marsupial had occurred . . . and from the Chimpanzee to the Bushman, and at length to naked Britons, all by a law of creation ending with the development into an Anglo-Saxon."

Charles Lyell complaining,
15 May 1860.[9]

But was the world of Darwin's ideological opponents *so* drastically different from that of young Darwin? The answer is a categorical 'yes' – more than anyone today appreciates. It turns out to be the diametric opposite of Darwinism, in both direction and intent. So, in the interest of straightening out apes, let us digress and cast a harsh light on some forgotten but no less fascinating men and their living legacy. Only this can clear the air before we reformulate fresh Darwinian goals.

Resurrecting preDarwinians to analyse their scientific intentions is not easy. Whom do we choose? I will leave Lamarck interred, even though he imagined the Angolan chimpanzee one rung below mankind and only prevented from rising in status towards Man by human repression. Lamarck's system might have served well; it was based solidly on the eighteenth-century ladder of nature with each creature stacked and ranked in a great chain from worm to man. Lamarck adroitly turned the ladder into an escalator, unleashing the 'lowly' to climb past their Providential station. But the system was never truly historical. His escalator was stacked with living creatures; thus our 'ancestors' could still be counted among the living – the worm was just starting his ascent to the human apex, the ape was almost there.

Instead I will focus on a fascinating amateur, Robert Chambers – founder in those glorious days of self-help of *Chambers' Dictionary* and a multitude of practical guides – who in 1844 galvanised the Victorian world with his *Vestiges of the Natural History of Creation*. His system capitalised on the boom in stratigraphy that had occurred since Lamarck's day: the "vestiges" of the title were fossil remnants entombed in the rock strata. What Chambers thought he was doing, how he went about it and why he thus differed from Darwin were the subject of an enlightening paper in the *Journal of the History of Biology* for 1972 by science historian M. J. S. Hodge. Too much Darwin had been retrospectively read into Chambers, complained Hodge, with the result that the *Vestiges* was treated as a premature *Origin*.[10] Nothing could be further from the truth. Because both were labelled 'evolutionists' no one doubted that they shared a common problem – to prove the descent of diverse species from a common ancestor, to locate the mechanism for life's tree-like spread. Wrong again, nothing could have been further from Chambers' mind. Removing the *Origin* from view to examine the *Vestiges* afresh, we might be startled to find not a tree in sight; in fact, there is no *common* ancestry, nor a spread of life. This was wholly alien to the *Vestiges* – indeed, to the entire preDarwinian mentality.

"No common ancestry" sounds palpably absurd with postDarwinian hindsight. Far from it. Chambers had read Darwin's *Voyage of the Beagle* and similarly took the Galapagos Islands as a case study. Now, Darwin concentrated on the striking diversity of Galapagos finches, each peculiarly specialised (since the Galapagos woodpecker niche lay vacant, one finch even assumed that role). He concluded that an immigrant South American finch had reached the islands, there to diverge into every niche. Chambers knew nothing of life fanning out, for him it was a linear ascent. Since the volcanic islands were devoid of mammals, he reasoned that indigenous life had only had time to rise to an avian grade. Thus, the islands were evidently younger than mainland South America, where mammals flourished. Life had started from scratch *independently* in Galapagos and South America, it lagged behind in the former for want of time. The older the landmass, the 'higher' life had risen.

This startling image of a million lifelines spread across the planet, all at varying levels of ascent, has equally disturbing consequences. First: life's creation was continual and not, as for Darwin, a once-and-for-all Precambrian event. As worms began their ascent, "globules" of living matter were incessantly generated to fill the vacuum. Second: animals on different continents were totally unrelated. Kinship between, say, Australian and South American marsupials was impossible: life had simply attained the same grade in both regions. It only looked similar because life followed the same upward path with uncanny accuracy. The contrast with Darwin is dramatic. Hence my statement that Darwin was the first man in history to see uniqueness as evolution's great gift; for everyone else life was regimented, channelled strictly 'upwards', its destination known and its path preprogrammed.

Chambers, of course, was composing a biological hymn to Providence. The *Vestiges* was his attempt to snatch back God from miraculists (who demanded He intervene every time some paltry mollusc was needed) and return the rightful sublimity due an Omnipotent Being. As such, law was conceived a Divine fiat which drove life inexorably towards man, "the true and unmistakable head of animal nature upon this earth".[11]

Throwbacks

Chambers thus illustrates the two leading preDarwinian tenets: 1) Life's inexorable ascent argues a preordained directionality, and 2) Mankind marks the goal, and thus the measure of perfection.

By this token, the ape squats immediately below man, his time having not yet arrived. Moreover, preDarwinians could prove this. Chambers himself imagined that gestation simply had to increase for a perceptibly more perfect offspring to emerge; in this way fish might give way to reptiles and apes to men (curiously, Chambers was himself an advance on normal men, being born a hexadactyl, with twelve fingers and toes). Thus the man who sat resplendent atop the evolution-aiy edifice was nature's latest child, the result of ever-lengthening gestation. He actually relived that ancestral ascent in his own foetal development, which was a kind of microcosmic telescoping of his history. This had a pleasantly obvious corollary – and evolutionists, frustrated by lack of fossil men, eagerly exploited it. If life rose through prolonging pregnancy, might it not sink by truncating pregnancy? The system was open to experimental sabotage. Even crusading Darwinians like Carl Vogt resorted to nature's sadistic tricks to prove man's ascent. In a sinister twist to the evolutionary story, Vogt paraded microcephalic (small-brained) "idiots" from asylums as actual throw-backs to the ape stage. These makeshift missing links resulted when pregnancy was terminated prematurely. Vogt sealed the unfortunate "idiot's" fate, giving him a hideous orang's visage, gangling arms, and the mute and brutish mind as well as the loping "knuckle walk of the ape".

The logic seemed impeccable, so much so that the "idiot" as a throw-back was excruciatingly difficult to prise from the popular mind. Yet, for those who troubled to look, the argument teetered on a defunct premise. Romantic biology was no longer in the ascendant; the re-capitulation 'clincher' had in fact crumbled. The one thing Huxley and Owen might have agreed on was that man never really was a fish in the womb; but simply less differentiated and thus at a somewhat piscine-looking phase of his growth. Nor was the much maligned "idiot" an arrested ape. Huxley's accomplice John Marshall dissected the 8½ oz. brain of a pathetic thirty-nine inch human "idiot" to discover not that it was frozen at some ape stage, but that it was built on an undeniably human plan.[12] This should have been a mercy killing, but the asylumed 'ape' lived on.

Indeed, later in the century the Darwinian psychologist George John Romanes was still trotting out "idiots" as a prime example of nature's "experiment wherein the development of the human mind is arrested at some particular stage".[13] By grading idiots, he urged, we can piece together a picture of human mental evolution. The 1878 British Association gave him a standing ovation for his excursion into "idiot" evolution. His intent, *The Times* fairly judged, was "to show that man and brute have much more in common intellectually, and, perhaps, even morally, than is dreamt of in popular philosophy". But again, in the infuriating absence of fossil men, all he could do was bend apes up and man down and hope they met in the middle. Thus, reported *The Times*, he concentrated on "savages, young children, idiots, and uneducated deaf-mutes". These were the prime evolutionary ingredients. In "low savages" he insisted that "the intellectual and emotional character approximates to that of the higher animals". In the mental development of a child he discovered "a condensed epitome" of human evolution. And in deaf-mutes the mind, stripped of language, rested "on a level of that of a brute in respect of its power of forming abstract ideas".

This was a common preDarwinian tactic, taking its logic from nature's great chain where these unfortunates stood ready ranked. The surprise was how easily Darwinism absorbed it. Darwin himself lapped up all that Romanes had to offer, crooning on the topic of the "thoughtless" deaf-mutes, "I should like to read whole chapters on this one head, and others on the minds of the higher idiots." He suggested Romanes keep a monkey, "so as to observe its mind". Darwin's son Francis chipped in with a less than practical amendment. "Frank says you ought to keep an idiot, a deaf mute, a monkey, and a baby in your house!"[14]

Flippancy masks the importance of Frank's suggestion. The ape, "idiot" and baby were three primes of human evolution in an age before *Pithecanthropus* and *Australopithecus*. The ape stood in as ready-made ancestor; according to preDarwinians it could *still* be in ascent. The "idiot" was a throwback, his mental development arrested at some ape level. Foetal growth was a microcosmic replay of an untold million years of ancestry. All three, jigsawed into a nonDarwinian picture of evolution, were officially discredited by the 1860s, but together they retained an immensely potent image, almost impossible to eradicate.

To this mosaic of ancestors and throwbacks a 'savage' was added, a frozen relic who had failed to advance out of the Stone Age. For centuries, aboriginals had slotted comfortably between white man and ape in the feudal hierarchy, being credited with scarcely more morality than a conscientious chimpanzee. Few rose to their defence, although one harsh critic of such defamatory statements was natural selection's co-discoverer, Alfred Russel Wallace. "The more I see of uncivilized people," he pleaded in 1855, "the better I think of human nature, and the essential differences between civilized and savage men seem to disappear."[15] And Wallace, unlike armchair Victorians pontificating on their own moral excellence, had lived happily among 'savages' in the Amazon and Far East. Today, cultural anthropology is feeling its way back to Darwin. While newspapers daily hail each new contact with emergent "Stone Age" tribes, anthropologists politely point out that Palaeolithic Europe ending 10,000 years ago was fundamentally different from modern jungle New Guinea. The barely common denominator among their peoples turns out to be stones; otherwise the habitats and socioeconomic bases of life are incomparable – we are not dealing with 'frozen' Stone Age relics. But old prejudices die hard. For this reason Columbia anthropologist Marvin Harris churns out book after book "to replace the old onwards-and-upwards Victorian view of progress with a more realistic account of cultural evolution". Thus he brilliantly reinterprets (see *Cannibals and Kings*, 1978) customs striking Westerners as bizarre or plain abhorrent in terms of cultural cost-effectiveness. Aztec cannibalism, for instance, or worldwide acts of infanticide, which only last century were dismissed as atavistic acts of animal criminality – *i.e.*, behavioural throwbacks to more bestial days – become cultural consequences of a play-off between human reproductive strategies and local, usually dwindling, resources. (The Aztec empire, for example, was run on a protein-deficient agriculture; the deficit was made up by the wholesale consumption of human meat.) Rituals are socially adaptive responses to ecological pressures. Even Christianity, according to Harris' adaptive canons, might turn out more "the gift of the lamb in the manger than the child who was born in it".[16]

But the fact that so eminent an anthropologist as Harris should need to hammer away in the late 1970s shows how ensconced the ladder has become. Of course, there have been powerful social and economic forces safeguarding it; colonialism needed nothing so much as a moral sanction to exterminate and enslave the 'weak' (= 'lowly'). The image of the retarded savage completed the quasiDarwinian superstructure, reassuring proof of the white man's definitive position, one step from immortality.

This preDarwinian ethic was not so much grafted on to Darwinism as absorbed by it (to cloud an already obscure issue). The assemblage of 'lowly' animals, 'subhumans' and 'inferiority' on the one hand, counterbalanced by 'progress', 'superiority' and the human 'apex' on the other,

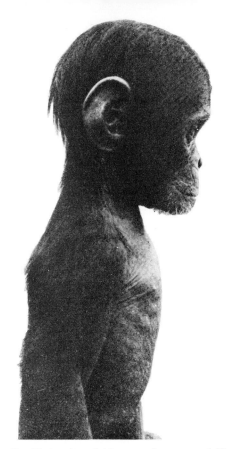 

David Greybeard (1), one of Jane Goodall's Gombe chimpanzees, displays the characteristic adult muzzle and receding forehead. By contrast, man's flat face, massive brain, reduced pelt and upright frame recall the features of foetal and infant apes (2). The embryonic chimp has in fact about the same brain-body ratio as an adult man, although as the ape matures its body grows disproportionately. Human ancestors may have slowed this body growth, freezing the high brain-body ratio, and leaving modern man a neotenous Peter Pan. Below: the contrasting crania of adult (3) and infant gorilla (4).

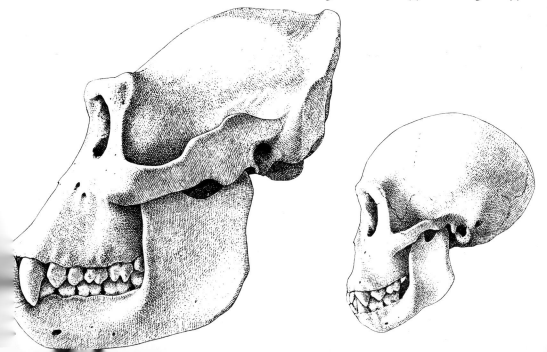

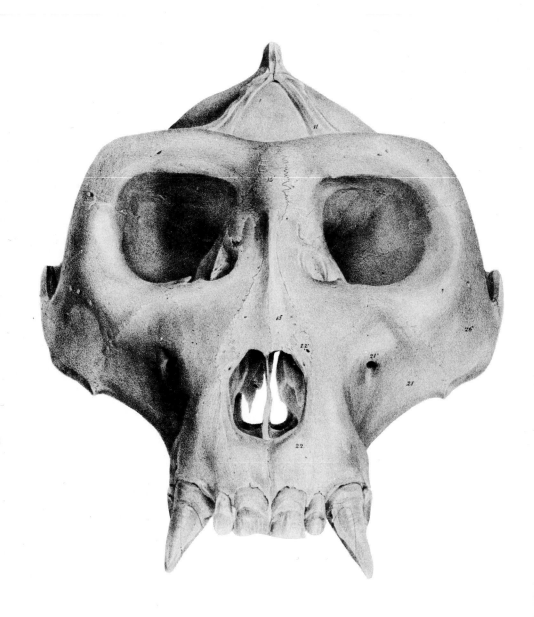

Taxonomists still group together man and gorilla (5) on physical grounds. Sooner or later, they must grasp the nettle and take into account the psycho-social realm, where matters are infinitely more problematic. It has long been the ideological imperative to make *Homo sapiens* a psychically distinct being. Indeed, it is still suggested that if mental development were any criterion, man would stand in a Kingdom by himself.

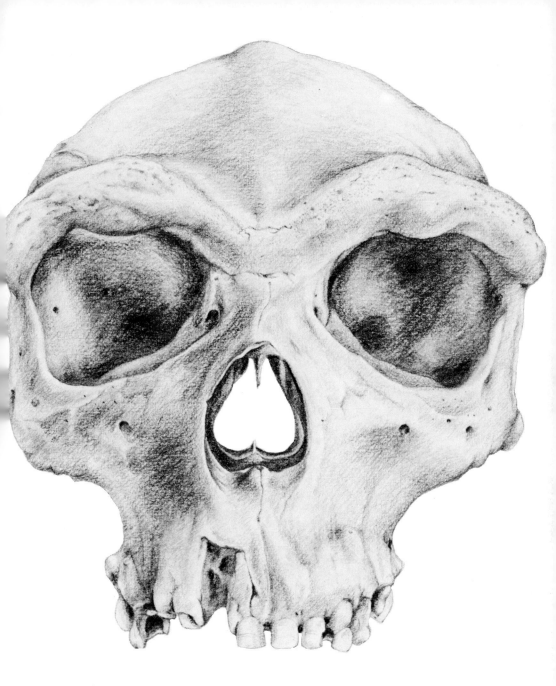

Rhodesian man (6), a Neanderthal perhaps 125,000 years old, showing massive skull thickening and sloping forehead – so much so that the finder first mistook it for a fossil gorilla. Later Neanderthal men betrayed their consciousness of death in lavish flower burials. Awareness of death presumably hinges on self-awareness, since a being has to "exist" before it can die. Mirror and self-recognition tests now suggest that apes may possess at least this preliminary awareness of self.

(7) Young Neam Chimpsky at Columbia signs "dirty" to his teacher Joyce Butler. Originally, this meant "I want to use the toilet", but finding it handy for breaking off boring lessons, Nim used it as a bogus excuse to escape his schooling. Here Joyce sympathises, signing "house", meaning "Do you want to go into the house?"

"YOU"

(8) A remarkable film clip: Koko points an angry finger at Francine Patterson and signs, "You dirty bad toilet".

"DIRTY"

"BAD"

"TOILET"

(9) "Flower" in artificial chimpanzee sign 'language'. Washoe interpreted this sign to refer to the smell, so she generalised it to pipe tobacco and kitchen fumes. This illustrates the problem of interpreting the *ape's* meaning.

(10) Patterson glosses this sign by Koko as "think". Yet there are awesome problems attached to this interpretation. Even assuming that the gorilla did mean something akin to "think", the word cannot possibly carry an identical meaning to our human word, simply because the brains and thus brainstates to which this sign refers differ in man and gorilla.

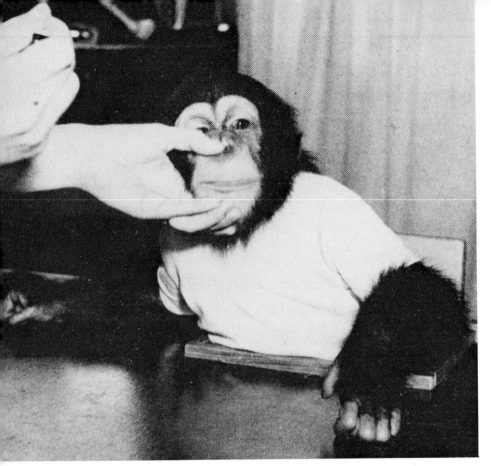

(11) Viki being coaxed to speak in the 1950s, with infuriatingly little success.

(12 below) At least part of the reason apes fail to speak is the lack of human-like vocal cords in the neck region. (13 right) The long organ-pipe air passages in adult man contrast (below) sharply with the truncated pipes in the infant (above) and ape (centre).

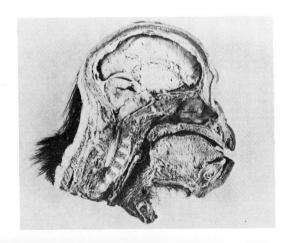

(14) David Premack's chimpanzee Sarah pondering the hierarchical 'sentence', *Sarah put apple pail banana dish*, meaning "put the apple in the pail and the banana in the dish". Is this language, or sophisticated problem solving? When human volunteers were similarly conditioned with plastic "words", they scored equally well on Sarah's tests, but had no idea that it was a language, nor were they able to translate into English.

(15) Elizabeth responding to the plastic "word" instruction: *Elizabeth give apple Amy.*

(16) Lana composing a "sentence" of lexigrams on her keyboard. Originally, her stock "sentence" *machine give . . .* must have been meaningless, or, at least, a ritualistic sequence necessary to precede her demand for candy. In fact, pigeons can be taught to peck colours in sequence in order to obtain corn, although no one dreams of adding the linguistic gloss "give pigeon corn". Lana, however, later began manipulating some of her "words" in intriguing ways. By 1978 the Rumbaughs were attacking the central question: "Can the ape understand the *symbolic* nature of the lexigram?"

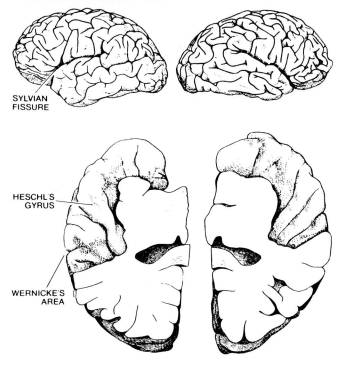

(17) In the human cortex, the Sylvian fissure on the left side is usually deflected downwards, and may even be a little longer than its right counterpart. This marks the development of Wernicke's comprehension centre, and thus indicates that speech functions have been assumed by the left hemisphere.

SYLVIAN FISSURE

HESCHL'S GYRUS

WERNICKE'S AREA

(18) In 1975 Marjorie LeMay and Norman Geschwind investigated the cerebral hemispheres of apes, discovering that orang-utan brains are also asymmetrical – though to a lesser extent than in man. (Orang above: human below.) The ape's left temporal lobe often has a deflected Sylvian fissure, suggesting that the "speech" and comprehension centres had already expanded. But why, if not for speech?

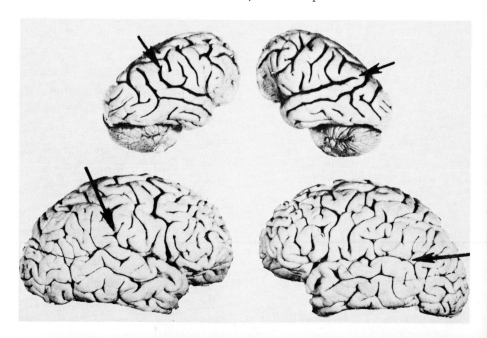

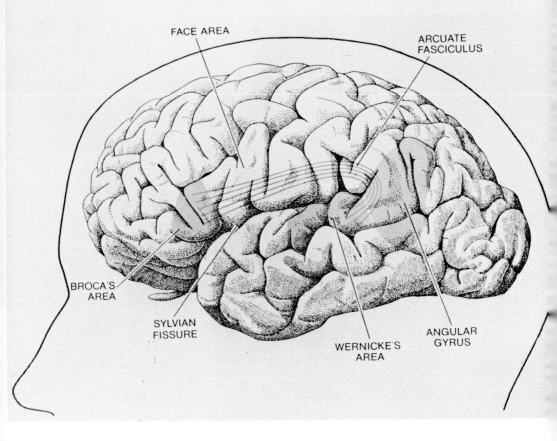

FACE AREA

ARCUATE
FASCICULUS

BROCA'S
AREA

SYLVIAN
FISSURE

WERNICKE'S
AREA

ANGULAR
GYRUS

(19) Broca's area is sited near the region of cerebral cortex controlling the lip muscles, mouth, tongue and vocal cords, and probably serves to coordinate their movement. Wernicke's area is primarily concerned with decoding and comprehension, and hence it borders on the auditory association area. The angular gyrus probably associates sight and sound, such as an object and a word – and thus could be an important precursor for the development of language. It is highly probable that all great apes have homologues of Broca's and Wernicke's areas, as well as the angular gyrus, much smaller than in man, but nonetheless of similar cellular architecture.

(20) Termite 'fishing' is a technical skill which may take the infant chimpanzee six years to learn. It is, in a real sense, a *tradition*, since the technique has to be copied and mastered by each new generation.

(b)

(21) Chimpanzees may carry probes over a hundred yards to the fishing site. The manufacture and "intelligent" use of tools was until the last decade thought to be peculiarly human: the practical product of something unquestioningly called "reason".

(22) The Hayes published this photograph of Viki in 1954 without comment. She is clearly using pliers to pull a tooth that she could only see using a mirror. Hence she was well aware that it was *herself* out there, behind the mirror. Gordon Gallup suggests that mirror self-recognition depends upon the presence of a self-concept. So far, only well-adjusted humans and apes past the age of about twenty months have learnt self-recognition, despite the fact that Gallup has saturated monkeys with over 2400 hours of mirror exposure.

(23) "Humanized" apes like Lucy delight in making crazy faces into mirrors. Here, Koko admires her chalk-marked features in a vanity mirror.

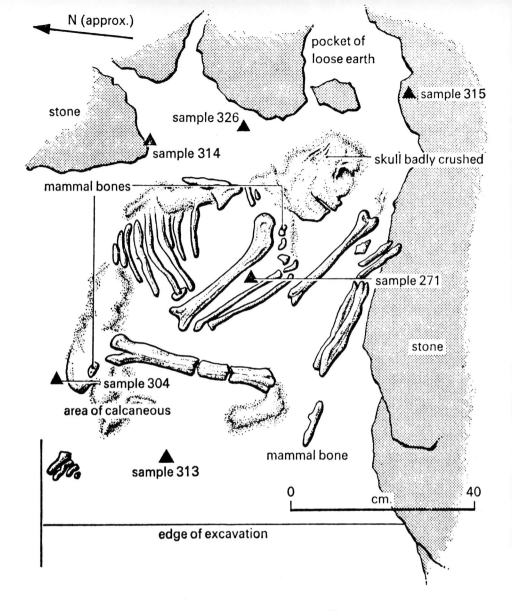

N (approx.)

pocket of
loose earth

sample 315

stone

sample 326

sample 314

skull badly crushed

mammal bones

sample 271

stone

sample 304

area of calcaneous

mammal bone

sample 313

0   cm.   40

edge of excavation

(24) Self-awareness seems a logical prerequisite for death awareness, which is first encountered at the Neanderthal stage. (Of course, the trauma of death-contemplation probably struck ancestral humans long before Neanderthal man; although this is not a fact easily determined from fossils.) At Ralph Solecki's Shanidar site in North-East Iraq, the Neanderthal corpses had been lain on mats of horsetail in carefully dug graves, then covered with blue and yellow bouquets of hyacinths and hollyhocks, freshly collected on a late Spring day, 60,000 years ago. Numbers 313 and 314 were soil samples which first showed up pollen clusters, suggesting that posies of flowers had covered the deceased.

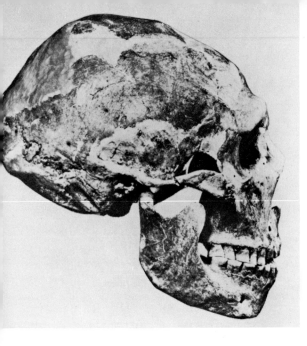

(25) The best preserved of the Shanidar Neanderthal skulls. Notice the 'swept back' cranium, receding forehead and massive brows. Curiously, the brain – at 1600 c.c. – was larger than existing man's.

(26) Twentieth-century programmes of ape humanisation have raised tantalising questions. How does a chimpanzee brought up by an alien species, a human family, see its self? (Still more intriguing, how would a human raised by chimpanzees?) Lucy (above, with her foster mother, Jane Temerlin) displays a degree of species confusion, and in oestrus is sexually attracted to 'other' humans – though not her foster father. She receives her own copy of *Playgirl* and positively drools over the naked men. Lucy has never seen another chimpanzee, although she instantly recognises her photograph in magazines.

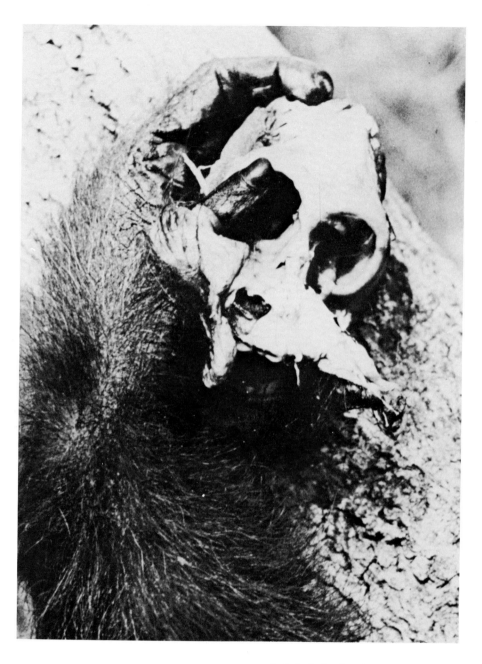

(27) Mike's thumb grips the partly devoured skull of a colobus monkey. Colobus were probably the Gombe chimpanzees' chief prey before banana provisioning brought them into competition with baboons in the later 1960s.

(28) Chimpanzee-baboon relationship is perplexing. Often the young of both troops play happily together – and there are even cases on record of genuine friendships blossoming.

(29) The chimpanzees were not above teasing the baboons. Here Figan butts Job, the old baboon, as a friendly provocation. On occasions, the teasing led to tempers fraying and minor skirmishes (30). On other occasions, male baboons have been seen requesting grooming from chimps, and even making amorous advances. This had led to a belief that the Gombe baboon-apes are a "mixed community".

(31) In the late 1960s the male Gombe chimps began systematically hunting baby baboons. As many as five males have been witnessed stalking in a coordinated fashion, jointly manoeuvring to catch their quarry unprotected. Here Mike strips away the shoulder flesh of a captured infant.

(32) Mike scalps the victim and sucks out the eyes prior to eating the brain, clearly a delicacy.

(33) Having stabbed a hole through the cranium with his canines, Mike inserts a leaf wad into the brain pulp, fingers it around, and then scoops up the tasty morsel. Although Leakey sits watching, highly-prized brain tissue, unlike the rest of the carcass, is rarely shared, and remains the captor's spoils.

(34) After a kill, the flesh is savoured with almost ritualistic thoroughness. Sharing clusters surround each individual with a joint, and anything up to a day may be spent dividing the kill. Chimps may beg, with hand held out, palm uppermost.

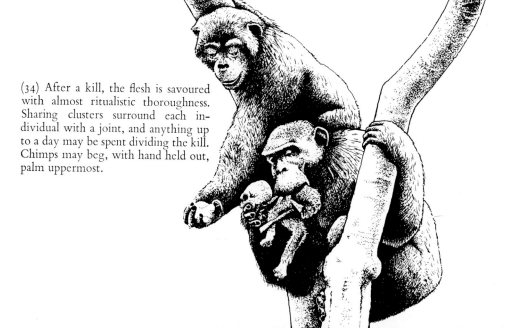

(35) Infanticide and cannibalism among wild chimpanzees were first systematically observed in 1971. The adult Gombe males cornered and terrorised an unfamiliar mother, snatching and thrashing to death her infant. Here Figan drags the baby's corpse into a tree, constantly beating it. The body passed from ape to ape, though most seemed confused, unsure whether to eat or groom it, some even treating it with the dignity due a dead community member. By the end of the episode, the infant was mutilated, but very little had actually been eaten. The Gombe has witnessed a gruesome spate of murders in the last few years, with members of a splinter group being successively butchered by the main troop.

(36) Since 1975, Passion (right) and her daughter Pom (left) have been seen snatching and killing three infants of lower-ranking (and partially crippled) females. Here they sit with Gilka's baby. They then spent five hours devouring it.

(37) Bandit (right, watching worriedly) had previously been shown a fake snake. He then led the group back to that spot. All knew that something frightening was hidden in the grass; in fact, some chimps had already run away in fear, and Belle cautiously prods about with a stick. Had food been buried, none of the apes would have hesitated from rummaging about with their hands. This was one of Emil Menzel's tests to determine the amount of information chimps can pass to one another using 'eye language'.

(38) Taking to heart early criticisms – that some ape trainers had forgotten that the function of language was communication – the Rumbaughs taught Austin and Sherman to communicate with one another using Lana's computer keyboard. If one was given food, the other (in a separate room with a connecting window) would request a piece. However, left to their own devices, the status-conscious chimpanzees played havoc with experiments which required them to mimic human reciprocal altruism. Rank-pulling Sherman asked Austin for a delicacy, chocolate, and the lower-status Austin happily complied. When Austin's turn came, he asked Sherman for a piece of his chocolate. Sherman, far from returning the favour, glanced at the unmistakable message, "gimme chocolate", pretended to misread it, and fobbed Austin off with unappetising monkey chow instead.

was a cultural package which so imbued Darwinism that eventually the tender revolutionary himself talked unselfconsciously in these terms. An age enraptured by scientific and technical progress – an age of bourgeois man rising unaided through the ranks – somehow screamed out for Lamarckian scientific sanction. Darwin slowly came to reflect this feeling of cosmic ascent as he migrated further from his 'purist' starting point. The *Origin*, for example, became increasingly Lamarckian as editions fell from the press, while *The Descent of Man* enters the following plea.

> Man may be excused for feeling some pride at having risen, though not through his own exertions, to the very summit of the organic scale; and the fact of his having thus risen, instead of having been aboriginally placed there, may give him hope for a still higher destiny in the distant future.

Count the number of preDarwinian value-terms jam-packed in that single sentence – "risen", "summit", "scale", "higher". Indeed, closing the *Descent* Darwin utters his famous downbeat phrase – that despite his noble qualities "man still bears in his bodily frame the indelible stamp of his lowly origin".[17]

An Ideal for the Age – Whose Age?

Thus the tenor of the *Vestiges* survived – nay, thrived. After realising the full horror of Darwinism, many like the Duke of Argyll happily fell back on a Vestigean-like flow of life towards its human apotheosis. At least the light of its Creative imperative dispelled Darwin's Lucretian nightmare. What of the *Vestiges* itself? Scientific ravages turned it into an overnight sensation. Adam Sedgwick, furious that Chambers could skip the finer points of nineteenth-century natural theology to make law a Divine mandate, launched a bitter personal attack in the *Edinburgh Review* on this "rank, unbending, and degrading materialism". Choked with emotion he began flailing wildly:

> The sober facts of geology shuffled, so as to play a rogue's game [he told Lyell]; phrenology (that sinkhole of human folly and

prating coxcombry); spontaneous generation; transmutation of species; and I know not what; all to be swallowed, without tasting or trying, like so much horse-physic!! Gross credulity and rank infidelity joined in unlawful marriage, and breeding a deformed progeny of unnatural conclusions![18]

Sedgwick did not like it. Yet the *Vestiges* dished up just enough of what titillated the public to command prodigious sales. By 1860 eleven editions had sold out, plunging professional scientists to the depths of despair. It may have sold still more copies after the *Origin*'s appearance. It did, however, teach Darwin one sharp lesson. By 1844 he had already reached his early 'purist' position, and sketched out two essays on natural selection hopelessly at variance with the *Vestiges*' intent. In this mood Darwin scrutinised the newly published *Vestiges*, then pencilled in a margin: "Never use the word higher and lower."[19]

But of course the *Vestiges* left a rut into which the *Origin* too easily slipped. Even elderly Sedgwick, Darwin's geological mentor, tried to explain to the Archbishop of Dublin the *Origin*'s leading tenet: "There has been a continual ascent on the organic scale," His Grace learnt from Sedgwick, busy Vestigianising the *Origin*, "till organic nature became what it is, by one continued and unbroken stream of onward movement."[20] This misreading could not have been more off target, yet who but faithful Huxley saw it any differently? The people at last had their scientific sanction of social progress, while preconceptions of Caucasian supremacy seemed justified. Only Darwin, at times exhibiting an almost misanthropic bent (noticeably in dealing that sharp blow to Lyell s "dignity"), saw natural selection refuse to sanction biological privilege. In 1837, he had jotted in a clandestine notebook, "It is absurd to talk of one animal being higher than another."[21] Man has one criterion of "highness" – he scribbled with an endearing Darwinian twist – a bee would have quite another.

Social pressure and scientific needling, especially from St. George Mivart, softened his anti-feudalism. Mivart was a man who, more than any other, captured the feelings of the late nineteenth century; a forgotten man who both reflected and shaped an age, whose views are arguably still the leitmotif of public opinion on evolution, even in the 1970s. He was a prominent if embarrassingly liberal member of the Catholic community. Taught ape anatomy by the maestro himself, T. H. Huxley, Mivart became an ape authority in his own right, and

Darwin's *Descent* drew heavily on Mivart's monkey dissections. For his part, Mivart loathed Darwin's tone. In fact, he found the *Origin* a total misnomer – it completely by-passed the cause of variations (true), concentrating on their preservation, once arisen, by natural selection. For Mivart, species variation was orderly and progressive, channelled towards man by some hidden law. (Mivart polarised the issue into law *vs.* chance, thus sanctioning his own lawful stand and reducing Darwin to a Lucretian absurdity.) Again, life was found streaming gently but inexorably towards its culminating type; man, in Romanes' metaphor, being the "topmost inflorescence of one mighty growth".[22] Gently, that is, as long as no radically new principle was called into play. In "A Limit to Evolution", Mivart concentrated on nature's traumatic breaks – the primal emergence of life itself and the quantum jump from brute instinct to human reason. Only these hurdles were overcome by a Creative push. The ape was seeded with reason, its ascent complete, and a qualitatively new kind of 'animal' emerged – man. The chasm had never gaped more widely. Man, as a "free moral agent", Mivart concluded, differed "far more from the elephant or a gorilla than do these from the dust of the earth on which they tread".[23]

It was undeniably an ideal for the age. It rested on a view of law as an Omnipresent edict – and that, I suspect, was a predominant nineteenth-century viewpoint. It has also imperceptibly guided twentieth-century thinking. Evolution is still vaguely imagined an irrevocable 'ascent', man is somehow 'superior' – the whole point to the process. The Mivartian tone still dominates non-philosophic (and not necessarily Fundamentalist) thought. Reason remains an Absolute. Mivart put the definitive seal on human 'uniqueness'. It was Mivart whom Premack was bludgeoning to death with his attempts to drum some flag-saluting, God-fearing respect into Sarah.

The Romantic legacy is an image of life wending its way towards the human goal. Nature became self-aware through man, and his awareness stretched out to God, thus completing the cycle by turning back to the source. The sundry other creatures, by contrast, were just stepping stones on the human path, the worm was starting out, the ape almost there; although many felt that when God seeded his chosen race with Reason, the evolutionary process abruptly terminated and apes were frozen on their penultimate rung. Pulling this evolutionary view out of its theological cradle, we find two enduring characteristics: (1) Man is the sole sovereign being; only he has severed his chains through an inturning self-consciousness. No other creature can experience such freedom. (2) Since all life is frozen in ascent towards the human apex, it can only have an incomplete *human* appreciation of the world, if it has any at all. Today, a 'progressive' Romantic might argue that precocious apes had "advanced" by acquiring human language; they had stepped up to our level of understanding.

This of course is a travesty and total misreading of nature. We can never with the best will in the world 'elevate' an ape beyond its station; the very terms we are using betray our belief in a wholly defunct picture of evolution. The ape is not one rung below man (that is, a 'frozen' ancestor) and therefore it cannot step up anywhere. Even if it could, it wouldn't be to a *human* understanding. To have human language the ape must have a human meaning for words and a human syntax for sentences; this is a bare minimum. So it would have to have a human social and psychological framework that would intuitively lend words a human meaning. We are going round in circles; the ape would *be* human. Robert Chambers was both Romantic and heretical enough to see the ape's upward progression leading ultimately to the acquisition of language: in fact, there was nowhere else for the ape to go. But Darwin gave us a new vision, where man was no longer the goal and thus completion of nature.

Darwin's Alternative

The real reason that Darwin forced the most disruptive shift in human thought since Copernicus has barely begun to percolate. It was not evolution, it was not even natural selection – it *was* the defiantly iconoclastic assumptions underlying the *Origin*. What Darwin demolished was not 'Creation', but the metaphysics behind The Great Chain of Being, as ancient and venerable as Aristotle himself.

True, Darwin the 'purist' later becomes tainted. He is unable to stick to his guns; infuriatingly, he lapses into talk of life's ascent, he wonders whether the test of tooth-and-claw battle might not decide "competitive highness" after all. But cut through all that, return to the young idealist starting out, and one gets an inkling of the egalitarian stand modern biology has recaptured. We might reconstitute the young Darwin as follows.

Two views were current in his youth. First: as the goal of Creation, man was the metaphysical standard of perfection. But second: on ecological grounds, as Archdeacon Paley insisted, *each* animal was exquisitely (and Providentially) adapted to its niche. Few commented on this double standard of perfection, although in 1843 Louis Agassiz, Darwin's implacable foe from Harvard, brought it to a head:

> There can be no doubt, that a polypus, or a worm, is more imperfectly organized than a mammiferous animal, or man – more imperfect on principle; but does it follow from that, that these creatures are more imperfectly organized for the situation to which they are destined? Is man a more perfect being in the water, than a fish is in the air? Certainly not.[24]

The worm did not rise too high on life's scale. But in its way of life it was supreme. Herein lay the dilemma. Which standard really fitted nature? An egalitarian Darwin denounced the first – the 'scale' was jettisoned. Then he modified the second, adaptation, to explain life's changes. Darwin had studied the work of Paley at Cambridge until he could quote him backwards. Still, he knocked out the very core of Paley's Providential adaptation of life. It was not *perfectly* adapted, only imperfectly. There was always room for 'improvement'. As environments changed, life was in danger of losing its synchronism; it therefore evolved correspondingly to remain anchored in (or increase its hold on) that peculiar niche.

Darwin's mechanism could explain this. Population growth always outstripped the food supply, resulting in a struggle for what little there was. Any fortuitous variation better adapted than its cousins would thus be "favoured" (the *Origin* anthropomorphises nature to an infuriating extent). Since competing variants self-select the best adapted, the net result of evolution was an increasing specialisation. The only criterion of progress was 'improvement' relative to that environment. Life was therefore a never ending adaptive spread. 'Higher' and 'lower' lost all meaning for Darwin the 'purist'. Even in the compromised sixth edition of the *Origin* he still challenged: "who will decide whether a cuttlefish be higher than a bee",[25] an inane comparison since they were both beautifully adapted to strikingly different environments. Life's teeming multitudes no more aspire to humanity's lofty heights than man to vermiform existence. All creatures merely seek to strengthen their grip on surroundings. Spokesmen for nature's rampant inequality, however, notoriously resort to question-begging in order to achieve their aim. Edinburgh geneticist C. H. Waddington once pronounced that "we will take seriously the worm's claim to be our equals when the worms come and present it, but not before".[26] Notice how Waddington slips the criterion of superiority into the premise – the worm has to present his credentials! In other words, speech is not treated adaptively, but as a universal measuring rod; since only man has it, he places himself on a pinnacle. Such wonderfully transparent tricks are absolutely necessary, though, because no degree of deductive reasoning – as far as I can see – can winkle this conclusion out of Darwinian premises. Mercifully, as long as Darwin rules biology, he rules "God's chosen race" tactics strictly out of line.

Accurately speaking, nature is no more a community of 'equals' than 'unequals' – both are insupportable and meaningless value judgments; in respect of disparate creatures like Darwin's cuttlefish and bee, or man and worm, it is a community of incomparables. Hence Darwin's image of life specialising into every nook and cranny solved a major biological riddle without recourse to 'perfection' or 'ascent'; indeed, selection was blindly indifferent to Aristotelian 'Ups' and 'Downs'. Nature's aristocratic veneer crumbled under the canons of adaptation.

Man is of course a more recognisably kindred spirit of the ape than the worm; much of the man-ape evolutionary journey was shared, and they possess a high degree of common inheritance. But I want to pass *beyond* the similarities. Once we jettison our cumbersome Romantic baggage and wake up to the tyranny of nature's feudal chain, we suddenly encounter beings not aspiring to manhood but unconcernedly travelling their own path. Darwin's vision was nature spread before him; the biological concern of each species was its comfort, not its proximity to man. And this is what makes the ape's symbol-use potentially so exciting; since its social set-up and mental faculties are adapted to idiosyncratic ends, the interpretation it puts on words will not necessarily be a human one. Even the ape 'self', the very essence of pongid being, might have begun adaptively drifting from the man-stock's after the ancestral split. Treating the chimpanzee as a half-finished human prototype quashes any last chance of using symbols to explore its 'inner space', reaching out to a part-alien mind, on the fringes of the known world.

In 1960 Frank Drake aimed his 85-foot Green Bank antenna at Tau Ceti and Epsilon Eridani to intercept intelligent radio signals; since then we have combed the skies for an intelligence which might put man in cosmic perspective. Jung pictured us alone and confused, a "unique phenomenon" on a planet lacking another "conscious, reflecting being, gifted with speech" who might act as soulmate. Only when we "establish relations with quasi-human mammals inhabiting the stars", he thought, might we meet our match.[27] Our arrogance has never been contained, but in our belief that life throughout the galaxy aspires to the human form (Romanticism stamped soundly on to the Universe) it reaches truly cosmic proportions. We stretch to the stars, crying that we are alone, while knowing next to nothing of the psychic dimensions of the life surrounding us.

Mivart gruffly conceded that as zoologists we had to recognise our physical resemblance to the ape; yet in the psychic realm out of zoo-logical bounds man so blatantly transcended all other life, apes included, as to warrant a kingdom for himself. In 1974 Dobzhansky echoed this to the letter: the human body warrants only distinctive family status, but "If the zoological classification were based on psychological instead of morphological traits, man would have been considered a separate phylum or even kingdom."[28] Sooner or later zoologists will have to grasp the nettle and tackle mental experiences and their adaptive value; when they do I doubt whether they will see fit to split multi-cellular organisms into a tripartite arrangement plants-animals-man. The psychic realm is still unexplored territory; but our preconceptions of it seem designed to lead us astray. It should be embarrassing just how much these preconceptions, fashioned by theological imperative and cultural consideration, have intruded. It is evidently adaptively re-assuring for recent Judaeo-Christian man to feel psychically distinct. Death-knowledge in early *Homo* or even *Australopithecus* subsequently made theologies a panacea, afterlives a reward, and gods too frighten-ingly real. But possibly only in recent millennia and then only for certain sects has the blow of mortality been softened by the knowledge that *Homo sapiens* was singled out for eternal redemption. Faith in our unique self-awareness with its consequent moral transcendence has been conditioned with such methodical precision as to seem self-evident. It is part of the metaphysical back-drop we take for granted. When we question metaphysics the foundations begin to rock.

8

Reflections and Ripples

"It may sound ridiculous, but to date better quantitative evidence
of self-recognition exists for chimpanzees than for man."
Gordon Gallup, at a conference
on primate socioecology, 1975.[1]

An uneasy stalemate exists, leaving that towering psychological
enigma, Self-Consciousness, hanging perilously between the
murky swamps of metaphysics and the lush but ininhabitable
pastures of introspective analysis. Trapped like some lost soul in this
awful limbo it admits of no scientific explanation; indeed, Huxley's
proud claim, echoing clearly through to the present day, was of its
untouchability – biology simply had nothing in its arsenal to deal with
the Self. And yet, totally forgotten is the fact that this psychic apotheosis is pre-eminently a *social* and evolutionary problem; one, moreover,
tied tightly to the symbolic skills. From this quarter, then, we might
expect a glimmering of light.

We inherited a strong ideological bias from our pious Victorian
forebears, for whom it went without saying that 'morality made man'.
But the whole question of morality was inextricably entwined with
self-consciousness. By exercising a 'free' moral choice, man transcended
mere physical nature; in other words, he could act freely in respect to
a 'higher' moral law laid down by the Almighty (a judicial law in the
sense that it was not binding; as sinners we all broke it). Free will thus
allowed man to operate outside physical and environmental constraints,
to make truly uninhibited decisions on 'higher' moral issues. (Even
today, Christian apologists still insist on this. David Lack, who did
spectacular work illuminating "Darwin's finches" and their Galapagos

guises, nevertheless wrote unashamedly in 1957 that: "A Christian, agreeing to man's evolution by natural selection, has to add that man has spiritual attributes, good and evil, that are not a result of this evolution, but are of supernatural origin."[2]) Hence man, and man alone, of course, was endowed with the god-like gifts of reason and self-consciousness, that transcendent domain where the Will exercised free rein and whose policy decisions determined one's eternal destiny. Moral man was thus self-consciously unique. It was not a physical or an evolutionary problem, man had transcended nature, he was no longer one with the irrational brutes. Few doubted this, even in the evolutionary aftermath of the *Origin*; indeed, it was the mainstay of Mivart and the 'ordained' evolutionists. Horrified by the prospect, Darwin pushed ahead with his *Descent of Man* – whose intent might better be described as "The Descent of Morality" – to make morals evolutionary phenomena, a move tremendously upsetting to conservatives. The upshot, which Darwin's labours left untouched, was that self-consciousness was considered unique to man – an ideological bias, despite its context being torn away, that has passed to us largely unquestioned. Robert Ardrey, for once not championing our bestial alter-ego, spoke for the pre-1970s generation when he admitted in a strikingly Victorian passage in *African Genesis* that glorious man, that "shining link in the chain beyond knowing", was "the first animal conscious of self".[3]

Just as tool-making was unthinkingly accepted as a corollary of reason, and was thus self-evidently 'explained' (it aroused little more than a yawn until apes muscled in on the act – *then* questions were posed in earnest), so self-consciousness has slipped past dozing biologists. As psychologist Gordon Gallup wrote recently, "Since it is introspectively obvious that most humans do have a sense of self-awareness, this has fostered an empirical and conceptual laziness about operationalizing the phenomenon."[4] There was a greater laxity (for still more obvious reasons) in testing the ape; only the sudden recent upsurge of interest in psycho-biology catapulted a complacent science into action. Victorian ideology made mental science a kangaroo court as far as the miscreant ape was concerned. Indeed, until the late 1960s the verdict passed on ape selves was still "absent until proven present" – hence the recent research geared to uncovering the chimpanzee self, with the laughable result that man verges on knowing the ape better than himself (operationally speaking).

Seeing Yourself as Others See You

Operationalising self-awareness (that is, setting up a standard repeatable test to establish its presence) sounds a ludicrously impractical task; but since I can only have introspective knowledge of *my* self, can I ever be sure that I am not alone in a sea of automatons? One glaringly obvious way to test the self's existence – so obvious, in fact, that it has been totally overlooked – is with a mirror. The profundity of what takes place in a mirror is in perpetual danger of being lost through familiarity. Yet it is an extraordinary experience. A man, an ape or a canary can be brought face to face with a physiognomy it could never have seen before – its own. I think it is a far greater paradox that we see ourselves than that a canary does not (after all, if you have never seen a face before, how can you *recognise* it?). In man, it only comes with practice and learning experience in infancy through prolonged exposure to mirror doubles. Infants up to eighteen or twenty months still see a playmate, and frequently peer or grope behind the mirror to catch out this someone else. But having inherited the capacity, the baby eventually learns to recognise himself 'out there'. Of course it goes far deeper than just learning; quite probably, as a necessary prerequisite to achieve recognition, we need an integrated self-concept which we can bounce off the reflective surface and identify with. But how do we build up such a *recognisable* self-image before we actually see ourselves in a mirror?

Self-awareness and self-recognition are not identical, they are better described as 'isomorphs', and hence one should indicate the other's presence. In the months before the self strengthens in a child he sees a mirror companion, and in the months when it disintegrates in a schizophrenic the person may stand and stare intently in the mirror, progressively losing all powers of self-recognition. Apparently animals, unlike children, never learn to recognise their mirror image. They respond socially, behaving as they would towards a member of their own species, threatening, submitting or contact-calling. A chicken high in the pecking order will fly into a frenzy at the sight of this mirror-intruder, attempting to beat it into subservience to retain its own rank (necessarily a self-defeating process). The same is true of dogs and cage-birds, despite the pet owner's insistence as a point of honour that the animal recognises itself; in fact it recongises only a like-minded companion. All ape researchers at some time or other have given a mirror to their charges, and left some lovely accounts of the ensuing battles. This is Romanes', concerning an ape amusing spectators in the Jardin des Plantes;

> At last someone threw in a small hand looking-glass, with a strongly made frame of wood. This the ape at once laid hold of, and began to brandish like a hammer. Suddenly he was arrested by the reflection of himself in the glass, and looked puzzled for a moment; then he darted his head behind the glass to find the other of his kind that he evidently supposed to be there. Astonished to find nothing, he apparently bethought himself that he had not been quick enough with his movement. He now proceeded to raise and draw the glass nearer to him with great caution, and then with a swifter dart looked behind. Again finding nothing, he repeated the attempt once more. He now passed from astonishment to anger, and began to beat with the frame violently on the floor of the cage. Soon the glass was shattered, and pieces fell out. Continuing to beat, he was in the course of one blow again arrested by his image in the piece of glass still remaining in the frame. Then, as it seemed, he determined to make one trial more. More circumspectly than ever the whole first part of the process was gone through with; more violently than ever the final dart made. His fury over this last failure knew no bounds. He crunched the frame and glass together with his teeth, he beat on the floor, he crunched again, till nothing but splinters was left.[5]

Yerkes witnessed a less destructive episode with his young female gorilla Congo in 1927 (perhaps she was less concerned with intimidating the intruder than a male might have been). She kissed and fingered the image, keeping one hand dangling round the back of the two-foot mirror feeling for this stranger. Perplexed, she shuffled round behind the frame, only moving back again to gaze through this two-dimensional space portal. Eventually, she too resorted to thumping. But like all experimenters, Yerkes only allowed her ten-minute sessions, totalling at the end no more than an hour. "I have never yet kept her in the proximity of the mirror long enough to let her get tired of it and go away," he wrote.[6] A pity – if he had done, disinterestedness might have been the last thing he would have seen.

If self-recognition is learned, and we only realise our potential after prolonged exposure to mirrors, then next to nothing is gained by giving the gorilla a series of ten-minute peeks at itself. Coming to this conclusion, Gordon Gallup, then at Tulane University, thought it only fair to test monkeys and apes under lengthy exposure, with quite unexpected results. I asked him early in 1978 specifically what his motives had been: "my original interest," he recollected, "was merely in knowing whether animals might be capable of recognizing themselves in mirrors. In all honesty, I must admit that my thinking about self-awareness has gradually evolved with the data."[7] He did not set out to record self-recognition in order to prove self-consciousness in chimpanzees; his motives were directed elsewhere, which is important. He simply wanted to duplicate conditions that led to man's self-recognition, which meant subjecting apes and monkeys to equally long exposure. As it turned out, he was not ready for the consequences. He commented, "I was actually more surprised by the inability of monkeys to recognise themselves, than in the chimpanzees' success."

In separate experiments, Gallup exposed four wild-born chimpanzees to full-length mirrors over a ten-day period (the mirrors remaining outside the cage bars), sampling their behaviour at intervals and dividing it into "social", such as bobbing, vocalising and threatening – as if reacting to an intruder – and self-directed. Since the chimpanzees were suddenly confronted by apes whose faces were totally unfamiliar, a good deal of threat-posturing was first in evidence. But within two or three days a quiet reversal had taken place. One of the females, Marge, began peering into her own mouth, protruding her lips to expose more teeth and gums in the mirror, evidently fascinated by this cavity into herself that she had never seen before.

Between the second and third day, there was a rapid rise in the number of self-directed actions as the apes came to grips with their self-images. As Gallup reported in *Science*:

> Such self-directed responding took the form of grooming parts of the body which would otherwise be visually inaccessible without the mirror, picking bits of food from between the teeth while watching the mirror image, visually guided manipulation

of anal-genital areas by means of the mirror, picking extrane-
ous material from the nose by inspecting the reflected image,
making faces at the mirror, blowing bubbles, and manipulating
food wads with the lips by watching the reflection. In all instances of self-directed behavior, the self is the referent through
the reflection, whereas in cases of social behaviour the reflection
is the referent.[8]

Doubters at this juncture would need more to convince them. "Even
though these data were impressive," admitted Gallup later, ". . . it was
felt that other investigators might not be particularly convinced by the
seemingly subjective interpretations of self-directed responsiveness in
the presence of a mirror."[9] What Gallup needed was a cast-iron test.
To this end, he pioneered a technique, later adapted for use on human
babies, to determine the onset of self-awareness. He anaesthetised the
chimps (this is not done to babies!), then painted bright red spots on to
the eyebrow and ear with an alcohol-soluble dye that can be neither
felt nor smelled when dry. The dots were undetectable, except via the
mirror. And with the chimps unconscious, there was no recollection of
the spots actually being dabbed on. Four hours later, fully recovered,
fed and watered, the chimpanzees were re-exposed to the mirror.
Perplexed by their transformation while asleep, they immediately
began fingering the red blemishes, guided by the mirror, occasionally
(and this is important, as Gallup was aware) smelling and staring at
their finger-tips. Gallup pointed out that "if the reflection was still
being interpreted as *another* animal there could be no reason for the
chimps to smell or look at their own fingers . . . because these would
not have been the fingers that made actual contact with the red spots".
Only because the apes concluded that their own faces were spotted,
and not those of intruder chimpanzees, was there "a reason to inspect
their OWN fingers".

The mirror test seems so obvious yet profound that one wonders why
no one had thought of it before. Partly, I suspect, because the incentive
had been lacking, certainly while antagonistic ideologies held sway;
but also because, before Gallup's operational tie-up between self-
recognition and self-awareness, the mirror was just too familiar for
critical appraisal. And yet, searching the literature for photographs of
chimpanzees at home, one finds superb examples of chimpanzees
engrossed in their own reflections. Consider the best, Hayes' 1954

photograph of Viki, armed with pliers and mirror and intent upon pulling a tooth. Clearly, she recognised herself (raised as a human, she had long enough exposure to her reflected self), yet the photograph was published without comment or analysis. Were it not for our contemptuous familiarity, we might have sat up startled when Washoe, asked whom she saw in the mirror, signalled instantly, "Me, Washoe."

Orang-utans identify with their mirror image, while Patterson's Koko goes one better than Lucy, whose own "crazy faces" are a never-ending source of self-amusement; Koko powders her dark face with chalk dust and stares at her ghostly reflection. Now, it is less of a surprise to learn that apes also recognise themselves in magazine pictures (that's what comes of being famous). Infant apes first recognise their mirror selves at about the same time as infant people: as soon as their maturing cortical connections permit it. In children it occurs at about twenty months. Young Nim watched his trainer blowing bubblegum in the mirror, then turned to the glass and stuck out his tongue and peered curiously into his own mouth; he was twenty-three months. His self-image was stabilising, indeed, not a month before, "me" had entered his vocabulary; while a month after his first self-encounter, he began talking of that person "Nim". So again, it looks suspiciously as though man and his 'uncultured' cousins share the same potential, and are perhaps psychologically closer than previous generations imagined even in their wildest Darwinian dreams. Gallup boldly closed his original *Science* piece by precipitously drawing a line across nature:

> [preliminary results] suggest that we many have found a qualitative psychological difference among primates, and that the capacity for self-recognition may not extend below [*sic*] man and the great apes.

This can only strengthen Mason's belief that "apes and man have entered a cognitive domain that sets them apart from all other primates".[10] As Gallup admitted, what really surprised him was that monkeys failed to identify their mirror twin. Not only monkeys, but gibbons also continued socialising into the mirror even after long exposure. By 1977, Gallup had saturated a crab-eating macaque with some 2400 hours of mirror exposure in an "attempt to salvage the conceptual integrity of monkeys".[11] But to no avail – still it continued its social display, grimacing and lip-smacking, as though incessantly confronted by a rival who refused to take the hint. Strange, since macaques were shown in classic experiments in the mid-1960s actually to deploy mirrors to pinpoint food morsels deliberately hidden behind screens. They appreciate that the food's reflection is inedible (or, at least, unattainable) since, having spotted the food, they smartly turn away from the mirror to feel for it.[12] But if a real food morsel can cast a ghostly image, and the mirror world is only one of bright shadows, why does the macaque stubbornly fail to recognise its own ghost?

This is a special case of Gallup's broader riddle (whose validity is itself open to question): "How are we to account for such an apparent psychological void between great apes and other primates?"[13] He hazarded a guess that monkeys lacked "an integrated self-concept"; meaning that there might be no cohesive inner 'self' identity to correspond with the mirror image. I wonder whether the evidence demands such harsh conclusions. If we can assume that even before self-recognition, socially reared chimps have a self-identity – and that it does not materialise on habitually viewing themselves – so it might equally exist in monkeys, regardless of recognition. All that mirrors do, after all, is "objectify" self-awareness: that is, give us the means of detecting it. We have not been able to detect it in monkeys, admittedly, but does it thereby follow that no self-concept exists? Absence of evidence is not evidence of absence. I further wonder whether monkeys simply fail to *learn* to recognise themselves, although Gallup finds this "difficult to accept and impossible to reconcile with the data".[14] If that is true, one is left groping in the dark, wondering what turn to make next; but Gallup, although he still clings to his belief that monkeys probably lack a self-concept, has begun to help. Writing recently in *American Psychologist*, he conceded less harshly that "the apparent lack of continuity in this instance may be a consequence of a failure to tap an underlying continuum. The [mirror] techniques described here were designed simply to assess the existence of self-recognition, not to quantify the capacity." As so often happens when dealing with monkeys, apes and men, we might be confronted by varying thresholds which Victorians stretched into gaping chasms. "It is possible," even Gallup admits, "that as yet undefined tests of the self-concept, which requires a lower threshold for recognition, might yield positive results for monkeys."

This takes the emphasis off those overworked 'chasms', and prods us to devise alternative tests of self-awareness. Before surrendering to the selfless monkey, every attempt should be made to fill Gallup's "apparent psychological void". Monkeys do their damnedest to try experimental patience, we should not give up on them too soon. Remember that cross-modal association in monkeys was only detected after a struggle. Moreover, formation of the self-image presupposes sophisticated modal crossing: if an animal cannot integrate its senses, it stands little chance of building a conceptual image of itself. One wonders if a similar struggle will herald the monkey's belated self-recognition.

Death

Closing their report on the LANA Project, Sue Savage and Duane Rumbaugh set man apart with the sobering statement that through language "he has been able to make long-term predictions", and that

> Perhaps, in the appreciation of the passage of time in that perspective, *he alone has become sensitive to his individual demise* and, to compensate therefore, has worked space to collapse the living of an eternity into the brief span of a single lifetime.[15]

This somewhat poetic fancy may or may not be true, but with little supporting evidence it simply reinforces another time-honoured prejudice, and enough of those have collapsed about us in the last decade to make us wary. Nor am I the only one who holds a modicum of doubt. Reviewing Rumbaugh's book in 1977, Gallup latched on to this crucial assertion, commenting that the ape's awareness of death "is still very much an open question".

> Such a capacity would seem to be a simple and logical extension of an awareness of one's own existence. The distance between contemplating your own existence and your nonexistence may be very small indeed, particularly when confronted with the transition from existence to nonexistence in a conspecific.[16]

Well, what does happen when a chimp experiences a companion's death? In his sensitive telling of *Lucy: Growing Up Human*, Maurice Temerlin left a poignant account of Lucy's trauma on finding her cat dead (a cat is not a conspecific, of course, but Lucy, like many children, treated her pet as one of her own kind):

> I was in the courtyard at the time and I heard a scream coming from inside Lucy's roof-top room. It was a different kind of scream from any I had ever heard and I rushed immediately to the roof of the house. The cat was dead. Lucy was at the other end of the room, obviously quite shaken. She was staring at the body intently, not moving a muscle. Lucy approached the body, reaching a forefinger towards it as though to poke it. But she never touched the body. She withdrew her hand rapidly and shook it, a movement indicating anxiety, just before making contact with the body. She appeared to have some sort of understanding that the cat was dead, never to return, for she never looked for it again nor seemed to expect to play with it.

> Three months after her cat died, Lucy was leafing through an issue of *Psychology Today*. She was turning the pages rapidly and casually as she usually does. This issue had an article on chimps and included a picture of Lucy and her cat. When Lucy came to the picture of herself and her cat, she stopped turning pages and sat transfixed, staring at the picture. She stared for about three minutes without moving, and then started signing in ASL "Lucy's cat, Lucy's cat, Lucy's cat – " altogether she signed "Lucy's cat" repeatedly for another ten minutes as she continued to stare at the picture. Her mood was one of thoughtful sadness.

The instant of death is rarely observed in wild chimpanzees; it is an intensely private time and they crawl off to die alone (from polio or old age), away from the gaze of the troop. For this reason, neither chimps nor their observers often have to face the harrowing experience of an ape's death throes. Geza Teleki, however, has fully documented one case in which the entire troop witnessed an horrific death. Certainly they could not avoid seeing it. It was 8.38 on a bright morning, 22 November 1968, when Rix lost his life. Two groups of Goodall's Gombe chimps located and joined a third after pant-hooting to one another across the valley, and the entire band now numbered about sixteen, including Goliath and Hugo, with Mike now as top-ranking male. There was a sudden burst of commotion and Teleki came running. Rix had apparently lost his footing while clambering through a fig tree, and crashed on all fours, to the valley floor, where a boulder caught him on the chin, snapping his neck. The forest exploded with raucous cries and screams and frenzied movement. The males initiated sequences of complex displays, "their hair erect, swaggering bipedally, slapping and stamping the ground, tearing and dragging vegetation, and throwing large stones".[17] At least half the group were shrieking at any one moment, with eerie *wraah* calls echoing down the morning valley. Each chimpanzee stopped, stared at the motionless corpse, then started calling again, all the while patting and embracing one another, as if seeking reassurance. Hugo began hurling six-inch stones towards the carcass, although none actually hit it. Mike, Goliath and Godi first sat within yards of the body, staring entranced at the corpse, with none daring to touch it.

> Hugo then steps closer still, stands right next to the body, and peers down at it for several minutes; he then launches into a vigorous display away from the corpse. Hugo and Mike also charge away in different directions, ripping down vegetation as they run. Meanwhile, Godi and Sniff have been steadily wraahing while staring fixedly at the body from a distance of several meters; others join in the calling more sporadically. The three males return from their displays, soon followed by others, and at least twelve individuals now gather round the body, forming a rough circle of about 5–8 m diameter; all but Godi, who wraahs steadily, sit in silence and gaze at Rix.

It is difficult to interpret this extraordinary episode; certainly we should beware our human feelings clouding the issue (though we too stare at a corpse, or diametrically away from it, refusing to touch it but reassuringly grasping one another's hands). The chimpanzees' distress lasted until past midday, when Mike led the troop away, although some were loath to be torn from their dead companion, and all peered over their shoulders until Rix was out of sight. Teleki very cautiously concludes that this distressing ritual raised "a fundamental question about the role of cognitive processes in an event of death witnessed by a chimpanzee group". Their agonised behaviour betrayed an awareness that some morbid change had overcome Rix, "but it remains uncertain whether any participant grasped the conceptual difference between life and death". Nonetheless, Teleki thought the chimpanzee reaction towards Rix's corpse "suggestive of greater insight" than mere curiosity about his peculiar, motionless behaviour. By itself, the evidence is equivocal, but as part of an emerging pattern, which acknowledges pongid conceptual and *self*-conceptual powers, it is highly suggestive, and adds one more piece to the puzzle which continues to reshape our understanding of the ape mind. The sum total of this cognitive and behavioural complex is far more telling than any one component, and itself suggests that we are invariably too conservative when interpreting isolated aspects of behaviour. Teleki concludes that "a potential to recognize the significance of death may have appeared long before Neanderthal men began to ritualize burial of their dead by the Middle Paleolithic".

Just how far we can trace man's death-fear into the palaeontological past is a challenge eagerly awaiting modern anthropology; inestimably further, I suspect, than current conservative estimates. Too often, for example, we are presented with Neanderthal man at the "dawn" of human history; struggling heroically into the spiritual age with a shadowy half-awareness. Ralph Solecki (whose brilliant researches at Shanidar cave in North-East Iraq have turned up a wealth of evidence bearing on Neanderthal's psychic state) felt constrained to admit that, "It is among Neanderthals that we have the first stirrings of social and religious sense and feeling."[18] One can quibble with this conclusion, though not his spectacular discoveries: for "first stirrings", he in fact meant something in marked contrast – "first evidence of stirrings", which is definitely another matter. Once again, absence of evidence is not evidence of absence; death-awareness and the associated religious awe may be rooted far deeper in human prehistory, despite the lack of evidence.

Solecki had broken into a vault, some 60,000 years old, containing "classic" Neanderthalers, more archaic-looking than their "progressive" counterparts in Mount Carmel, Israel, but still (paradoxically) bigger brained than living man (by about 200 cc). Of course, death-fears do not fossilise, but burials do, and they provide the most intriguing evidence. The numerous corpses in Solecki's vault told similar stories, but one was of especial interest. Given the impersonal tag "IV", this cadaver had been laid in a dug-out depression and covered with loose earth. By great good fortune, Solecki had routinely taken soil samples, dispatching them to Dr. Arlette Leroi-Gourhan at the Musée de l'Homme in Paris. In 1960, when the bones were disinterred, she could do little with the 6000 soil samples, at least until a comprehensive pollen atlas of local plants had been drawn up. By 1968 this was complete; and almost at once oddities began turning up. Whereas most showed sporadic pollen grains spread through the sample, two soil cores contained pollen clusters, in places matching the pollen arrangement on the anthers of living flowers. Leroi-Gourhan leaked the news to Solecki, but did not publish herself until 1975, when she announced in *Science* that not only were blooms once present, but "seven were found in clusters. Some of the clusters contained two or three different species of agglutinated pollens. Thus we may conclude that complete flowers (at least seven species) had been introduced into the cave at the same time."[19] Pollen had not blown into the cave, but had been deliberately introduced as bouquets of flowers. Still, Leroi-Gourhan had absolutely no idea where in the cave her samples (known only by their numbers 313 and 314) had been collected. She contacted Solecki, who pinned down their precise location; working back through his records, he located the samples at either side of Neanderthal IV's corpse. Leroi-Gourhan diverted her attention to the grave proper. She began detecting uncarbonised wood splints. She further identified the flowers, which were dominated by daisies, hollyhocks, horsetail, brilliant blue grape hyacinth and striking yellow groundsel. The woody horsetail had flexible, dividing stems which, she suggested, lent themselves beautifully "to the making of some sort of bedding on which the dead could have been laid". The relatives had then ranged the summer mountainside, gathering hyacinths and hollyhocks; these, bound into posies by shrub saplings, were probably laid as a bed on top of the horsetail stems for the deceased to rest on. From the pollen types, the time of year can be pinned down precisely to late June or early July, some 60,000 years ago.

Solecki was taken aback; as he admitted in 1975, "the evidence of flowers in the grave brings Neanderthals closer to us in spirit than we have ever before suspected".[20] He conceded that even he had perhaps done Neanderthal man an injustice in his own earlier writings. But Solecki noticed another tempting fact: that seven of the eight flowers in the bouquets were listed in current herbals as being of medicinal value. Yarrow is widely used in herbal medicine, like groundsel, hollyhocks and hyacinths – even the woody horsetail is a cardiac stimulant. So it is not inconceivable that herbal lore was passed down through Neanderthal generations, and that plants were known both aesthetically and medicinally (it is suspected that Neanderthal man cared for his crippled sick).

But was this really the *first* flower burial? Had man really never before laid out his deceased on beds of hyacinths and hollyhocks, ringing them with the serene blue and yellow beauty of nature? And if they had, why have flowers not been detected? Solecki himself unintentionally answered this: probably, he admitted, because "no one had ever thought of *looking* for pollen in graves" before. There's the rub: it is the first evidence, not necessarily the first funeral. All collectors know the hazards of fossil location. It seems unfortunately to be the palaeontological prerogative to alight by chance on a fossil (especially a hominid), then elevate it to a "first" something or other. How far back funerary rites in truth go, no one can say.

I believe that it was less the flowers that draw Neanderthal closer to us "spiritually", than the burial itself; an act of profound implications indicating not only that the forbidden fruit, the knowledge of mortality, had been tasted, but that the resultant death-fear made potential an entire restructuring of our metaphysical universe. Actually, I cheated a bit, introducing flowers before death. Neanderthal graves are by no means a recent discovery. They have in fact been known for seventy years. In 1912, while the Paris Museum professor Marcellin Boule was 'brutalising' his La Chapelle Neanderthal man, a group of more sympathetic palaeohistorians digging at La Ferrassie (in the Dordogne) signed a declaration to the effect that unequivocal funerary rites had taken place about their Neanderthal humans, whose cadavers had been lowered into special graves; and *that*, so far as they were concerned, closed the matter.[21] The two corpses were interred in vaults covered by stone slabs, while nearby a child rested in a trench, whose roofing slab was ornamented by cup-like scoopings. Even Boule's La Chapelle man, made out to be a thick-skinned, insensitive brute, was buried by his kin with a good deal of pomp; venison was laid on his chest, and cooked morsels of game accompanied him on his journey. Elsewhere, funerary foods, dyes, jewels, arms and tools have been used to adorn the corpse. Family vaults suggest a kinship, even in death. Bear skulls have been carefully arranged to guard the deceased, who might be ringed by a stone circle, and the tomb ritualistically littered with innumerable canines from slain bears.

Sudden death (there is no other kind) is the ultimate trauma for mankind; and it has long been recognised, on good grounds, that this trauma is closely correlated to belief in other-worldly existence. To invest some meaning in the emotion-crippling experience when a friend's life is suddenly snatched, indeed, to comfort the distraught left to cope in this life, there naturally emerged escape-valve universes where the 'dead' continue to live. The 'last rites' conducted over the deceased were less a fond and final farewell than the deceased's initiation ceremony into this dark and alien spirit realm where mortal senses fail to penetrate: it was the last deed the living could perform for the dead. To lay food, tools and ochre (which has been considered a magic blood-substitute) in Neanderthal's grave hints at precise beliefs in a future journey, with future needs. In Neanderthal, we seem to meet almost a definitive stage in this ritualistic process, requiring untold aeons for its evolution. Why, originally, did man start burying his dead – why did he not walk away and leave hyaenas and bears to their human pickings? (Wild pigs can devour an entire orang-utan corpse in a matter of hours; this explains why in five and a half years Biruté Galdikas of Indonesia's "Orang-utan Project" has only ever stumbled on two corpses, one of which was audaciously dragged off by Bornean bearded pigs as the observers looked on.[22]) If interment was designed primarily to thwart the scavengers, then there must have been a reason. Even if originally it was simply less harrowing to keep the corpse hidden, burial eventually acquired significance for keeping the body intact (at least in Egypt back to PreDynastic days) in order to secure against violation of the soul. The six pairs of mountain-goat horns circling the head like a diadem in the Teshik-Tash Neanderthal child grave have been thought a symbolic defence of the 'sleeping' occupant against earthly predators.

There can be little doubt, then, about Neanderthal's death awareness; nor, as a corollary, of his appreciation of 'self', and perhaps that this 'self' can pass out of the body to continue its ethereal existence elsewhere. Burial is an outward indication of an elaborate metaphysical component in Neanderthal man's cultural package. Further, the meanings of these rituals had to be passed on, placed within their precise metaphysical or spiritual contexts, which makes incredible Philip Lieberman's early statement that Neanderthal man was a linguistic cripple, whose vowel use was severely curtailed. (Lieberman, who deduced this from Boule's La Chapelle fossil cranium, has subsequently

suffered a torrent of criticism, leading him to retreat slightly of late.[23])
The precision required to convey complex abstract notions of time and
space – not least in alternate dimensions where the 'soul' resides –
cannot be imagined in the absence of articulate language. Neanderthal
man may thus have reached the essentially human philosophical
predicament, in which the surface seems illusory, while 'reality' lurks
disguised beneath, either as spirit or formless matter (depending upon
one's ideological standpoint). The cerebral realm of this rugged Ice
Age human could therefore have been that explanatory precinct today
inhabited by equally mysterious quantum forces and relativistic
relations.

How long hominids have entombed their dead, and how long before
that a death-fear existed to play havoc with their temporal understanding, must remain magnificent imponderables. One third of a
million years ago, *Homo erectus* bands constructed huts along the Mediterranean shores at Nice and drank from wooden bowls (whose powdery
remains can be detected[24]); and at the same time they were engraving
ox ribs, which suggests to Harvard's Alexander Marshack that the ribs
are part of a symbolic tradition.[25] If these hominids were seasonally
encamped and not nomads then disposal of the dead must have traumatised them into some contemplation of death's meaning. Likewise, it
seems inconceivable that hominids whose psychological awareness had
already displaced itself into the universe of written symbols should not
consider the self's demise; the more so, since symbol manipulation (as
we will see) may demand a degree of self-identification – and *that*, of
course, is also the prerequisite for an awareness of death.

If self-awareness is necessary before self-destruction can be contem-
plated, then even great apes may have the mental capacity to understand
this one awful truth. Premack, as always, is first to face the obvious
moral quandary, resulting from his language tuition. "Can I tell the ape
that it will die?" By "the ape" he meant *his* ape, Sarah or Peony, which
gives the problem a dreadful immediacy. It is a moral quandary of
astounding proportions. Man ploughs endless philosophic energy into
contemplating his pending death; round it have coalesced rituals,
magic and religion. Few humans have quite accepted death, and are
brave enough to reject the tenuous threads to some paradisical afterlife
and face the numbing consequences of total annihilation of the Self.

Premack's worry is not that his apes will not understand him, but whether he has the moral right to tell them. And if understanding the annihilation of the Self follows from some fundamental awareness of its existence, Premack's fears no longer seem so wildly misplaced. Mercifully, he is fully aware of his moral obligation as self-imposed custodian of the chimpanzee mind.

> If we succeeded in communicating [the notion of death] to even one [chimpanzee], saw its hair stand on end, heard it moan, we would know we had provided the necessary conceptual elements which the animal combined to make this knowledge possible. And we would have proved that the limits of the ape's concept of self approach more closely our own than had been thought. But we cannot take such pedagogy lightly. What if, like man, the ape dreads death and will deal with this knowledge as bizarrely as we have? (It is fascinating to consider what human history would have been like if the representational capacity of man had not been linked so urgently to the solution of one problem – the knowledge and dread of death.) The desired objective would be not only to communicate the knowledge of death but, more important, to find a way of making sure the apes' response would not be that of dread . . . Until I can suggest concrete steps in teaching the concept of death without fear, I have no intention of imparting the knowledge of mortality to the ape.[26]

Man's Crisis of Identity?

It is ironic that the two social psychologists who first melted and forged the 'Self' in a social mould should be personal renegades from the systems they proffered. Late last century, Ann Arbor sociologist Charles Horton Cooley, in the words of one commentator, took "up sociology as men once took up theology or socialism",[27] to reconcile and submerge individual aspiration in the greater social good. In America's wilderness age of rugged individualism, with its vogue of wheeler-dealers, steel magnates and entrepreneurs, sociologists rose like prophets. Self and society were an organic whole, Cooley proclaimed (for which perceptive biographers branded him not so much a sociologist as a "seer"[28]). Cooley elaborated his influential theory of the "looking-glass self" – the looking-glass being not a mirror, but the reflected glances and appraisals of one's peers. The self is fashioned from these reflected judgments; in a very real sense, we come to see ourselves as others see us. The irony is that Cooley himself was shy and introverted; a recluse whose childhood was marked by malaria and fifteen years of stomach disorders, leaving him a self-conscious semi-invalid with scarcely any friends, petrified of how others saw him. Yet from this tormented perspective emerged the brilliant insight that the self actually emerges during childhood out of these very reflected appraisals.

The sense of irony heightens with George H. Mead, Cooley's disciple at Chicago University. Mead's 'self' was similarly rooted in society; again it was social reflection, in stark contrast to mystical Christian tradition, in which the self, liberated at death or during its Rosicrucian galactic wanderings, struck out on a determinedly independent path. Mead found the individual inadequate to explain the self's genesis: "it is impossible," he wrote in *Mind, Self and Society*, "to conceive of a self arising outside of social experience."[29] The self was transmuting from a fiercely independent god-like entity into a social reflection, the point of intersection between man and society. So the answer to our advance-guard question earlier in this chapter "how do we build up a recognisable self-image *before* we have actually seen ourselves in a reflection?" emerges from the work of Cooley and Mead. The individual sees itself not directly (as in a mirror) but by analysing "the attitudes of other individuals towards himself within a social environment". Mead imagined that the socially moulded self emerged from role-swapping and talking back at oneself in childhood. Children play *at* mother, or at policemen, or at burglars, getting right into their skins and looking back to their own shadow. That shadow metamorphoses into a butterfly-like self as the child's role-taking allows an objective appraisal from multiple vantage points. Not only looking, but talking back to itself – this was Mead's departure point: the child eventually internalises this dialogue with himself into thought. Thus the self emerges, as a reflection of the social viewpoint, with an inbuilt sympathy for the pains and pleasures of others (almost, we might add, an empathy or intuitive knowledge of their thoughts and actions). Like the flights of a seer, this description loses something through encapsulation. But two factors loom large. First, for Mead language was intrinsic to the self's emergence; moreover, once the self matured, it was cast back into the social mêlée providing the feedback to ensure continuing social progress. The personal irony? Where Cooley shied away from the very appraisals essential to his self's well-being, so Mead the man remained equally diffident about publishing, or throwing himself back into the social fray. His students had to resort to collecting his lecture notes, out of which they published some three philosophical treatises *after* his death in 1931. And even then his style was rarely the happiest. As philosopher John Dewey said over Mead's grave, his laboured prose "was often not easy to follow",[30] and more so today one finds Mead an excellent tonic for insomnia.

It appears almost rude to interrupt Mead with chimpanzee talk, yet the unfortunate moral consequences of the weakest part of his system makes this all the more urgent. While humanely stitching together individual assertion and social welfare, he was concomitantly tugging man from "brute" nature. Since animals remain dumb, they lack the mechanics for forging a brute self and thus develop no social responsibility. With no socially reflective self "animals have no rights. We are at liberty to cut off their lives; there is no wrong committed when an animal's life is taken away. He has not lost anything . . ."[31] It is an age-old argument given a new twist; untestable, too, until now. The Mead-Cooley system has been savaged, praised, and used as the rubble for later sociological thought; but always it stood in peril of falling foul of that definitive Popperian line distinguishing science from pseudoscience – testability. As one critic complained of Mead, it was near impossible "to cast his statements into operational forms so that they can be tested, and so rejected or revised".[32] And today nothing is more damning than that.

But is it untestable? Since Mead's *ad hoc* amendment, the absence of language in animals, allows us to slaughter without moral compunction, the stakes are now too high to let him pass unchallenged. It would be marvellous to sort out the strengths and weaknesses of the Cooley-Mead model of self-emergence and extract the inner pearl; to determine – especially in light of our post-Goodall appreciation of chimpanzee society – whether language really is essential to self-realisation. Another critic wrote, with Mead freshly in his grave, that his social psychology and philosophy "were connected by his personality rather than by his logic".[33] I must admit, especially in regard to language, that this worries me too.

The final irony which caps all others is that the helping hand is being extended not by man, but by one of the selfless apes. Ethics (and the law) understandably forbid us from forcefully isolating children in order to sabotage and thus comprehend their self-development. The pay-off of Gallup's elegant mirror experiments was his power actually to test Mead's impressive theory of the social self. Gallup's early ideas necessarily evolved with the data (they had to, because the results battered everybody's preconceptions, his included), but his subsequent work on the effects of social isolation on self-recognition, he told me recently, was "quite premeditated and based on explicit predictions derived from Cooley-Mead concerning the effect of social experience on self-conception".[34] Captive chimpanzees had known normal social upbringing, with chimpanzee peers for playmates and formative appraisal from parents. Whether or not this interpersonal experience allowed the chimps to mould their self-concepts, they certainly had no trouble later identifying their mirror twins. Research laboratories, however, were stocked with apes reared in total isolation. From the Delta Regional Primate Research Center Gallup obtained three chimpanzees who had been taken from their mothers shortly after birth, then reared in small cells out of contact with fellow chimps. One had been left in this state for twenty-one months, the other two had been introduced at eighteen months and left together for the remaining three months. After this "remedial social experience" these two youngsters did show some belated signs of self-recognition after ten days of mirror exposure. On the Cooley-Mead model (disregarding language), however, the lone isolate should not have identified his mirror double. *And this is precisely what Gallup found.* Like a schizophrenic, his mirror gazing was obsessive, though it was never himself he was watching. He failed to identify the red spots as being on his own eyebrow and ear – he just sat there, neither displaying nor recognising.[35] And there were other peculiarities reminiscent of the schizophrenic's condition. Whereas mirror-watching waned in normal chimps once they had thoroughly explored themselves, the isolated ape remained obsessed by this weird mirror beast.

While the evidence is dramatic, its interpretation is not cut and dried. Still, the Cooley-Mead model does have a great deal to recommend it. Indeed, a self forged in a social mould might well explain why the Hayes' Viki, asked to sort photographs into animal *vs.* human piles, unhesitatingly placed her own photograph atop that of Joe DiMaggio; and why Washoe contemptuously dismissed her own father as a

"black bug", or why Lucy is sexually attracted to 'other' humans –
though not her foster father, Maurice Temerlin. It is staggering to note
the lengths to which Lucy in oestrus will go to avoid Temerlin,
assiduously shunning even platonic physical contact, though she is
normally an irrepressible bundle of hugging-and-kissing affection.
Despite wild apes never knowing their fathers – which makes Temerlin's revelation still more intriguing – incest avoidance is evidently as
strong between foster father and the "humanized" chimpanzee daughter
as the real daughter. These apes, of course, are all home-raised, suggesting that their inner selves are forged from reflected human appraisals,
resulting in total ego confusion in the chimpanzee's mind. Perhaps, in
one sense, we really have "humanized the ape".

One remaining puzzle is why these home-raised apes should identify
with that prognathous, brow-ridged face in the mirror, when all
interpersonal data were collected from flat-faced, long-nosed human
physiognomies. One clue, undoubtedly, is that all humanised apes had
free and ready access to mirrors from birth, and quickly became
familiar with their own looks, despite their self-concept being forged
from ape-human contact. One is only left to wonder how a "pongised
man" might view himself in chimpanzee society. Judging from
Donald Kellog's adoption of Gua's food-barks, I suspect that a man or
woman raised from birth by chimpanzee foster parents would socially
acclimatise without trouble, provided that no social deprivation was
involved, learning to accept the apes' status system. How would that
chimp-fostered child's self-identity emerge? One can only quote the
anecdote relating to Steve Temerlin, Lucy's foster brother. Although
he was already ten when Lucy entered the Temerlins' life, he developed
a strong emotional bond of friendship with Lucy, as his father relates.

> His self-concept once had been confused and chaotic. Often, he
> said, he could not tell the difference between himself and Lucy.
> External differences were obvious, of course; but they had been
> so close emotionally he had experienced a confusion of ego
> boundaries. There were times when Steve, with his eleven-year-
> old mind, felt that Lucy was human but that he was not.[36]

Gallup's thought-provoking experiments, then, provide our first
real insights into that untouchable of untouchables, self-consciousness;
and to the acute embarrassment of yesterday's moralists, it is again

seemingly impossible to prise apart man and ape. Chimpanzee self-awareness is no longer a cranky, insupportable notion. Every time a healthy, well-adjusted ape dies (to bend a famous philosophical lamentation about man), a universe blinks out of existence. It might lack the magnificence of our quantum cosmos; it might lack the mechanical splendour of even a rusty cogs-and-wheels Ptolemaic cosmos. Nonetheless, consciousness of the self – arising in every case out of a unique social interaction – endows every man and ape with a peculiarly subjective understanding of the self's relation to the universe.

With that said, it seems almost treacherous to turn and apparently argue the diametric thesis: that apes and men do differ crucially in just this one respect. But they do. The difference, of course, is on another plane. At a fundamental level, both apes and men agree in possessing self-consciousness, but the chimpanzee self must differ from its human counterpart precisely because the self is a psycho-social product. The chimpanzee self will be conditioned in part by the subtleties of ape society; it must be a peculiarly pongid appreciation. Self cannot (perhaps I had better say should not) be conceived as some metaphysical entity transcending species but, as social psychologists insist, as a culture-relative phenomenon. So long as societies differ, as those of ape and man emphatically do, *then selves must be adaptively distinct.* This effectively answers Gallup's conundrum, reflected in the title page of his recent review paper, "A Mirror for the Mind of Man, or Will the Chimpanzee Create an Identity Crisis for *Homo Sapiens?*" The answer remains a decisive "no", not while selves are partly social products and societies are adaptively distinct. (One major distinction between human and chimpanzee society, which bears strongly on this point, will be drawn out in the final chapter.) The inadequacy of the closing statement made by Gallup and his Albany colleagues is now transparently clear: "that perhaps someday, in order to be logically consistent, man may have to seriously consider the applicability of *his* [my emphasis] political, ethical and moral philosophy to chimpanzees." Only, of course, at the expense of defying the very Darwinian canons which promise truly to liberate the ape from human value judgments.[37] Extending our ethical domain might crown the humaniser's efforts with our ultimate anthropocentric jewel, creating a new order of second-class humans, but it blatantly ignores the unique social foundation of the creatively adaptive chimpanzee mind.

Mead's dogged insistence that language feedback is essential to generate self-identity has been gravely jeopardised by Gallup, whose illiterate wild-reared chimpanzees happily reflect on their mirror selves in the clear absence of overt symbolism. The "reflected appraisals" which forged this social dimension to the ape-child's self were not verbal but subtle and expressive facial and postural gestures, and the gentle vocalisations so richly enhancing chimpanzee relationships. Thus, despite the solemn warning of science and philosophy in all its might, the antithesis is far more attractive: that self-awareness supports symbol-learning. An animal that cannot contemplate itself, that is, see itself as subject and object ("I" looking inwards at "me"), probably lacks the cognitive equipment to likewise relate itself to the world through external symbols.[38] To generate the everyday sentence "I am looking at you" first of all requires an introspective familiarity with the subject "I". I cannot think it heresy to imagine the self-concept as one of the cognitive staples preadapting the ape for symbol-manipulation. Indeed, it is almost impossible to visualise language flowering in the absence of self-awareness. Unarguably, self and language share a strong social component which can only derive from early social activity (not necessarily with one's own species). It is not hard to see why, with all social contact severed, deprived children like Genie and Kaspar Hauser fail to speak, just as the isolated ape fails to recognise its own mirror image.

9

Introspection

"Me cry there": Koko signing in clear sympathy as she
fingered a photograph of the albino
gorilla Snowflake resisting a bathtub
scrub.[1]

Self-knowledge has been greeted like some long-lost heir, after
decades in exile during the rule of the tyrant Behaviourism, and
readmitted with a good deal of pomp into the psychological
citadel. If the 'self' could survive, social psychologists like Cooley and
Mead might be smiling from beyond the grave; but, of course, self-
survival was an impossibility given its social nature. One might be
forgiven for believing that the Cooley-Mead insight was *so* far ahead
of its time as to be totally forgotten (assuming some inexorable march
towards final 'truth', in this instance, foreshadowed in the 'wrong' age).
Otherwise, how could Nick Humphrey of Madingley Hall, Cambridge
University – while delving into "the social function of intellect" –
admit without so much as flinching: "I had not previously given much
thought to the biological function of the intellect, and my impression
is that few others have done either"?[2]

Indignant scientists are quick to champion heroes from history,
especially in face of some modern upstart who audaciously proposes
the 'same' theory under a new cloak. Darwin hated it when Lyell
insisted that his "Descent" was just an updated Lamarckism (of course,
it wasn't). It rarely pays to fight priority battles on the fields of history,
and this example illustrates why. The cardinal rule of science history
is that theories only make contextual sense when their inventor's

motives and intentions are fully understood. Hence, despite producing 'convergent' theories, innovators often set out to perform diametric deeds. Cooley and Mead were openly combating the harsh (but dying) Social Darwinism and its champions, the Carnegies and industrial tsars, who placed the highest premium on individual ruthlessness. New-breed sociologists reasoned that no man was an island, precisely because the 'self' was fashioned in society's image. It was a blatant attempt to harmonise individual aspiration and social good. In so doing they hit on the brilliant idea that the self, through its mode of formation, had an insider's understanding into the workings of like minds. Today, however, Nick Humphrey is searching for something past biologists considered a will-o'-the-wisp, if not a logical absurdity – the adaptive function of self-consciousness. He is optimistic that this will provide some semblance of an explanation of social behaviour. Yet he too arrives at a similar position: that through self-knowledge emerges "the possibility of intuitive knowledge of others",[3] a point which – para-doxically – I find crucial in order to appreciate why the ape *lacks* language.

In men and apes a prodigious amount of energy and sympathy is expended just dealing with one's relations. It is no overstatement that by far our strongest 'environmental' influence comes from kindred creatures with whom we must socialise: and socialise *properly*, with decorum, sympathy, understanding, ritual and a thousand other behavioural frames, each with its time and place. This welter of social practices with which we are all inundated means, as Humphrey writes, that "the ability to model the behaviour of others in the social group has paramount survival value". In other words, in this tangled web of relations, we have to judge the other's disposition in order to respond correctly so that social accord will prevail. With such pernickety and unpredictable beasts as men and apes, cross purposes can quickly upset the social equilibrium leading to explosions of anger, rage and worse. Humphrey continues reasonably:

> I believe that the modelling of other animals' behaviour is not only the most important but also the most difficult task to which social animals must turn their minds. The task of model-ling behaviour does indeed demand formidable intellectual

skill – social animals have evolved for that reason to be the most intelligent of animals . . .

Social structuring is not to be confused with gregariousness, which has probably been the lot of herbivores from *Iguanodon* to the huge herds of Serengeti wildebeest, massed for protection. Ants, too, are excused, despite their eminently social ways; with such a striking physiological division of labour no introspective insights are demanded from the scurrying individuals. The essential difference is one of behavioural flux. Social apes indulge in long periods of infancy, when they *learn* to handle complex and shifting personal relations. This is critical since, as Jane Goodall's two decades of Gombe research have shown, close-knit chimpanzee troops may have a membership spanning more than three generations (with their attendant gaps), and may contain little less than a dozen matriarchal families, each centred on an established female. Besides the problems of shifting statuses and the inevitable ego entanglement, juveniles build and maintain steady lifelong friendships, much as humans do, as well as opportunistic and sometimes fleeting alliances for overtly political motives. The wealth of personal relationships intertwined with this constant social climbing and tumbling, so sensitively recorded by Jane Goodall in *In the Shadow of Man*, is revealing. Take the case of companions Mike and the testy old J.B. Mike had risen to dominance through his flamboyant charging displays, during which he gathered up and flailed Goodall's kerosene cans, thus terrifying his one-time superiors into submission. Now, with Mike firmly ensconced in a position of power, his friend and associate J.B. began basking in his reflected glory. He even started social climbing; when Mike was in earshot, J.B. was actually able to lord it over Goliath, previously his superior. As Goodall recalls:

> I well remember one day when Goliath threatened J.B., who had approached his box of bananas. J.B. at once moved away but began to scream loudly, looking across the valley in the direction that Mike had taken earlier. Mike must have been quite close, because within a few minutes he appeared, his hair on end, looking around to see what had upset his friend. Then J.B. ran toward the box where Goliath sat, and Goliath, with submissive pant-grunts, hastened to vacate his place – even though Mike took no further active part in the dispute.[4]

As his status began to plummet, Goliath was bullied by an increasing number of males. One day three came charging down the mountainside like "a gang of thugs" intent, presumably, on laying into Goliath, sitting quietly with his bananas. Goliath vanished like a shot into the bushes, pursued by his would-be assailants "and for the next five minutes they bustled about noisily in the undergrowth, obviously searching for Goliath".

> They were unsuccessful and ultimately emerged and began to eat bananas. Suddenly Hugo [van Lawick] pointed. There, a short distance up the slope, I saw a head peeping cautiously from behind a tree trunk – Goliath's. Every time one of the three looked up Goliath bobbed back behind his tree, only to peer out after a few moments.

Yet at first light next morning the very same Goliath burst into camp, dragging a huge branch, and mercilessly beat up the leader of the three. And there, giving Goliath moral support, stood *his* companion, the "magnificent" David Graybeard, whose presence was, by Goodall's reckoning, sufficient for this all-too-human transformation.

To back someone's move calls for an inordinate degree of sympathy between two primates – one 'feels' for the other's predicament; empathises, in fact, precisely because one can summon up a similar experience through introspection. Modelling the actions of others on our own introspective insights, we know intuitively they are *feeling* pain, thus we actually share in that painful experience and try to alleviate it. In the old classic, *The Mentality of Apes*, Wolfgang Köhler left a searching account of the group's reaction when one of its members was singled out for punishment. "The moment one's hand falls on [the wrong-doer], the whole group sets up a howl, as if with one voice." But rather than run away, they tend to converge on the place of punishment. Some ape onlookers were even stirred to intervene, "little weak Konsul" in particular. He would "run up excitedly, and, in the way little chimpanzees have of expressing their wishes, with a pleading countenance, stretch out his arm to the punisher, if the ape was still being punished, try to hold one's arm tight, and finally, with exasperated gestures, start hitting out at the big man!" As always, Köhler's conclusions are perceptive. "Unquestionably," he wrote, "the animal 'was affected' by what was happening to his companion, but it would be impossible for him to assume himself in danger."

Perhaps dogs do likewise, but in apes such sympathy stretches to poignant extremes; and shows up as something like 'guilt' for another's sins. The neuroses of captive apes (and men) are well known; bodily mutilation is one manifestation, but in less extreme cases it results in eating their own waste. Since well-adjusted humans find this distasteful, Köhler would punish a chimpanzee whenever its whiskers showed traces of its "odious" meal.

> My approach sufficed to make it feel fear for what it had just done. At times the animals are sufficiently naive to give themselves away by their restlessness, when you yourself come up to them quite unsuspecting. Thus Chica once began to hop agitatedly from one foot to the other, when I happened to come up unexpectedly; I had noticed nothing unusual. As I got nearer, her agitation increased, and all at once she let a mess of rubbish fall out of her mouth.

There is nothing strange in this – simple conditioning had induced her shakes by associating her "odious" habit with a beating. But listen to what happens next:

> one day Chica received me with the same disquieted hopping and would not stop, although I could not discover any guilt in her. Thus made attentive, I became aware that her friend Tercera was missing, or rather that a piece of her black fur kept disappearing behind a box each time I came round the other side of it. Nearer investigation showed clearly that this time *she* was the sinner.[5]

But as Köhler said, "Since one animal [he means, of course, chimpanzee*] will often plead for another who is going to be punished, Chica's behaviour on this occasion was after all quite comprehensible." Such

---

* Since "animal" would be a positive slight if *man* was meant, I deplore the term when chimpanzee is meant. In Victorian days, when men were men and everything else was an animal, from chimpanzee to flea, this term might have served some useful purpose, since it implicitly bolstered the Mivartian chasm between cosmically distinct creatures. Today, even taking a *Homo*centric perspective (and why not in this Relativistic Era?), chimps loom large and stand boldly next to us, while fleas can just about be made out on the distant horizon. Substituting "animal" for chimpanzee belies the Darwinian importance of this visual metaphor.

an extraordinary incident of the transfer of guilt to oneself has an obvious human parallel, hence our legitimate fears for celluloid super-heroes unfairly framed for murders they did not commit, the script-writer's staple for thrillers. They *know* the formula works, that is why we see it dished up *ad nauseam*. Also, because guilt can be shifted around this way we can apportion blame, not merely to the immediate perpetrator of a crime, but to those who put him up to it, egged him on, and so forth. No longer chained to the immediate present, we can search out root causes and spread the guilt. Perhaps this was what happened when Jane Goodall observed one chimp infant hurting another in play; instead of thumping the offender, the mother of the injured party settled her grievance by assaulting the culprit's mother, as though the sins of the daughter were visited on her mother.

Sympathy for one's struggle to attain some goal can apparently elicit social cooperation even in monkeys, whose cumulative perform-ances result in one member finally reaching the prize. The best case on record comes from Chicago Zoo's harem of captive hamadryas baboons. Benjamin Beck spends the still, early morning hours – before visitors flock in to disrupt the proceedings – devising experimental tests of baboon cognitive ability using Chicago's subjects. In 1973 he published in *Science* some quite astonishing results. One ten-year-old male baboon was an accomplished tool-user – nothing extraordinary in that. But now Beck placed him in an impossible situation – not only was the dish of morsels placed outside the bars, beyond arm's length but his usual recovering rod was deliberately left in the next-door cage. The connecting door was too narrow for him to squeeze through, though not his slimmer mate. After a stroke of what Beck unashamedly calls "insight", she slipped through the door and fetched the tool (though she had not touched it before in these tests), returned and deposited it at his feet.[6] Her grateful mate immediately raked in the food and both consumed it. His behaviour contrasted sharply if another baboon idly picked up the rod and unintentionally brought it within grasping distance. The male would try to seize it through the bars, which led to fearful fights when its owner persistently refused to surrender it. Rather than similarly snatch from his mate, he waited until she laid the rake before him, and did so on each occasion she retrieved it.

Insight is the sudden appearance of a complete solution, with no apparent learning phase or previous trial-and-error practice (impossible in this instance because the female had not handled the rod before).

Although an anthropomorphism guaranteed to rankle behaviourists, "insight" in apes and monkeys cries out for explanation. Hence the value of Humphrey's "introspective modelling" and its product, the insight into another's desires. Until this can be explained in man, it strikes me as singularly unfair to ignore it in chimpanzees and baboons – or worse, to deny its existence in them when the behavioural evidence seems to warrant it, by direct analogy with man.

Emil Menzil's group of paddock-living young chimpanzees developed equally fascinating collective endeavours. After one ape learned to pole vault to escape the electrified wire round their enclosure, the trick quickly spread through the group.[7] But they also learned to prop poles against trees above the shock wire and climb to forbidden regions, and in some instances (of which an excellent photographic record exists) one chimpanzee, after tapping another on the arm to solicit its help in orienting the heavy branch against the tree trunk, then held the base fast with its feet as this other chimpanzee ascended the pole (after another tap on the arm, the signal to "go"). And there he sat obligingly as a third chimpanzee positioned himself ready to climb up and avoid the electrified wire.

The Strategic Importance of Lying

This modelling of another's behaviour by means of introspection in men and apes is necessary to cope with the subtlety and flux of social interactions. But just as this sympathy can be put to altruistic ends, so an intimate knowledge of the temperaments and desires of colleagues can lead to grand deceptions. We know this only too well in man and we have the added advantage of being able to lie verbally; but the behavioural equivalent also occurs in apes. One has only to think of scheming young Figan. Gazing into a tree one day, he spied a banana (placed there by Goodall, to give mothers and young a chance of some fruit, since males jealously appropriated the main caches). Unfortunately, Goliath was squatting beneath the tree, quite unaware of the prize lodged above his head. Goliath's rank meant the banana was his by rights – so Figan 'denied' the tasty morsel's existence. He *knew* Goliath would snatch it if he climbed for it there and then. He also knew if he sat and stared at it (admitting its presence), Goliath would be alerted. So for fifteen minutes until the old male had sauntered off,

Figan sat round the far side of a tent biding his time. "Quite obviously," wrote Goodall, "he had sized up the whole situation."[8] Like William Mason stuck for a scientifically acceptable substitute for "figuring out",[9] I cannot come up with an alternative to Figan's "scheming" (neither, by the looks of it, can Goodall). It was a 'behavioural' lie, as understandable as the typical ploy developed by the ringleaders of Menzel's captive group, who would deliberately lead others away from bananas, only to return later and personally appropriate the lot.

Given the advantages of a linguistic education, apes can lie like the best, or worst, human – not wholly unexpectedly, judging from Figan's antics. And not only lie, apparently, although that is controversial enough. Patterson believes her gorilla has a developed sense of humour, which manifests itself in linguistic trickery. Koko may or may not be the first funny gorilla, but it is Patterson's presentation of the evidence that is causing linguists palpitations. Words give man tremendous scope for subtle twists of meaning – a good deal of humour is, of course, a play on words. And like lying, this can take the form of truth bending, but for a markedly distinct social purpose. All apes can be naughty, often for the sheer devilment of it: on one memorable occasion, as Laura Petitto was flying round the kitchen trying to prepare a meal, a cantankerous Nim began systematically hiding saucepans in drawers. But in Koko's case – according to Patterson – this devilment has taken quite a linguistic twist. After her trainer once pleaded unsuccessfully with the recalcitrant gorilla to sign "drink", Koko finally turned and signed it perfectly – in her ear! Asked specifically for something that was "funny", Koko replied, pointing to a green plastic frog, "That red."[10] Few linguists or ASL experts accept this at face value. And this is not sour grapes at the prospect of gorillas having 'usurped' something preciously human; there *are* sound methodological criticisms being levelled at Patterson. What on earth does a gorilla understand by "funny", and how exactly could its *human* meaning have been conveyed by a symbol? This is the crux; if an ASL-derived sign for "funny" is listed in Koko's lexicon, we are lured into the assumption that she understands its English meaning.* Patterson

---

* Ostensibly the same "funny" sign (index finger touching the nose – which Washoe carries off with panache by adding a snort) is listed by the Gardners. But the *context* here suggests that Washoe is soliciting play, or asking to be "tickle-chased".

hinted in *National Geographic* (where her most sweeping claims appear) that Koko herself implies she's being funny by giving a broad grin, into which one must read a child's impish smile. Why would a gorilla, though, knowing that a frog is green, *want* to call it "red"? (Why would a child? you retort. My answer follows.) Patterson infers from Koko's grin that she enjoys such linguistic tricks precisely because they *are* funny. But without human feedback to assure her of this, it implies that she possesses an *innate* and uncannily human-like sense of humour. How could this be when children have to learn the humour character-istic of their culture and the social situations when it can be employed (what joke may be said to whom and in what circumstance). Humour is a matter of convention. Hence there is nothing intrinsically funny in a green frog being red. One must learn that this is acceptable as humour, but one can *only* learn what is funny by studying reactions. Perhaps, then, Koko has been conditioned by her trainers. But by admitting human feedback, we are drastically altering the situation. Now we are conceding that Koko might generate mistakes deliberately, without necessarily understanding their meaning, simply because it amuses her trainers and results in social praise for her (hence Koko's grin).

In short, is Patterson reading too much into Koko's apparent hilari-ties? One way to tell is for Patterson to publish transcriptions of Koko's complete utterances, not just anecdotal 'gems' prised from a background which alone gives them significance. Such transcripts will show the frequency with which she makes mistakes, and their circumstances. How many times, for example, does she make idiotic combinations (genuine mistakes), like *frog is banana*?, which might otherwise be taken for a joke. More importantly, we need a list of things she finds "funny" in order to understand what she *means* by "funny". Even deliberately generated mistakes in response to "funny" would be impressive, showing that she interprets it to mean that she must switch symbols ("red" for "green"). But there is nothing funny in that. Linguists are never going to accept a joking gorilla without a rigorous study of her failures as well as successes. Mistakes *are* legion in *all* ape "convers-ations"; as Laura Petitto says, what we often see in published accounts are the 'cleaned up' utterances, picked out from the less coherent back-ground precisely because they make sense to us. Parapsychologists have been crucified for doing exactly this.

Conditioned symbol-switching is a far cry from constructing an alternative reality, as when humans deliberately lie. Most humanised apes, cornered after performing some dirty deed, can and do try to shift the blame. Koko will categorically deny having eaten lunch, though everybody knows that she has. Lucy lies too: if there is a mess to be explained, she will point an accusing finger at those about her before finally owning up. This is creating a false reality, but it is much more. Lying is an outright attempt to mislead, hence it is a wholly social act. But it is an absolutely useless strategy *unless* the liar can place himself in the victim's shoes to ensure that he will be sent astray. Hence it shows an advanced ability to "introspectively model" another's actions.

While Lucy's white lie might stand some distance from an associated 'conscience', which develops in man to give deception its moral colour, that distance certainly does not stretch to a theological eternity. Still, the wild ape's (dare I say it) 'ethical' feelings are quite dissimilar from man's, as are the social needs which explain them. True, the desire for 'forgiveness' seems strong in chastised apes, wild and humanised. After a reprimand, home-raised chimps demand constant social rassurance: hugging, hand-holding, and grooming. True, gorillas and chimps *do* readily learn the word "sorry". But again, we must shout *beware*: "sorry" signed by an ape (palm of hand circling the chest in Nim's case) does not necessarily imply remorse, as does *sorry* said in English. Yet the sign is invariably catalogued as part of a linguistic ape's vocabulary, with little explanation of what it might mean *to the ape*. This is downright misleading. To understand just what Nim meant, Herb Terrace scrutinised the video records to determine the social situations. It transpires Nim signed "sorry" most frequently while under imminent threat of punishment, hence his emotional state was the chimpanzee equivalent of man's 'trembling with fear': Nim pouted with a worried half-grin, and screamed or whimpered in fear. Feeling threatened, he signed *sorry* as though a hand circling his chest were a ritual device to thwart an attack, not a symptom of deep remorse. The same problem occurs with *please*, which also appears in numerous published accounts of ape lexicons; yet Seidenberg and Petitto ask:

> Does the [ape] who signs *please* understand the human system of social interaction . . .? Does it understand the concept of politeness? Or was the sign a meaningless [*sic*] behavior which the apes learned to emit because it would be highly reinforced . . .?[11]

I doubt that it was exactly "meaningless", but if it was solely used to speed the arrival of food or whatever, then it might certainly bear little relation to the English word *please*. Seidenberg and Petitto conclude that apes like Nim (even if they used ASL signs correctly, which they do not) are not necessarily investing them with *human* meanings.

The pregnant *sorry* puts in a nutshell the profound problem of meaning and its social significance. In man it is an expression of remorse, for Nim at least it was a means of manipulating his trainer; Nim's "sorry" has few, if any, of the properties of the English *sorry*. Perhaps Nim is peculiar in this respect. Anyway, it shows the extreme caution needed in handling such emotive words or assuming that apes give them identical interpretations. If they did, it would imply that apes manage what man apparently cannot, to enter the world of an alien species to grasp *its* word-meanings!

Again, it is all a question of ape sovereignty; and of our having the unmitigated gall to assume that human meanings are universal. Word meanings mirror the social structure, so if chimpanzee society differs from ours, words will reflect the divide. We still seem hell-bent on proving that we can truly "humanize" the beast, as if this made Darwinian sense; thus ASL as a tool has scarcely been used to tap the ape's social or psychological reality. Is this too ambitious? I don't think so. Consider this approach to the problem. One reason "sorry" might mean something different to an ape is because of the pongid dominance structure (the fact that dominance cannot be completely flattened out even in "humanized" apes suggests that it is partly innate). The ape would therefore be *predisposed* to understand "sorry" in light of pongid social manners, not human. In wild apes, seeking reassurance (what we might label "forgiveness") has little to do with the rights or wrongs of the situation *as we see them*. Because of the hierarchical social order, a subordinate ape will seek "forgiveness" *i.e.*, social reassurance, from a high ranker regardless of who was, in human terms, "at fault". A female thumped for eating a male's food, a female whose own food is rudely stolen by a male, a female bowled over by a charging male: each of these subordinate females will nonetheless subsequently seek reassurance from the male in question. So although the male can be "at fault" and the female herself hurt, she still seeks "forgiveness"! It is only nonsensical because we are grafting our own ethics on to an alien social situation, the way we graft our meanings on to ape signs. For a change let's try to understand ape meanings. At most, Nin might simply be acknow-

ledging the status of a high-ranker by signing "sorry". This interpretation also fits Washoe's case. According to the Gardners, she signed it
"After biting someone, or when someone has been hurt in another way
(not necessarily by Washoe)." So they gave "sorry" the human meaning
of "Apology, appeasement, and comforting".[12] Yet notice that
Washoe signed "sorry" *though she was not to 'blame'* just as subordinate
females in the wild seek reassurance from males regardless of where
'guilt' lies. Perhaps a statistical analysis of Nim's use of "sorry" in every
context may tell us a little more about chimpanzee 'ethics', even in an
alien environment.

If we ignore genetics, innate predispositions and potentials, and carry
on intently "humanizing" the ape, we might expect to see Lucy, Koko
or her offspring learning to embed lying in a socially induced moral
context – which would make human sense of "sorry". I dare say that
with a master-stroke of conditioning something *resembling it* might be
attained. But that scenario resolutely ignores the one per cent genetic
differential, which seems the root cause of the marked contrast in
human and ape potential. Conscience in man *may* be only a partly
social phenomenon. It seems to be a universal feature of mankind,
which suggests a genetic basis – even the Mafia has a conscience, socially
malformed, but nonetheless hyperactive. Whatever the truth in this,
its living embodiment is culturally determined. We learn what is good
and bad and to whom this applies, hence the widespread practice of
regarding outsiders as racial inferiors, against whom often no atrocity
is reprehensible: an evolutionary strategy to space groups at arm's
length. (A mechanism for the evolution of conscience, irrespective of
whether it is learned or innate, is presented in the final chapter.) But
gorillas and chimps have not shared our recent history, thus this social
or genetic component may be absent or functioning differently; and
hence the extreme care needed in handling something of such feather-
light delicacy as 'conscience'.

In a broader perspective, ape lies do have potentially shattering
consequences for the theologically minded teetering on the brink of
philosophic respectability; those who persist in seeing man as a cosmos
apart, as unlike the ape as the dust of the earth. The ape's potential to
lie (either by word or deed) comes as a timely reminder that not even
in our sublimest act of displacement – distorting reality by bending the
"truth" – are we totally alone.

Through introspection, the tapping of that intensely private reservoir of knowledge, we can extrapolate to predict the actions of colleagues and competitors. We can thus collaborate, checkmate or thwart them – or lie to lead them astray. Figan's scrupulously controlled strategy, averting his eyes from the bananas in order to deceive a senior and experienced male like Goliath, was based on precise knowledge of how Goliath would have reacted given an inkling of the bananas' existence. Equally impressive are Figan's tactics against Flo, his ageing mother. She would termite fish for hours, sitting contentedly with her rod bowed into the termite hill, even though her miserable catch rate barely exceeded one termite every couple of minutes. Figan was a fidgety youngster, always determined to leave – which meant dragging his mother from her interminable termiting. But he always failed. He would walk away determinedly, peering over his shoulder, but still she refused to follow. So he would return. At this time Flo had a tiny baby, Flint, who was wobbling about on top of the hill thumbing termites. Figan approached an unconcerned Flint and mimicked Flo's posture when she wants Flint to climb on her back to be carried. Flint now scrambled aboard his elder brother, who promptly hastened from the scene with the kidnapped infant. Suddenly waking to the loss of her baby, Flo dropped her fishing rod and rushed after them. The ploy was successful. Eventually, this became a seasonal hazard for old Flo as other offspring took to kidnapping the compliant Flint in order to prise the old female from her wretched anting.

Modelling another's behaviour thus permits prodigiously complex manoeuvres on our part to force another's hand. Strategic scheming like this also places a selective premium on the extension of foresight. At some time in our own past the elaboration of such meticulously planned social ploys probably led to a growing concern for future time, the key to so much human thought, which has ultimately reached across vast temporal wastes to the final conflagration and Kelvin's heat-death of the cosmos. Koko, by contrast, has the greatest difficulty with time – in words, anyway. She is flummoxed by signs for "yesterday", "tomorrow", and indeed "now".[13] Since chimpanzees employ moderately long-term strategies and bear personal grudges which may erupt into vengeance much later, an extended memory, at least, does exist. The same is true of Koko, as is evidenced by a conversation recently reported by Francine Patterson. Koko had angrily bitten Patterson, and three days later she tried to get Koko to talk about it:

"What did you do to Penny?" asked Patterson.

"Bite," came the somewhat truncated reply. Penny looked inquisitive and tried to winkle out a reason.

"Sorry bite scratch," signed Koko. Yes, but why had she bitten?

"Because mad," came the logical reply. Okay, said Penny, what made you mad?

"Don't know," said Koko.[14]

This gem tells us little about an ape's perception of time, beyond an ability to remember. But it does suggest that Koko's difficulties with time *words* might stem in part from the training programme. After all, it is infinitely easier associating a sign-word with a tangible ball or tickle than with something as intangible as yesterday or tomorrow.

When an ape or man can model another's behaviour and use this as a basis for his own actions, the simplest contact assumes the infinite complexity of a chess match. And for exactly the same reasons: both parties can anticipate the other's move. Hence the constantly shifting goals and variables as the social game proceeds. As Humphrey says, like "Alice's game of croquet with the Queen of Hearts, both balls and hoops are always on the move".[15] This intellectual battle of wits puts a tremendous premium on the cognitive honing of causal inference, something Premack and Figan have demonstrated in their inimitable ways. By kidnapping young Flint from his mother, Figan knew that old Flo would be forced to follow. In fact, it is a common chimpanzee and baboon ploy for a low-ranking male under attack by superiors to sweep up a tiny infant and hold it forward as a pacifier. This tiny hostage assures the chimp or baboon of immunity since males are inhibited from assaulting youngsters. The components of causal inference in the psycho-social realm seem well established in the chimpanzee mind. Is it any wonder Sarah managed to bend her cognitive faculties round that tortuous conditional, "If Sarah take apple, Mary give chocolate Sarah/If Sarah take banana, Mary no give chocolate Sarah"? And Figan's behaviour leaves us every reason to believe that Peony *will* identify that missing frame in her story book.

The Gombe: From Hunting to Holocaust

To Ardrey devotees, indeed to a whole generation, the "hunting-made-man" hypothesis was staple fare. Ardrey was eloquent; the thesis attracted supporters because it apparently unravelled so much. In his racy scenario, the focus falls sharply on tools as *weapons*. Today, the thesis is a fascinating fossil, battered by seventeen years of scientific ravages, though its modified progeny live on. He reflected and shaped an era, one which saw the pieces apparently fall neatly together and man the enigma stand exposed to the glare of scientific light.

A 1960s mainstream picture of man's emergence might be telescoped into the following scenario. With incipient conceptual powers, hominids began reasoning and the geniuses among them invented tools. While this occurred they were being pushed by climatic and associated habitat changes out on to open savannas, where scouts learned to stand bipedally to achieve greater visual range. Standing erect, and with hands freed and armed with spears, the diet switched to flesh when they found themselves able to tackle midsize game. But this necessitated cooperation among hunting males. Strategies had to be developed for hunting and killing the game. This put a premium on advance planning and scheming; in short, it boosted intelligence, which again looped to make cooperation more sophisticated, enabling really big game to be taken. Now the kill provided enough flesh for the whole community, so it was carved up and carted home, to be divided among the family heads. This reinforced a growth in social relations and sexual division of labour (the womenfolk worked the neighbouring shrub, gathering fruit, roots and seeds – pair-bonding was already in evidence to keep the lower-ranking hunting males in

line: the women were bribes from the top man to ensure cooperation).
Law enforcement, property rights – all manner of cultural events
flowed from the hunting act. Indeed, the whole economic and social
base of hominid life was revolutionised. With the social web rapidly
entangling, cognitive powers burgeoned to keep pace, permitting
further tactical complexities in the hunt, enhancing gestural and finally
spoken signals, which completed the transformation of social life. The
circle was anything but vicious, it proved the most benign spiral to
modern man. The logic behind this galloping scenario seemed impeccable. By a system of complicated feedbacks, the whole, neat, onward
rush to manhood was accomplished as a result of the hunt and a
weapons technology. But most important of all, hunting was unique
to, and actually defined, the hominid line leading to *Homo sapiens*.

Nobody denies that social and technological acceleration were
initiated and sustained by powerful feedback loops (like a slow-motion
retroplay of the Industrial Revolution, when 'take-off' was only
achieved by successes feeding back to fuel the source, leading to exponential growth). But today's inter-disciplinary approach makes it
hazardous to single out one factor causing mankind's emergence.
(Even though an archaeologist like Glynn Isaac can cautiously use meat-
sharing as the lynch pin around which he builds the spiralling complex
of behavioural, social and economic developments leading to man's
meteoric rise.[1])

Under closer scrutiny, the sixties fossil chronology begins to appear
less neat, less logical. For example, the brain's astronomic expansion
occurred largely in *Homo erectus*, the original Java Man. During his
earthly sojourn (one million to 300,000 years ago), it almost doubled in
size, from 750–1300 c.c. Yet for millions of years hominids had been
walking erect. *Australopithecus*, according to Raymond Dart, occasionally wielded bludgeons and slaughtered baboons for their flesh and
brains, while two million years ago, Glynn Isaac maintains, East
African hominids were already transporting joints back to base camp
and probably apportioning them (using cutting edges fashioned from
imported stone). So this was achieved by protomen with brains that
were small compared to that of modern *Homo sapiens*, although larger
than that of a chimpanzee. (*Australopithecus*' brain size is often mis-
guidedly equated with that of the living ape. But this misnamed "Southern Ape Man" was small in stature, and the slighter physique made him
relatively brainier. For example, to find an ape of the same weight as

Australopithecus africanus – about 70 lbs – we have to look to the female pygmy chimpanzee, whose brain occupies only 330 c.c. In *Australopithecus* it was 450 c.c.[2]) Since chimps fashion twig and leaf tools, it comes as no surprise that hominid tool manufacture predates the cranial explosion. In fact, there is no telling how far back in time tool-making might eventually be traced. So technology, at least, probably emerged long before *social* factors forced that massive cerebral expansion.

The real reason it was imagined that hunting made man was because it was thought that hunting among primates was unique to man. In "The Evolution of Hunting", their influential paper of 1968, S. L. Washburn and C. S. Lancaster concurred that food-sharing was peculiarly human and highly characteristic of sapient social relations. As they said, technical skills, meat-dividing, cooperation, division of labour, indeed "the whole human pattern is new, and it is the success of this particularly human way that dominated human evolution and determined the relation of biology and culture for thousands of years".[3] By the time of *Homo erectus* the hunting/sharing patterns had emerged "which separate man so sharply from the other primates". Looking back further, they speculated that *Australopithecus* was already ranging widely, having broken out of the primate territorial prison, and had begun to broaden his horizons – a necessary and challenging step for a future big-game hunter. (To this last we might add that the chimpanzees living in the savannas and woodlands of Western Tanzania are now known to have home territories quite "remarkable for being of similar extent as the home ranges of hunting and gathering peoples such as Bushmen". So in all probability this escape from cramped prison territories stretches back way past *Australopithecus*.)

At the reverse end of the spectrum, the later 1960s – obsessed with Vietnam and witnessing among the young, for the first time in history, global disobedience and the demand for peace – happily accepted apes as innocent vegetarians, blameless creatures surviving untainted by mankind's fall from grace. Theirs was a peaceful coexistence, Africa was their Eden. Because of this radical man/ape psychological and behavioural dichotomy, it was easy to make napalming and its hunting antecedents exclusively human. As Washburn and Lancaster concluded, "The biology, psychology, and customs that separate us from the apes – all these we owe to the hunters of time past." To fringe biologists like Arthur Koestler, those primal hunters had transmuted into a race of psychotics, madmen driven to mutilate one another and ultimately sacrifice the entire world. Only one creature murders and tortures his own kind over a plot of land or article of faith; clearly the unprecedented cortical explosion had generated wiring anomalies with nightmarish implications. Long-standing anti-reductionists like Koestler adopted the ultimate reductionist strategy and blamed berserk man on an evolutionarily amateurish piece of cortical cross-wiring.[4] We were nature's pathological freaks and she was laughing sadistically at us.

Troglodyte 'hunter-gatherers'

The dichotomy was absolute: man was self-styled "the hunter", while poorer relations were fruit gorgers. As such, we were unparalleled in the primate world, a not wholly unexpected or unpleasant conclusion nor one worth much with wild apes only watched for odd hours, a day or two at most. On both counts – man and ape habits – we were blinded to the true situation. Because we *do* kill game, we managed "with one stroke of a conceptually bloodied brush"[5] to obscure our real eating habits – we are omnivores. More alarmingly for the traditional anthropological scenario, chimpanzees, as Jane Goodall was amazed to learn within months of arriving at the Gombe, were also skilful hunters. (This is not a distortion of the term: chimps do actually engage in hunting as it is commonly defined.) But more important, as it turned out, was the unexpected behaviour accompanying the hunt, which all but turned the prejudices on their head. On her first encounter, Goodall caught the big male David Graybeard pig in hand. He was, she dutifully recorded, "holding a pink-looking object from which he was from time to time pulling pieces with his teeth".

> There was a female and a youngster and they were both reaching out toward the male, their hands actually touching his mouth. Presently the female picked up a piece of the pink thing and put it to her mouth: it was at this moment that I realized the chimps were eating meat.[6]

It was not long before Goodall actually saw the chase, with the adult males cornering a colobus monkey and snapping its neck before wrenching it into portions. Chimpanzee predation is now so well documented that, as Teleki said mockingly, we might reasonably "launch a career for 'chimpanzee-the-hunter'".[7] Silly as this might sound (it is supposed to), the rationale for making man "the hunter" rests on little less. Both chimps and men subsist largely on non-meat foods, augmented by flesh. During Teleki's stint of Gombe chimp watching (March 1968 to March 1969), thirty cases of predation were seen, of which forty per cent were successful, the unfortunate victims being largely baboons and red colobus monkeys.

Tales of chimp-hunting with their attendant horrors generated something of a startled backlash among humans when it was first announced. It was dismissed as opportunistic, or unimportant because flesh supplied a negligible percentage of chimp diet (both points are still being furiously hammered out). Teleki insists that similarities between human and chimp hunters outweigh the differences. True, man gets a higher percentage of meat (which in African tribes may average about thirty per cent of the diet; in chimps it undoubtedly falls below five per cent), but then man uses spears and poisoned arrows to bring down the occasional wildebeest or giraffe, something only permitted by a weapons technology. Chimps catch nothing larger than 20 lbs, so even the bushbucks and pigs killed are pretty young. Nonetheless, human hunters do take a preponderance of such smaller fare. And despite popular lore about the "communal hunt", in many tribes the hunters prefer to stalk quietly alone or in pairs. Even among Colin Turnbull's gentle pygmies of the Ituri forest, one hunter armed with only a short-handled spear will tackle an elephant. Given the strategic similarities between chimp and human hunters, the social outcome, and that chimps (and baboons) hunt without tools and in silence, Teleki believes that we should look critically at current scenarios for human evolution. Specifically, he wonders whether flesh-eating might not be deeply rooted in primate behaviour. He ventured further in *Scientific American* in 1973:

> Suppose that predation, co-operative hunting and socially structured food-sharing did become habitual among certain primates long before the first hominids arose. If that were the case, it would throw doubt on a number of current evolutionary hypotheses. For example, the sequence of erect posture, free hands and tool use as prerequisites to the emergence of hunting behavior would no longer appear to be valid. The same is true

of the hypothesis that the open savanna is the habitat where hunting most probably developed. Moreover, whether or not predation is a far more ancient primate behavior pattern than has been supposed, at least one hypothesis must be abandoned altogether. As the actions of the Gombe chimpanzees demonstrate, socially organized hunting by primates is by no means confined to man.[8]

While certainly intriguing, there is no ancient fossil evidence for or against his first proposition. At most, chimp hunting shakes our once rock solid faith that man was *necessarily* a recent killer and flesh-sharer. It cannot prove that we are directly related to chimpanzees by bloodlust, since that would imply a shared behavioural (hunting) inheritance from a common ancestor, which seems unlikely. We might have a potential packaged in that omnivorous inheritance, but hominoid hunting proper is probably a highly fluctuating, learned behaviour, almost – in some respects – taking the guise of a custom or ritual, which is unlikely to have had a persistently uniform history back into dryopithecine antiquity. Even today, it differs widely among chimp troops – as indeed among humans – and has not been seen in the gorilla, let alone the solitary, fruit-eating orang-utan.

The Kill

Teleki amassed a detailed list of chimp prey, which broke down into thirteen species, including seven monkeys and four ungulates (*e.g.*, bushbuck and bushpig). But the clear preference was for monkeys. Teleki failed to include man in his list, but chimpanzees have been known to snatch human infants from neighbouring villages. Jane Goodall kept her own son, Grub, under lock and key when the apes were about, fearing for his safety. But then man cannot claim any moral superiority in this respect; both chimp and gorilla flesh are great delicacies among some tribes.

Chimpanzee hunters hold out considerable surprises for us. Although the charge of "opportunism" was levelled to disgrace them, even where an unexpected opportunity arises, a sophisticated tactical procedure may be adopted, characteristic of some human hunters. Bushmen, for example, travel in pairs and adopt a "pincer" stratagem to cut off the prey's line of retreat. Listen to Teleki's first-hand account of chimp tactics.

> After walking for some kilometers along a woodland trail behind two adult chimpanzees (Faben and his brother Figan), we stopped on the path to rest; upon hearing the rustle of vegetation nearby, I stepped toward the sound to investigate, and both males immediately stood and started toward the sounds, one fanning out on my left and another on my right their movements typical of predatory stalking; as we approached the sounds they both turned inward, closing the pincer formation; this action flushed a large monitor lizard which threatened and fled the scene.

This account appeared in an elaborately detailed report, drawn up by Teleki for *The Journal of Human Evolution* and published in 1975. Teleki's observations have totally discredited charges of "opportunism", showing chimp hunting to be planned and deliberate in many instances. At the onset of the hunt, an uneasy silence breaks out among the usually raucous apes. They assume a glazed, fixed stare, aimed at the targeted prey. Reading this facial signal, other males join in, concentrating on the "game", usually a colobus monkey or a vociferous baby baboon. If the targeted monkey is nearby, the chimp participants may silently "premeditate" on the situation before striking: "premeditation" is Teleki's term, but it does seem most appropriate. He says "Premeditation is most likely to be apparent prior to chasing and stalking, when one or more chimpanzees may spend more than half an hour while setting up the conditions for a particular mode of pursuit." If a chase rather than a stalk is called for, from two to five male chimps (usually a pair) will converge on the prey, with other males, females and infants trailing some distance behind in anticipation of a kill. The males can dash over a hundred yards, although they usually cover no more than ten or twenty. When the several manoeuvring males are unable to get a strategic advantage over a baboon, or if they cannot get the better of its ringing protectors, they might spontaneously disband, giving up the hunt – a situation unashamedly labelled by Teleki as "decision-making", and apparently collective decision-making at that.

If these mental processes are indeed integral features of chimpanzee predation, their performance as collector-predators begins to approach the sophisticated cognitive processes allied to subsistence by human gatherer-hunters.

On other occasions, after targeting the prey, the males might stalk their quarry for over an hour.

Furthermore, the chasing and stalking modes are performed in a more deliberate and controlled manner, and in many instances involve complex strategies and manoeuvers to isolate and corner the targeted individual. Two or more chimpanzees (maximum seen: 5 adults) may co-ordinate their actions with great precision, their movements to position and reposition themselves being deliberately complementary.

I have quoted Teleki at length to dispel some of the lingering doubts. Chimpanzees can be deliberate and systematic hunters, as man is on occasions. Obvious factors stand out immediately as requiring explanation. Why, as in humans, do only *males* hunt? Also revealing, the opening gambits – up to the point of prey capture – take place in total silence. More than that, gestures apparently play no part, despite tricky manoeuvring and even the leadership switching midway through a tactical strike, if one male finds that he must suddenly take the initiative. By contrast, at the kill there is a sharp burst of vocal hysteria, alerting all the neighbouring chimps, and bringing them scurrying to the site of the kill.

Now a still more unexpected episode follows. After the baboon or colobus monkey is slain (by breaking its neck with the hands, biting it, or – and this is interesting – by the chimp running bipedally and wildly flailing the victim, dashing it against a tree), the male participants tear the corpse apart manually. This seems to be a no-holds-barred phase when the kill comes up for grabs, although it is sectioned with little or no hostility between the participants. With the carcass torn up property rights set in, and each male 'owns' a piece by right of possession (nine-tenths of the law, as Teleki quips). Possession is recognised by others, and little theft now occurs. Rather, round each male in possession of a chunk of flesh a queue or 'cluster' forms, largely drawn up from relations (sexual, social or kindred), who *beg* with palms out-

stretched, sometimes touching the male's lips. In this relaxed atmos-
sphere, anything up to an entire day may be spent apportioning the
carcass in increasingly smaller sections, and leisurely consuming the
spoils using leaf-wads as flavour enhancers. On one occasion, after the
dominant male caught a colobus monkey about 8 in the morning, the
sharing went on among thirteen individuals until 5.30 p.m. Teleki was
able to draw up a 'flow chart' of flesh distribution, which showed that
portions found their way, via numerous intermediaries, to almost every
ape present. At this begging phase, dominance is at least partially
suspended, and high-ranking males will usually beg rather than
intimidate, and accept rather than appropriate the morsel. Only highly
prized brains seem too good to share, and the captor usually reserves
this delicacy for himself.

Food sharing (which Glynn Isaac demotes to "tolerated scrounging")
the hallmark of human hunters, thus plays an important part in chimpanzee social life. Isaac, of course, is right; meat exchange is done far
more willingly among humans, and gathered seeds and roots are also
divided up. But I would not want to press the differences too hard.
There are other equally obvious dissimilarities. Chimps do not kill with
weapons. Yet on occasions they will dash baboons to death, fracturing
skulls against tree-trunks. How much innovation is needed to switch
the procedure, and dash the tree against the baboon (that is, bludgeon
its head with a hand-held log)? At some point our ancestors made the
switch. Moreover, tools are employed in the mopping-up operation.
Brains are savoured by chimps and man, and have been presumably
back as far as *Australopithecus*. A number of ways have been devised for
getting at the brain. The foramen magnum (at the base of the skull
where the spinal nerve cord enters) might be enlarged and the brain
poked out with the index finger; it might be poked out through the
nose, breaking the nasal bones; or the chimpanzee, using its elongate
canine, might stab a hole through the dome (man, including perhaps
Australopithecus, uses an axe for this). The chimp captor will then carefully pick off the bone splints and insert a wad of leaves into the brain
mass, moving them round with his finger to soak up the juices, before
retrieving the wad and savouring the tasty pulp. Finally, though Isaac
carefully stresses that man actually carries portions of meat back to
base, chimpanzees will carry a carcass, slung over the shoulder; it is
sometimes carried up to the nest, and maybe again transported the
following day. The difference, obviously, lies not in what a chimp or

man does, but *why* he does it. And here, I suspect, Isaac might make a case for differences in intent. For example, while the chimpanzee holds on to his joint for a more leisurely consumption, man transports it specifically for sharing or storing.

The social ballet of begging and clustered sharing furnishes some baffling clues whose interpretation is sure to provide the foundation for some future anthropological furore. Just listen to the veteran C. R. Carpenter, who was observing monkeys in the wild years before anybody saw the worth of systematic field studies; reading Teleki's report, he rhapsodised, "the images of ritualistic and ceremonial behavior urge to be included in the descriptions, analyses, and interpretations of this phase of predation episodes".[9] Both he and Teleki were quick to see possible implications of this languorous flesh-parcelling period when dominance all but collapses. Scientists searching for the roots of sociocultural events, finished Carpenter, "are invited to consider in all aspects the terminal acts of chimpanzee predation and their significance as regulators and indicators of community structure". Others gave short shrift to Teleki's newsworthy "scoop" and Carpenter's melodramatic announcement of the sociocultural roots of mankind among living apes. Nonetheless, the begging-sharing episode *is* tantalising, as much for what it hides as reveals.

Goodall's first encounter was with a chimp begging flesh by gently touching David Graybeard's lips as he chewed. Chimpanzees will also finger another's meat, peering intently into the owner's eyes, or simply extend an open, upward-facing palm (as in the ASL gesture "gimme") and "ask" with a soft *hoo*. It is even known for a male to voluntarily tear off a chunk and offer it without being requested. This elaborate socialising as the carcass is dismembered and distributed, and the inordinate time and energy lavished on it, hint that the episode is invested with some unplumbed "social" meaning. It is *more* than a food-getting habit; at the very least it has become incorporated into social customs which strengthen kinship and friendship bonds. So too the kill is elaborately ritualised in many modern and prehistoric human societies; it is a tribal, sometimes magical, event which has passed far beyond simply satisfying hunger.

Sharing, albeit a telling aspect, only completes hunting behaviour. Yet the whole predatory episode is riddled with peculiar quirks suggestive of a social event. Chimpanzees may bypass potential prey even when within easy reach, again stressing that it is not solely a matter of

greedy opportunism. The young Japanese primatologist Akira Suzuki
has seen a young bushbuck flushed out under the noses of three male
chimpanzees moving in procession across savanna. But rather than grab
it, they moved on. Likewise, he spotted a startled colobus dash away
from foraging chimpanzees straight past a female chimp, who stretched
out a calming hand and touched it. The apes seem to need some sort of
social preparation, a kind of adrenalin-raising excitement which
spreads through the hunters, before each positions himself ready to
block the escape of potential prey. Suzuki concludes:

> The motive force which drives them to hunt animals is not the
> mere fact that the prey happens to be within their easy reach,
> but it is also related to social excitement caused by the situation
> of the group in their nomadic life.[10]

In fact, hunting may not be initiated by hunger at all. Indeed, the
Gombe chimps, in the heyday of banana provisioning, were often
satiated with fruit when a pair from the core group of male hunters
began stalking. So what is the prime drive? More interesting, actually
offered meat or a corpse, they will not touch it, even if it is laid on a
chimp path for them to find. Apparently, it is not looked upon as food
unless it is killed by the group. Strange, then, to find chimpanzees not
averse to snatching bushbuck carcasses from baboons; in fact, they
frequently steal baboon kills. On one occasion, the chimp Melissa –
hair on end and *waa*-barking – was witnessed charging into a group of
some eight baboons, grabbing a carcass and escaping unscathed, flailing
about with her fists and warding off the fearsomely toothed male
baboons. So, strictly speaking, chimps do not have to be the actual
killers. The baboons, with whom they share a baffling relationship,
can do the job for them; the chimps are instantly aware of a baboon
kill by the bleating or screams of the victim, and rush to the scene. But
although they sometimes show almost kinship behaviour towards
baboons, and at times even groom one another (see below), the apes
never beg flesh from baboons, but *steal* it (something protocol forbids
their doing from even the lowest-ranking chimpanzee female in
possession of flesh). Then again, while happily socialising with baboons
one minute, chimps will turn and prey on them the next.

When the Killing Turns to Murder

"Baffling" really is the word for chimpanzee-baboon relations.[11] Not only will they intermingle when drawn together by the prospect of bananas, but they will even socialise, individuals from the two species acting with strange familiarity towards one another. Play groups comprising youngsters are not rare, and in one touching instance an actual cross-species friendship blossomed. Fed up with being ignored by her mother during those interminable termiting sessions, young Gilka became attached to the baby baboon Goblina. On hearing baboon-troop movements or the old baboons barking, Gilka would climb a tree and after spotting her playmate, rush off to greet her, when Goblina too left her kind and patted and cuddled her chimp friend, tickling her ribs and rolling over in play. Young chimps and baboons often play together, but the tussles can end in threats when the irascible chimps begin teasing. Not so with this pair, who for a year played gently and dearly favoured one another's company.

While adults tolerate each other, for some it went further. One elderly baboon known as Job often lingered in camp long after his troop left. As the chimps wandered in, he would sidle up to Fifi or one of the females, turn sideways and demand to be groomed. More unexpectedly, Fifi actually complied, after which it became a common occurrence to see old Job begging to be groomed and juvenile apes agreeing (the baboons rarely reciprocate). It is not unknown for the males of one species to take an amorous interest in the females of the other. They not only respond to each other's signals (many game animals pick up on one another's "danger" signals) but here they actually *answer* as if they 'understood', taking interspecies communication a stage further. For example, one day fearless Mr. Worzle was startled by a female baboon stealthily creeping by. He jumped in the air and barked, at which the female cowered submissively, and in realisation of his hasty act he patted her reassuringly; thus calmed, she sat nearby and began eating. It looks to all the world as though intermixing and responding jointly to signals have led to a mixed-species 'community'. One could even imagine a blurring of ego boundaries. Consider the chimpanzee reaction to a baboon killed after a fight with its own kind:

rather than snatching it to eat, the chimps examined the corpse, then began grooming it as if it were a dead comrade.

This makes all the more perplexing the sudden hunting down of a baby baboon by male chimps. Tragically, Goblina's firstborn fell prey to chimpanzees during a predatory episode, an act which predictably stretched Jane Goodall's sympathy to the limit. Teleki twice saw chimps seize baby baboons that only moments before had been playing in mixed play groups, watched over by female chimps and baboons. Moreover, the big male baboons, although strong enough to kill a leopard (and on one occasion in the Gombe they were observed mortally wounding a serval cat suspected of preying on young baboons), rarely hurt chimpanzee attackers. Male baboons *do* rally round targeted youngsters, they do retaliate with yawning threats and scuffles do occasionally break out. Yet they seem inhibited from ganging up and killing the chimpanzee aggressor the way they did the serval. After an ape snatch, the old male baboons retire, leaving a mourning female. This peculiar psychological ambivalence between chimpanzee and baboon (one might justifiably term it schizoid behaviour) calls to mind the parallel of man and his pets (dogs, sheep). We too move freely and amicably among them; we even groom them and are groomed in return, while children form strong attachments to rabbits, for example, frequently investing them with human attributes. Yet with almost schizoid disinterestedness, man suddenly turns to butcher them and devour the carcasses. Our predatory ways are gradually learnt during childhood, as they presumably are for the chimp. At the same time, we receive maximum exposure to cuddly pets and somehow manage to accommodate both killing and loving traits without mental friction.

An intense debate is currently raging on the distinction in man and apes between intraspecific aggression (displaying, charging, stamping, and generally terrorising one's peers into submission) and true predation. Konrad Lorenz said in *On Aggression* that he feels no hostility towards roast turkey, to which I add neither would he try to cannibalise the driver who rammed the back of his car. In true social carnivores (wolves and lions), prey killing is kept absolutely distinct from aggression towards one's own kind, with strong inhibitory drives operating to stop social displays degenerating into orgies of blood. But according to Lorenz, since unarmed man was unable to slaughter big prey, failsafe devices were never incorporated into his social behaviour to ensure against manslaughter. Weapons, however, severely upset the equilibrium, giving mankind an enhanced killing power like true social carnivores while still leaving him devoid of restrictions on its use.[12] The chimpanzee – pictured by Lorenz as a "social and friendly creature" – suggests all is not so simple; even though unable or unwilling to kill with weapons, cousin *Pan* seems equally to suffer a blurred distinction between prey killing and social aggression. In the only photograph taken at the precise moment of killing by a chimpanzee, the hunter sports a terrifyingly aggressive facial and gestural expression as he thrashes the young baboon to death, something quite unknown in true social carnivores. The ape was 'intimidating' its prey into fatal submission: showing off, as it were, something which equally terrified onlooker apes, judging by their grins of fear. Kortlandt thus infers that ape predation is a form of redirected aggression, aimed at a member of one's own 'community' (with mixed ape and baboon members). "The killing technique is the same one as is often used in child killing in concentration camps," says Kortlandt. It is a "form of racism since, to chimpanzees, baboons are a sort of semi-conspecific [conspecific= member of same species]".[13] Despite the distressing and melodramatic analogy, Kortlandt said what many felt. It goes without saying that this does not prove man's supposed innate aggression, for two reasons: (1) It is probably not phylogenetically-linked to ape intra-community aggression, *i.e.* it has not been proved that a common ancestor shared the same behavioural trait, and (2) it is undoubtedly drawn out by peculiar social conditions in both man and ape (where, it seems, hunting is also learned). Roger Peters studies wolves, and for him too chimpanzee hunting just does not fit the true carnivore pattern. He notes curious anomalies like "a chimpanzee brushing other baboons aside, *i.e.* physically coming into contact with baboons, in order to attack a specific baboon". Not only that, but "The chimpanzee may chase him for a while and then sit down next to him."[14] But if it *was* redirected aggression, how to account for those calm stalking episodes? Clearly, we have to do an awful lot of disentangling.

It seems no use denying that aggression can turn with horrific consequences into predation upon one's own kind. In the last few years the Gombe has been racked by the most horrifying violence. Murder, it seems, has become commonplace to the extent that many well-loved apes made famous *In the Shadow of Man* have been slaughtered by their own kind. Others have turned killer. It is no longer a question of wilfully denying that such events happen; the onus is now to look to their psycho-social causes. Nor can we blame it on chimp psychopaths, mad apes run amok, since normally well-adjusted males now have blood dripping from their mouths.

Twin cases of infanticide and resultant cannibalism were first reported in 1971 and 1972, suggesting from the outset that it might not be an outrageously freakish act. Suzuki witnessed the dominant male of his Budongo Forest troop in Uganda gnawing a mutilated but alive newborn infant. Then in September 1971, J. D. Bygott, an observer sent from Cambridge University, recorded an incident among the Gombe individuals whose life histories and social predicaments were well known.[15] A group of males quietly feeding chanced upon two silent females, one known to them, the other presumably unfamiliar (since Bygott failed to recognise her) carrying a child. Five males launched into a vicious attack on this female, and ran off screaming, with Humphrey holding the struggling infant. Its nose was dripping blood and Humphrey was beating its head against a branch; then he started eating its thigh muscles and the poor infant went limp. Mike was allowed to tear off a foot. But now confusion seems to have overcome attendant apes. They watched intrigued, but none begged a portion. They did however inspect the carcass, and Humphrey too began poking and sniffing rather than eating it. He even groomed it, then dropped it and walked away (*prey* is devoured by the group with not so much as a scrap wasted). Others retrieved the small corpse, only to play, examine or groom it, often giving it the respect accorded a dead community member. The carcass changed hands six times and, although battered beyond recognition, very little had been eaten.

Teleki and Bygott began rationalising the cannibalistic act. Teleki saw it as a case of "pseudo-predation" caused by social stress (Humphrey and Mike were vying for dominance at this time).[16] Any leadership tension was certainly sublimated, since Mike and Humphrey showed no evidence of stress. Besides, the episode was paralleled in October 1975, when observers caught Figan in the act of pounding a dead infant, with an accomplice, Satan, chewing a detached hand. Again, curious apes walked up to sniff and poke the corpse, seeming confused and torn between reponses. Since the infant's mother was presumably unfamiliar certain inhibitions were lowered, and aggression 'sparked over' into predation. Such was Teleki's theory. Bygott thought chimps were recent predators, and that aggression and predation had yet to come fully under independent motivational controls, as they had in wolves. Both agreed, in short, that extreme aggression had spilled over into predation. In such infuriatingly complex social and psychological creatures as chimpanzees there are no simplistic solutions to murder. Even less so in man, where sophisticated, institutionalised learning and habituation to culture, mores and customs make any snap comparison with apes hazardous. Nonetheless, murder might not be a "pathological" anomaly unique to man. Certainly the chimp parallel is too overpowering to ignore, though we must beware of naïvely assuming identical causes.

The latest spate of gruesome chimpanzee killings is largely unfathomable, rooted presumably in deeply entrenched social and psychological causes, so far as impenetrable and mystifying as man's own. In very recent years, a high-ranking female, Passion, and her adolescent daughter, Pom, have been seen on three occasions beating up mothers, then stealing, battering and devouring their tiny babies. Violence of such horrific intensity violates even Teleki's cool judgment that the victim must be unknown. In August 1975, Passion seized Gilka's three-week-old baby after a scuffle and began sharing its flesh with her own offspring. Gilka was a low-ranker; weakly and partially paralysed from a polio attack ten years earlier, she also suffered a fungus infection which gave her a sadly comic nose. Gilka was no match for Passion and Pom. In 1976 they snatched her next baby. They caught Gilka at the feeding site and launched into an attack. Gilka crouched over the tiny infant, trying desperately to shield it. Passion bit into Gilka's face until blood streamed while Pom seized the infant and cracked open its skull with her teeth. Again, they shared the meat for five hours, devouring most of the feet, arms and head. Unlike the males' attacks on strangers, there was no thrashing of the infant, no confusion, nor any reluctance to gorge themselves on the flesh. Other apes wandered up and some sniffed the infant's entrails; one female touched a scrap of flesh then disgustedly wiped her fingers clean. Later in 1976 another mother, Melissa, was savagely assaulted by the Passion family. She too crouched low over her baby, and the tug-of-war for the three-week-old baby lasted several minutes, during which time Passion gouged Melissa's face. Also a polio victim, Melissa was quickly outflanked and exhausted. She watched helplessly as Passion's family devoured her baby, and even submissively stretched out her hand for reassurance from Passion, who embraced her 'forgivingly'. "Of the five babies born in 1976," Goodall wrote in sorrow to *The New York Times*, "only one survived its first month."[17] Gilka and other mothers with newborn infants now seek out protective male company. And the males have been seen chasing off Passion after being alerted by a mother's screams of fear.

In retrospect, it appears possible that Passion herself was a disturbed mother whose daughter Pom suffered severe neuroses as a result. While normal chimpanzee mothers guard their offspring from contact with other chimps (except siblings) for up to six months, Passion laid Pom on the ground from her first day of life and allowed all and sundry to touch and groom her. From then on, she was nothing if not callous. Pom had to ride her mother's back far too early in life; she was often denied adequate milk; when learning to walk she struggled unaided, while whimpering for her mother to wait. By contrast, old Flo would guide and support Flint. Eventually, it is not surprising to learn, Pom became so neurotic that she gripped her mother tightly with one hand while playing with Flint or Goblin with the other. Goodall's explanation of Passion's insensitivity is that she had already lost a number of babies. Perhaps, then, Passions' is a peculiar case; of neuroses building to negligence and cruelty. Whatever the causes, cannibalism is certainly not unique to her. Even gorillas, it now appears from Dian Fossey's field studies, not only indulge in personal violence, but actually practise infanticide. This is inferred from an analysis of feces of the high-ranking female of her study group, which contained the bones of a vanished baby belonging to a low-ranking female. This may shoot to pieces another piece of Teleki's jigsaw, since he first speculated that cannibalism occurred in hunter-gatherers, by getting carried away in the heat of the moment and switching over into their prey-killing pattern while aggressively displaying. Yet gorillas are apparently not systematic hunters like chimpanzees.

The 1970s was evidently a decade of tremendous social stress for the Gombe chimpanzees, aggravated (or perhaps reflected?) by Passion's baby battering. Jane Goodall visibly stunned her academic audience during her 1978 L. S. B. Leakey Memorial Lecture given at the British Museum (Natural History) by relating the full horror of the bloody spate of panicides: a recent and disturbing feature of the escalating and brutal gang warfare between Gombe chimpanzee residents and a southern splinter group.[18] Trouble began brewing about 1970. One guess was that, of the thirty to forty troop members, there were too many males (eighteen) and this sparked off the violence. Whatever the cause, following a social rift seven males and three females broke away (or were ostracised?) to form the southern splinter group. Chimpanzees *can* be aggressively territorial, more so than was previously realised. The males will patrol their home range, moving along the boundaries; occasionally (and silently) climbing trees to stare intently into a neighbouring group's domain – they will sit vigilantly peering in one direction like this for up to ninety minutes. Occasionally there are hostile encounters, they might rush in to molest a 'loner' if all seems safe. But nothing on record rivals the treatment of the splinter group which seceded in 1972.

In 1974, males from the main group launched at least three "vicious" attacks on solitary males from the southern community, beating them unconscious, leaving them bloody and dying after twenty minutes of merciless pounding. Thus died Goliath. The pattern was repeated with nauseating precision; from three to five males moved in for the kill, taking usually twenty minutes to finish their deed. Goodall was near to tears as she told of an old female who managed to escape by crawling into thick vegetation, only to die five days later. Her ten-year-old daughter kept vigil with her, brushing flies from her mother's wounds and waiting for the end. Goodall's assistants broke the 'non interference' field policy and took her bananas and water, but there was nothing they could do. Chimpanzee compassion was conspicuously absent in these dark doings; one old male was actually seen hurling a rock at a victim already prostrate and dying on the ground. The main group annexed the southern home range as spoils of their thuggery. All southern members were butchered bar one male. In 1977 this sole survivor was attacked, his legs were broken and he has not been seen since.

Predictably, chimp brutality raised vital questions about man's own warring "instincts". Of course, this haunting episode leaves prodigious scope for fallacious reasoning, as *The New York Times* discovered. An atrociously misguided editorial, headed "A Theory of Devolution", rallied to the "bright side" of Goodall's disclosures:

> If the chimpanzees, who presumably preceded mankind in evolution's plan, were indeed purely gentle and harmonious, that would suggest that mankind's evolutionary drift has been steeply downhill. So Miss Goodall's latest observations offer

grounds for optimism. If we can trace our bad habits to the animal kingdom, there is hope that becoming more human need not mean becoming more murderous.

It is hard to envisage a more muddled hotch-potch of ideological and philosophical anachronisms. (1) The chimpanzee as man's 'predecessor' in evolution's "plan" (even though it lives alongside us today!) might have recommended itself to an ahistorical Lamarckian, or even a Romantic like Louis Agassiz, for whom man was life's ultimate manifestation and the "plan" God's proof that we were in His thoughts from the outset; (2) the nonsense of murder heralding our evolutionary slide "downhill" smacks of nothing so much as a demystified version of the Fall; (3) belief that our "bad habits" can be happily explained as atavistic traits to be blamed solely on our animal ancestry befits late nineteenth-century extremists, who actually saw criminals as literal throwbacks in their acts of "animal" brutality. Ashley Montagu, whose investigations into the social causes of man's occasional inhumanity had only recently resulted in his definitive book *On the Nature of Human Aggression*, politely pointed out a few of these facts in a follow-up letter to *The New York Times*. He explained this act of chimpanzee mass murder as probably the result of

> a peculiar set of social or ecological conditions. If this is so, then it is clear that under certain conditions chimpanzees behave more like humans than humans behave like chimpanzees. . . . The fact that chimpanzees and humans are capable of slaughterous behavior proves neither their kinship with us nor that they are innately programmed so to act. What the study of each species reveals is that each is capable of learning a wide repertory of behavior.[19]

But war genes are only as laughable as a *tabula rasa* on which society can scratch "love" or "hate", and genetic determinists only as ludicrous as pure culturalists. Nature/nurture has degenerated (or rather polarised) into the pseudoproblem of the decade. It is not a question of genes *versus* environment, since the two conspire to act as one. Genes in fact only bestow an action potential; in other words, they cannot dictate that man or ape will turn killer, or indeed *is* a killer by nature. They permit an enormous leeway in behaviour, action within wide margins –

thus permitting the inordinate flexibility so essential to big-brained primates. Social or cultural conditions then channel this potential, pinning it down forcibly into one actual behaviour to suit those conditions. Look at the chimpanzee murder case more closely. Numerous workers now believe that chimpanzee flesh-hunting is a recent innovation, perhaps evolving from simpler plant-gathering actions. Probably little or no genetic distance separates these holocausting apes from peaceable plant-gathering chimps (any more than between Nazis and their victims); even though the Gombe group had *learned* to harness old ways into savage baboon-hunting practices. No hunting genes specifically exist (it would be naïve to believe they did), but a genetic matrix permitted one highly specific murderous behaviour in this peculiar instance because social-psychological conditions narrowed the potential: family histories, social friction, ecological conditions, personal psychologies, plus learned hunting ways – all *conspired* at this point. The consequence was racial extermination.

It would be premature to assign causes to the chimpanzee holocaust, which anyway must be imponderably complex. But consider the following, just one among many tentative approaches. Ten to fifteen years ago, many of the males indulging in these recent barbarous attacks were impressionable adolescents or young adults setting out to make their mark on chimpanzee society. Yet this was a highly abnormal time for Gombe apes. In order to keep track of these shy creatures, Goodall had been banana provisioning since 1962. This drew chimps to camp for study and recording. But bananas also drew baboons, and as provisioning increased baboon-chimpanzee aggression escalated. During the period when vicious competing was at its worst (1965–1968), the banana provisioning system was explicitly modified three times to alleviate the situation but keep the chimpanzees coming. By 1967 there were more chimps at the feeding site than observers could keep track of. By 1968, recorded Richard Wrangham of Cambridge University, who produced these very telling results, "The number of attacks rose rapidly as baboons became bolder, and eventually created so many problems that observation was almost ended."[20] The crisis reached a head and Goodall ordered a drastic and selective reduction of banana provisioning. But had this already left psychological and social scars in the male chimps? I ask this because Teleki's study immediately followed this crisis period, and he was staggered by the number of baboons hunted by chimpanzees. (During 1968, the chimps killed nine infant baboons near the artificial feeding area. From 1969 to 1972 only one such incident was recorded each year. If provisioning had ceased altogether, it might have been nil.)

Banana provisioning had forced chimpanzees and baboons to compete, even while forming a mixed 'community' where youngsters played happily together in integrated creches and adults mutually groomed. This forced association had strange repercussions. Chimpanzees switched their hunting on to baboon targets. Only now it was not *pure* hunting since there was an aggressive element in their clashes. The association, I hastily add, did not *initiate* chimpanzee hunting tendencies; in fact, when Goodall stopped provisioning, the apes returned to hunting colobus monkeys. This suggests that the Gombe "hunters" are flexible flesh-takers; all Goodall did was furnish a new supply of limbs and torsos. Moreover, chimps in non-provisioned areas also hunt and share the spoils. Akira Suzuki saw his chimps in the Budongo Forest hunting colobus monkeys and blue duiker antelope, as well as dividing the spoils and carting chunks of torso slung over the shoulders.

Even the Gombe chimpanzees may show a fine but critical distinction between hunting proper (characterised by surreptitious stalking, manoeuvring, silent coordination, with no aggressive signs at all) and violently aggressive and noisy competition; although high density (which itself intensifies ape to ape aggression around food) and forced association with baboons had 'unnaturally' blurred the demarcation lines. The presence of vulnerable infants under these conditions sparked off hunting techniques, but the sudden and awful realisation on catching these community infants snapped the pattern into an aggressive act. The hideously intimidating facial grimaces of apes killing baboons emphasise this. Despite this knowledge that it was a clan member, emotions were too highly charged, and aggression, rather than ritualistically channelling the violence, degenerated into terrorising and flailing the infant to death (using a well practised charging–display thrashing movement). Behavioural confusion towards cannibalised chimpanzee victims, when the killers were not sure whether to eat or groom them, well illustrates the psychological chaos that can result.

The young male apes, then – the future leaders – were reared and receptive in this tense and confused period of the 1960s, when carrying out guerilla raids against their own 'community' members was commonplace. They had witnessed, perhaps even assisted in, the skirmishes against baboon fellows. They had certainly tasted the flesh of these one-time chimpanzee playmates. In this sinister air, they became habituated to intercommunity killing, familiar with the insidious blend of violent aggression and refined hunting which targeted one's own kind and marked it for death.

This is by no means an exhaustive explanation. Myriad other factors must be brought into play if ever we are to present a three-dimensional picture of chimpanzee mass murder. And at the risk of repeating myself – necessary so long as theories of man's "killer ape" ancestry are legion – we must delve deeply into individual and family histories of the deceased and victors, social stresses and the superabundance of males, personal psychologies and ecological pressures, for all played their part in this gruesome event. We may never understand the complete story. Nor the full extent of the atrocities. But as the only case of non-human murder on record it deserves a penetrating study. At least, it demonstrates vividly the absurdity of reductionist logic: that man's amateurishly exploded brain was accidentally rewired for perpetual warfare. If anything, the ape atrocities suggest that 'aberrant' man acts as naturally as his Gombe cousins under extreme environmental provocation. Even chimpanzees have enough genetic leeway for murder.

II

The Mechanics of Morality

In 1973 the Dutch chimp-watcher Adriaan Kortlandt echoed the prevailing feeling when he answered his own question: "Why do chimpanzees *not* talk?"

> Part of the answer [he replied] is, of course, that fruit-pickers have less to discuss with one another than cooperative big-game hunters who must engage in sophisticated stalking and ambushing strategies.

Today's systematic research has shown life in the Gombe (psychosocially speaking) to be inordinately more complex than yesterday's term "fruit-picker" suggests. Figan's is far from the vacuous, idyllic existence so admired by previous human generations; indeed it is as rich as we might expect *a priori* for so close a relative of man. To this social end, apes have a convoluted cortex which seems out of all proportion to their merely technological needs. The reasoning and scheming abilities so in evidence in psychological laboratories permit chimpanzees to grapple with the psychological complexities and political chicanery of community life. And as with man, the razor's edge balance of the social equilibrium established by such massively unstable intellects can be quickly shattered, leading to chimpanzee madness or treachery and mass murder. Original belief in the chimpanzee's 'vacuous' existence stemmed from watching zoo apes idling away their interminable prison years; even though a human criminal behind bars studied with the same superficiality would suggest a species of equally vapid ape. To do justice, Kortlandt himself was not implying that the ape cranium was a hollow cavity, far from it. Watching Washoe reading, and thinking out loud to herself in signs as she flicked magazine pages and recognised gin or toothpaste advertisements, he reasoned that "these apes have a lot more to think than to say".

True, yet false; left there, it belies the real subtlety of the chimpanzee's social predicament. After all, Figan *was* desperate to tell old Flo that he was *bored* with interminable termiting. Indeed, every social act is an act of communication. The point is that apes have numerous other means besides true symbolism with which to get the message across: the art of subtle eye and lip movements, and not so subtle body postures. As long as these standard systems cope, there will be little pressure for behavioural novelty – like signs or speech. I would go so far as to claim that apes are far better equipped than most mammals, for they can augment facial expressions with a new system obviating the need for communication: introspective modelling. Figan's scheming proves the point. He got round the dire need to say to old Flo "For God's sake, hurry up!" by kidnapping Flint and forcing her move. Figan made language redundant; so in the sense that he had more to scheme because he could not speak, Kortlandt was right.

But how do you pass from plenty to think to something to say? What *will* overload the conventional mammal communication system and precipitate a novel language is a growing division of labour. Not the inflexible physiological kind found in ants, where each form is programmed – soldiers, workers, queens, *etc.* – and thus chained to its station in life. Rather, mankind has created its own positions of soldier, worker and queen, but has 'randomly' parcelled them out to community members (in the sense that each could learn the other's skill). This labour-splitting generates a steep communication gradient between specialist groups, which calls for a system with a high-information content. If an artisan excels in flint-making, the others obviously leave him to it; he then makes axes and knives for the community in exchange for furs, food, services or whatever the others can provide. *Now* there is a need for explicit signed or spoken instructions. Engels followed up the obvious corollary of his socialist theorem: labour, he reasoned, generated the need for articulate speech. Only after the social unit cohered and individuals became engaged in joint activities had "men in the making arrived at the point where *they had something to say* to one another".[2] I disagree only on the fine but nonetheless critical contention that working together (*i.e.* towards some common goal) is necessary and sufficient to encourage speech. Chimpanzees have taught us that when objectives are common – as in collective colobus-hunting – they can and do coordinate brilliantly with scarcely more than a periodic glance at one another. Introspective modelling is still functioning to offset the need for language.

The chimpanzee hunt has its lessons. It is finely coordinated, involving stalking and advance manoeuvring to cut off the target's line of retreat. Most importantly, though, it is evidence for incipient dominance breakdown, both during the hunt – when the leadership switches in a flash – and especially during the ensuing begging phase. Stalking is conducted with the conspicuous absence of sounds or symbols, despite the information that must be shared: pinpointing the target, devising a stratagem, switching tactics in full stride. Such eerie hunting silence gravely jeopardises decades-old speculations on how artificially to set up a self-sustaining language in captive chimps. Yerkes long ago set the trend. In his 1943 book, *Chimpanzees: A Laboratory Colony*, he told of an experiment in which caged chimps had helped one another haul in a heavy crate. The crate had deliberately been left out of arm's reach, but two ends of attached rope were within grabbing distance; one chimp tried pulling, gave up, and was seen entreating his cage-companion for help. With an ape on either end of the rope, the crate was dragged towards the bars and within dismantling distance.[3] Such collusion is also shown by Menzel's chimps, where one will tap his companion on the shoulder and request him to orientate the escape ladder. Soliciting help in a common endeavour, Yerkes thought, was a transitional step to the invention of language. Of late, the Fouts' group in Oklahoma has investigated the prospects for establishing a band of sheep-hunting apes, in an attempt to trace man's (supposed) early footsteps by encouraging teamwork among the young male chimpanzees. The group hopes this all-out attempt will provide the reinforcement required for language 'take-off', when signing becomes self-sustaining. (They intend to cheat by teaching ASL to the hunters beforehand – the goal is not to mimic language evolution but aid its perpetuation.)

This venture rests on the presupposition that a common striving will catalyse language. Yet I imagine quite the reverse to hold: that the diverse interests of specialist groups, each with a certain sovereignty, generate the conditions for informative exchanges. Anything less is adequately dealt with by chimpanzee 'eye language'.

The 1970s are at last coming to terms with the real power of 'body language'. The claim that it merely backs up words smacks of naïvete. Humans use twin primary systems in complementary fashion, each with its own power base – postures and gestures as against words – and it is often difficult to tell which s the emotional intensifier. Kortlandt laughed that extraterrestrials visiting Earth and scrutinising the Latin types scattered around the Mediterranean might not "wonder whether the primary biological function of human speech is to add emotional emphasis to gestural language". So often, facial expression can render words superfluous; only a poem could match the slight raising of an eyebrow for subtle evocation. It should not be surprising, even to a human blinded by the coarseness of speech, that chimpanzees can detect such nuances in a facial expression, since it is their communicative forte. Nim read Laura Petitto's feelings like an open book, which made life with him occasionally precarious. She could even explore hidden aspects of her emotional self simply by trusting to Nim's heightened perception rather than her own coolly rational judgment: "he made me *wary* of my body," she confides, and relates an incident which explains this cryptic statement. Laura was angry with someone; it was, of course, bottled up – decorum rarely allows for heated exchanges in our society. Perhaps, more than bottled up, it was actually sublimated to the extent that she was no longer consciously aware of it herself. By all human accounts, there was not the slightest sign of anger when she next greeted the person who had caused the upset. Yet no sooner were pleasantries exchanged than Laura unknowingly triggered Nim's sympathetic aggression, and with hair erect he flew into an attack on the culprit. Laura is first to admit that she learnt more from Nim than he from her, even though she devoted three years to language-training him. If anything, pidgin-signing cramped Nim's style, squeezing him into a conversational straitjacket. He was alive to new discoveries, and just had to share them; he would drag his flatmate outside to point out planes or birds. But always he conveyed so much more without his mock-ASL: signs which were largely made redundant by real ape communication.

Indeed, Emil Menzel has brazenly claimed that none of the ASL-trained and home-raised chimps "could tell each other any more than wild chimpanzees are capable of conveying to each other with their 'language of the eyes'".[4] And he backed his claim with some telling experiments. A group of young chimpanzees was released into a field a little over an acre in size, 'seeded' with hidden treasure: toys, food and fake snakes. One ape was carried round the field and shown the whereabouts of each cache, then returned to the group, whereupon they were all released. Menzel's problem was to determine how much precise information the initiated chimp could pass to the others. The results convinced Menzel that the leader conveyed details such as the food's location, since his 'uninformed' companions would rush ahead of him to the cache. An ape could even relate the *amount* of food: so, for example, two leaders, each previously shown different sized caches, would each attract a number of followers proportionate to the cache size. And if the object was dangerous (the toy snake), then all the chimps knew it well before they cast eyes on the snake; when the leader returned with his comrades, he would stand well clear while others felt for the snake with a stick, poking about in the grass – if food had been the prize, none of the young apes would have hesitated from rummaging about with their hands. If the snake had vanished by the time they returned, the group would fan out in a search pattern, as if a live snake had been spotted but had crawled away. "In sum," concluded Menzel, "the chimpanzees were able, and without any deliberate training on our part, to convey to each other the presence, direction, probably location, and the relative desirability and undesirability (if not the more precise nature) of a distant, hidden goal which no one had directly seen for himself."

Menzel's claim that untutored chimpanzees could convey more with their eyes than could house-trained apes with all the educational advantages of a twentieth-century sign system must have rankled, to say the least. The challenge was recently met by Rumbaugh's team (now comprising psychologists Sue Savage and Sally Boysen), whose elegant experiments capitalised on chimp-to-chimp cross 'talk'. Rumbaugh raised two laboratory-born chimpanzees on Lana's computerised fare, the dominant Sherman (four and a half years old) and Austin, his junior by a year. Using Lana's keyboard, the two apes were first taught to name and request foods, and also to read sentences punched in by the human operator (telling them, for example, what a sealed container was baited with: usually chocolate – a food they could then request). At this stage the real testing began. Without training or practice at "talking" to one another, one chimp was led away and shown the container being baited with one of eleven foods, from beancake and banana to Coke and milk. Led back to his companion, he punched in the food name – which appeared on the illuminated screen – effectively passing on the news of what he had seen. The silent watcher then took over the keyboard and placed a formal request for just that food. They quickly perfected the procedure, telling one another in turn of the food they had spotted. Sherman and Austin "exploited and expanded upon previously acquired skills in the successful communication achieved here," affirmed Rumbaugh, Savage and Boysen in *Science* (August 1978), "and the transmission of information regarding the contents of the container was between two chimpanzees, unmediated by any human being".[5]

This information was highly specific. Would Menzel's boast stand the test if eye language, or indeed any non-symbolic clue, was all that was permitted Sherman and Austin? Could one tell the other it was Coke not milk; could subtle postural clues disclose that it was one highly favoured food (chocolate) and not another (banana); or that it was boring beancake rather than equally unappetising chow? To find out, one ape was shown the food, led back and allowed any means at his disposal *except pressing the keyboard* to pass this information to his accomplice. But to no avail, his uninformed colleague resorted to guessing as he sat down at the keyboard. If, that is, he bothered with the keyboard at all. Showing typical chimpanzee guile, he first tried worming the answer out of nearby humans by forcing them to press the right keys!

That the challenge was issued at all testifies to the strength of Menzel's position: eye language is efficient for low-level information. Menzel commented in *New Scientist* that experienced chimp leaders – those conveying maximum information – were surprisingly those who least showed any visible sign. These were masters of gestural subtlety, perfecting techniques which juveniles with all their haste had yet to learn. On the contrary, "the most dramatic and humanoid-looking signals," judged Menzel, "were made by the most infantile and least efficient leaders." Using eye language expertise, chimpanzees can not only wring out maximum information or convey it, they can use the system to subvert or thwart, throwing followers off the track. We saw that behavioural liars might actually lead off the gullible in the wrong direction, only to return alone to the food cache; they might, alternatively, stubbornly refuse to lead others to the hidden food. What I did not point out was that this sort of deception cuts both ways, since it encourages disbelief, and followers keep a sharp look out for suspicious

behaviour in the leader. And having guessed his lying strategy, the
sceptical retinue will home in on his every move. "The less eager and
obvious he *tries* to act," said Menzel watching the leader, "the more
closely the followers might keep him under surveillance."

Natural chimpanzee communication can thus handle a vast amount
of general information. But at some point in our own ancestry a similar
chimp-style system must have overloaded: the social situation created
the pressure for greater and more precise information flow, one which
neither eye language could handle nor unaided introspective modelling
could by-pass. Goodall's Gombe chimpanzees confirm that body
language systems probably began showing stress given a greater
division of labour; for even in chimps, when roles are sharply
differentiated and the rewards great enough – as in the case of flesh-
owners and beggars – the "gimme" gesture is used to augment eye
language.

While from *Homo habilis* to *Homo erectus* brain size doubled, the
human tool-kit managed only a painfully slow advance; evidently, the
brain 'explosion' was mated less to technology than to social factors
which failed to fossilise. In the last two million years mankind's social
practices have become so elaborate, his kinship patterns so complex and
his labour division so complete, that the overloaded 'eye language'
system flipped (to borrow a highly appropriate model from René
Thom's Catastrophe Theory) into the novel language of symbolism to
which the hominid was exquisitely preadapted.

Sherman's Treatment of Austin: Or Why
Dominance had to Erode for the Genesis of Kindman

The flip to symbolism necessarily occurred when labour was rapidly
specialising and thus reciprocal altruism was emerging as one of the
formative influences on human society and mind. Reciprocal altruism
(you scratch my back and I'll scratch yours) is a salient characteristic of
mankind – it is also the long promised means to disentangle the human
and chimpanzee 'selves' confounded in Gallup's psychological 'new
deal'. If the self is forged out of social relations, then society and self are
inextricably linked; so the social peculiarity of any species will be
mirrored in its psychic realm. And as long as these social reference

points are unique, words – although ostensibly shared between species – will retain idiosyncratic meanings for both.

Reciprocal altruism has melted so deeply into every aspect of human social relations that we barely recognise even its outline any more. The bartering system, in which we employ money to cover delayed exchanges, even the ready and reciprocal access to knowledge we all enjoy, these are all examples of two-way altruism we take for granted. Meshing the conclusions from today's chimpanzee research with Robert Trivers' ingenious theory of reciprocal altruism, which explains the evolution of guilt, remorse – and, indeed, morality itself – we can link language, morals and altruism in parallel and mutually reinforcing evolution; and thus set forth the social conditions in which the human conscience emerged.

Morality is a topic of prodigious interest, the more so for the violent ideological disputes which swathe it. But it is of more than peculiar theological concern since, for a century, it has seemed squarely at odds with the tenets of Darwinism. In his declining years, Huxley waded deep into ethical waters, his endeavours culminating in his famous Romanes Lecture on "Evolution and Ethics" delivered at Oxford in 1893. Huxley's was the definitive formulation of the classic Darwinian dilemma. He saw an irreconcilable clash between "the ethical process", summed up by the injunction 'do unto others as you would have them do unto you', and the opportunism which seemed best to promote personal survival and increase one's wealth: an opportunism brutally necessary as part of Huxley's caricature of nature's gladiatorial free-for-all. Summarising his problem, Huxley admitted that "since law and morals are restraints upon the struggle for existence between men in society, the ethical process is in opposition to the principle of the cosmic process, and tends to the suppression of the qualities best fitted for success in their struggle".[6] How can the fittest endure when they are not allowed to show themselves the fittest? How can the weak be weeded out when human compassion made their preservation a priority? He never solved this momentous problem; and he even foresaw, in morality's curtailing natural urges, a genetic rusting of mankind's adaptive armour.

Today, critics of natural selection shake their heads with incredulity as exponents of Darwinism struggle with a recalcitrant altruism. The "survival of the fittest" seems incapable of explaining personal sacrifice, like a man jumping into a river to save a drowning child, or the 'sacrificial' urge of a bird rising into the air with warning shrieks as a hawk hovers overhead – or even why we should find it disagreeable to lie when it would result in personal gain and thus increase survival value.

The forces of light plunging Huxley's topsy-turvy universe into Cimmerian blackness have finally fallen to an elegant Darwinian rationalisation. Morality, the ultimate refuge of the gods of natural theology, has at last a plausible explanation.

Robert Trivers of Harvard's Biological Laboratories has devised a model for reciprocal altruism in which 'cheats', those who take but never give back, are harshly scythed down by standard Darwinian selection – a move which paradoxically *increases the total fitness of individual members of that population*. Huxley's expectations have been stood on their head. He knew morality banished the 'cheater' and encouraged self-sacrifice, but he could not have predicted that this actually fortified the sacrificer.

The first step is easy to grasp. The model proposes that anyone performing a good deed will be repaid a hundredfold, not in the kingdom to come, but in this life. It is largely a matter of balancing the cost-benefit columns. A man diving into a river to save a drowning child does so at far less cost to himself than benefit to the child. The child's *life* has been saved: the man is merely wet and out of breath. There was danger for him, it is safer to stay on land; but the immense life-saving benefit far outweighed the cost. Of course, it was not *his* life, the man himself has not benefited. However, if the deed were one day reciprocated by the grown youth, then each party would have expended relatively little energy to save the other's life.[7] So far, so good. But as long as there are do-gooders ready to help one another, 'cheats' might be expected to cash in profitably. After all, to have one's life saved and fail to reciprocate hits the jackpot as far as personal benefits are concerned: no danger, all the rewards – even if others suffer or die as a consequence. In a society of reciprocators, cheaters would have a field day; always being saved, never putting themselves in danger, their numbers would clearly explode at the expense of duty-bound do-gooders. Soon, they will vastly outnumber reciprocators. In fact, they will totally exterminate all others, leaving a heartless society of non-helpers.

Now enter the third party: Richard Dawkins in *The Selfish Gene* calls him a 'grudger'. If reciprocators wised up quickly, they would bear grudges against anyone not helping them out (assuming their survival: although I have talked of life-and-death dramas, these are swamped in real life by such mundane acts as reciprocal food-sharing, lice-picking, aiding the sick, and swopping tools and expertise). In short, cheats would be helped once, though never again after their cover was broken. But grudgers will always come to the aid of other grudgers, knowing them to be trustworthy. What happens overall in a population of cheats and grudgers? Dawkins ran a computer simulation to check his intuition that grudgers would prevail, and indeed they do.[8] So long as enough grudgers exist to start (to ensure they run into one another with a certain frequency), then by helping one another out they will eventually push cheats to the verge of extinction – the more speedily as grudgers proliferate and encounter one another with greater frequency. So although the population had few grudgers to start with, the net gain of their helping each other far outweighed the once-only exploitations of a larger number of cheats. Grudgers have greater survival value. The process is more easily pictured if one imagines parasite removal as the reciprocated act. Grudgers would always remove parasites from another grudger (parasites on the neck, say, where it cannot see); hence they will always be free of infection. But cheaters would be deloused only *once* by any grudger. With grudgers refusing to be tricked a second time the cheater would find fewer and fewer willing to help, eventually none; and so even though it was marginally gaining by not wasting its own precious time by delousing others, it will eventually suffer or die from parasitic infection.

This, then, is Trivers' model with Dawkins' embellishments. The exquisite mechanics of the situation explain how jeopardising oneself for the good of others ends up strengthening one's own survival potential. It highlights with computerised simplicity how the counter-intuitive can exist within Darwinism. The model provides an equally impressive demonstration of how social relations among humans are necessarily cemented and complicated, putting the onus on time factors, like the remembrance of grudges and debts. However, nothing has been said so far of how the grudging system might have evolved.

Certain specified conditions must be met before Trivers' model can cut in; primarily, where for example food-sharing is considered, 'theft' by high-rankers must be quashed and even the dominance structure itself must be substantially levelled. A rigidly hierarchical system with ingrained 'divine rights' acknowledged and bowed to by all – where alpha males can appropriate any morsel they so fancy – will thwart selection for grudgers. Menials will be browbeaten into servicing the lordly ranks, despite the lack of reciprocation. Hence the extreme interest shown in the incipient dominance breakdown in chimpanzees during clustered sharing. In baboon troops, fresh meat of the hunted Cape hare does find its way round from individual to individual, but only by being snatched or picked up after a satiated high-ranker has thrown it aside. The nearest to sharing is seen in consort pairs, who might chew on alternate ends of the same corpse.[9] This is in utter contrast to chimpanzees, where hierarchical restraints break down; the social atmosphere is freer, and alpha males tend to beg a portion of colobus monkey rather than snatch it. Hence we can legitimately talk of altruism – the donor volunteers flesh to the lower ranks as well as higher, thus incurring some personal loss.

This provides an approximate model for the route early man may have taken. But genetic-based ranking has crumbled substantially in man (despite Lionel Tiger's & Robin Fox's deduction in *The Imperial Animal* of the subtleties of human society from baboon behaviour). In chimpanzees, apart from this all-important clustering episode, it still exists to impede the free social relations which might otherwise permit grudging. In a superbly designed experiment (though planned for a different end to the one to which I am putting it), Rumbaugh's team simulated the chimpanzee flesh-sharing episode, but switched a polite request written in lexigram language for the less specific natural begging. Rumbaugh sat Sherman and Austin on either side of a glass screen, presenting one with a tray of assorted food items while the other watched attentively. Without a second thought (and certainly without training), the empty-handed ape punched in a food request to his companion, who after reading the message was free to respond by slipping some of his food through a hatch in the window. Roles were then switched and the other ape was handed a tray of delectables and the process repeated. Right from the start, things went wrong in a very apeish way, forcing Rumbaugh to step in and persuade Austin and Sherman to act more considerately, by mimicking the social customs of human reciprocators. What happened initially was that rank-pulling Sherman asked Austin for the best he had, a piece of chocolate, which Austin happily parted with. But when Austin then requested a piece of candy in return, Sherman glanced at his sentence, an unmistakable "Gimme chocolate", and deliberately misread it, going through the comical motions of diligently passing poor Austin an unappetising piece of dry chow instead[10] (under other circumstances, a classic 'cheat' strategy). Had Rumbaugh not stepped in to terminate this dreadful inhuman protocol, Sherman might have gone on forever swindling Austin out of his beloved chocolate. 'Returning the favour' reciprocal altruism, which is the bedrock of human social relations, is unworkable as long as the threat of domination hangs over the lower orders.

In our labour-divided society, a chimp-like giving and receiving of flesh has expanded and intensified into the reciprocal trading of specialist wares, in which exchanges must be scrupulously balanced. And it was a similar though more specialised asking-and-giving situation, which in the chimp clusters engenders the "gimme" gesture, that may have catalysed the invention of human language. But although incipient status fracture characterises chimp sharing, the resilience of ranking – manifested in Sherman's unabashed swindling of Austin – inhibits the peculiarly human ethic of 'fair play'. One can speculate why dominance continued to weaken in our ancestral stock. The human hallmark is cooperation rather than coercion, and protohumans were undoubtedly more willing to help in big-scale ventures, and help more enthusiastically, without the threat of the rod hanging over their head, and without the fear of being browbeaten every time into surrendering their share of the spoils.

The grudgers who gained a foothold once dominance weakened would have hastened the system's collapse. Individuals still trying to pull rank amid the growing band of grudgers would find themselves treated like the cheats and banished as Dawkins' computer predicted. Fraternal grudgers would now reap far greater rewards by preferentially dealing with fellow grudgers, leading to an exponential growth of social commitments. Furthermore, it is amongst grudgers that language is far more likely to flower, since in a labour-split society individuals had services to offer for reciprocated deeds, and specialist manufactures for exchange. This engendered the formalities of asking – requests had to be precisely and politely formulated, specifications had to be exact (impossible without words or signs, as Sherman and Austin, refused access to their keyboard, so graphically demonstrated) and the tally of exchange goods kept for a precise reckoning.

With the enormous benefits accruing, grudgers would be thrust to the forefront, their genes penetrating rapidly into the human population.

This could be human history in microcosm. A million years ago the brain was already in the throes of its impressive slow-motion explosion – uncorrelated to any known technological breakthrough, but presumably reflecting the prodigiously increased input as social responsibility and commitment multiplied. Reciprocal altruism had cut in as the major driving force of economic and political change.

With a flattening out of dominance by grudge-bearing and a cementing of social relation, the base-line was established for the peculiarly human-style moral society. Not only moral, but mathematical; our whole existence has been so geared to pounds, feet, litres and seconds that it is not surprising Pythagoras actually saw reality in numbers. The first prediction from the grudging model is an extended memory, often reaching back into early childhood. On this are chalked up grievances and debts – and hence an ability for mathematical reckoning to balance the scores, as demanded by 'fair trading' practices. But that use of "fair" already shows how radically we have departed from Huxley's understanding. In today's model, morality is an adaptive device to keep reciprocating society stable for the distinct benefit of each member. One has only to listen to Colin Turnbull's pygmies to see the earthy incarnation of all these rather abstract ideas. Turnbull was travelling with his forest people when they netted an antelope too large to be taken to camp whole. They decided to section it then and there, and he recorded the ensuing exchanges:

> the womenfolk crowded around as Ekianga hacked away, each claiming her share for her family. "My husband lent you his spear . . ."; "We gave your third wife some liver when she was hungry and you were away . . ."; "My father and yours always hunted side by side . . ." these were all typical arguments, but for the most part they were not needed. Everyone knew who was entitled to a share, and by and large they stuck to the rules of the game.[11]

But then we all do this every hour of every day of our lives. It is so close to home we invariably overlook it in explanations of mental evolution. We barter and trade; we take tokens for promises, money to mediate, and issue credit notes and receipts.

So far, the model looks naïve, almost idealist; and Trivers took account of this. He ventured that as relations became more subtle and inextricable, it might pay to cheat occasionally, especially if there were no come-back. To check this, selection would have honed our frail faculties for ever finer detection of minor infringements. Enter still more perceptive and sensitive grudgers. What Trivers terms "moralistic aggression" is vented against the deceitful, in an attempt either to reform or banish them; this is a form of aggression scarcely noticed by Lorenz, yet it seems to be overwhelmingly prevalent. Small, niggling issues of unfairness or failure to return a favour rapidly lead to angry episodes with overtly moral overtones. In Bushmen, aggressive exchanges are most frequent over the protocol of gift-giving and work rotas; pacts are quickly formed as sides line up in the dispute. As Trivers says, "A common feature of this aggression is that it often seems out of all proportion to the offences committed. Friends are even killed over apparently trivial disputes. But since small inequities repeated many times over a lifetime may exact a heavy toll in relative fitness, selection may favour a strong view of aggression when the cheating tendency is discovered."[12]

One extremely vivid first-hand account of the roots of antagonism was recorded by Turnbull. Among his Ituri forest pygmies incidents can escalate alarmingly after the initial deceit and the villagers' counter-measure. The accused might then act with sham piety, playing hurt while wriggling to shift the blame, the episode ending in drastic censure by the group. Nobody knows what sparked off this particular ugly scene. Anyway, old Cephu, an experienced hunter, refused to contribute to the daily feast – a cardinal sin among pygmies. In return, he was of course ostentatiously refused a portion of the first antelope caught during the day's netting. Cephu's own hunting had gone badly, leaving him nothing for the table. But that, he insisted, was not *his* fault: the womenfolk had deliberately frightened away his game. Such shallow excuses were pooh-poohed and Cephu started whining to enlist sympathy, which exasperated everybody. Both sides now felt slighted and a gloomy pall hung over the village. They all set out for a second try, only this time Cephu stealthily crept ahead of the nets and caught the first animal driven by the beaters. Unable to slip away in time, he was caught red-handed. It was his undying shame. Cephu claimed loudly that he had been lost; nobody believed a word of it. The long tirade began against this pygmy reprobate. One male took to the floor: "Cephu is an impotent old fool. No he isn't, he is an impotent old animal – we have treated him like a man for long enough, now we should treat him like an animal. ANIMAL!" The cacophony of critical voices rose as old grievances were aired: he mistreated his relatives, he was deceitful, his camp-site was dirty, even he was dirty. The social scorn was evidently intended to intimidate the old hunter, and it worked. Cephu started a counter-blast: he was one of the oldest and best hunters and "it was very wrong for everyone to treat him like an animal". He was sternly reminded that he had gladly accepted "help and food and song" when his daughter died. Another jumped to his feet. "He said he hoped Cephu would fall on his spear and kill himself like the animal he was. Who else but an animal would steal meat from others?" At this strong moralising show, almost overkill for the crime, Cephu burst into tears. His shaming was getting him nowhere, so he switched tactics, insisting that he *deserved* first place. This only blotted his copy-book further because pygmies have no chiefs. Drive him out was the cry, let him be a big chief of his own band. Turnbull takes up the story.

> Cephu knew he was defeated and humiliated. Alone, his band of three or four families was too small to make an efficient hunting unit. He apologized profusely, reiterating that he really did not know he had set up his nets in front of the others, and that in any case he would hand over all the meat. This settled the matter, and accompanied by most of the group he returned to his little camp and brusquely ordered his wife to hand over the spoils. She had little chance to refuse, as hands were already reaching into her basket and under the leaves of the roof of her hut where she had hidden some liver in anticipation of just such a contingency. Even her cooking pot was emptied. Then each of the other huts was searched and all the meat taken. Cephu's family protested loudly and Cephu tried hard to cry, but this time it was forced and everyone laughed at him. He clutched his stomach and said he would die; die because he was hungry and his brothers had taken away all his food; die because he was not respected.

Retribution was swift and severe. It left Cephu's family wailing while the villagers gaily chattered and planned the next day's hunt. In the end, Turnbull watched as the hunter Masisi finished his meal and, feeling sorry for Cephu, slipped out of camp with a full pot of meat in mushroom sauce and headed in the direction of Cephu's camp-site. The moaning ceased, and within hours Cephu was back in the midst of the villagers, singing as though nothing had happened.

This characteristic episode stretched across a number of days and was the major focus and talking point of the entire village. It monopolised the collective psychological domain in the same way Nixon's personal game of sham piety and bluff riveted the American (and world) mind, almost to the exclusion of the original crime. Issues have a way of blowing up out of all proportion through a tangled hierarchy of moves and counter-moves. For genuine remorse or piety, sophisticated cheaters can conjure up a sham version, so society has to be on its guard. But notice that the situation among humans is now quite different from Dawkins' computer simulation. If one member fails in his 'duty', *the entire group feels slighted* and punishes or even banishes him. In other words, grudges are shared; personally uninvolved members will take on a grudge – itself a reciprocal act – from the hurt party and so spread its effect. The community coalesces into a single grudging organism, ostracising the cheater like an amoeba jettisoning a bubble of waste. This advanced level of reciprocal grudge-sharing maximises the cheater's problems, but to a lesser extent it is also unhealthy for the community, since expelling a member means the loss of a potential reciprocator. Hence both sides have a desire to make up, the cheater more than society. To ensure this, natural selection has strongly favoured a deeply ingrained guilt complex; human conscience, the good angel's voice whispering in one ear, is a socially adaptive device to perpetuate grudging. Social outcasts seek remission for their sins in some reparative gesture – old Cephu donates his meat to the others, Nixon relinquishes his high office. Then society, like some beneficent heavenly father, absolves the sinner for the good of all. (Forgiveness only follows when all suspicion of shamming has finally disappeared. Cephu's crocodile tears met with the same hostility as Nixon's attempt to 'come clean', embellished with television tears and "Fellow Americans, Pray for Me" impieties.)

The dizzy upwards spiral where cheats learn to fake penitence and society takes steps to detect the charlatan leads to an infinite regress of enormous social and psychological complexity. Trivers sees still further repercussions:

once moralistic aggression has been selected for to protect against cheating, selection favors sham moralistic aggression as a new form of cheating. This should lead to selection for the ability to discriminate the two and to guard against the latter. The guarding can, in turn, be used to counter real moralistic aggression: one can, in effect, *impute* cheating motives to another person in order to protect one's own cheating. And so on. Given the psychological and cognitive complexity the system rapidly acquires, one may wonder to what extent the importance of altruism in human evolution sets up a selection pressure for psychological and cognitive powers which partly contributed to the large increase in hominid brain size during the Pleistocene.[13]

Since selection has honed exquisite backdrops of reciprocal expectancy on one hand, and remorse and guilt on the other, we cannot wilfully divorce the deep-rooted meanings of words such as *please* and *sorry* from this altruistic context. Apes like Nim and Washoe must redefine these words according to their own socio-ethical understanding if ever they are to use them significantly.

Melissa, partially crippled by polio and brutally beaten by Passion and Pom, extending her hand to Passion for 'forgiveness' and reassurance – even as Passion eats her still-warm infant – is not an act we readily understand. A million years of social and ethical reconstruction have given us the peculiar conception of 'fair play'. Thrusting this value-system on to non-human nature in an effort to 'interpret' it would be a biological perversion (though conveniently permitting us to sit in final judgment). Melissa's seeking forgiveness shows how any attempt to graft human values is doomed to failure. In its way, 'explaining' ape behaviour by human mores and values is as insidious as 'explaining' *our* alleged murderous "traits" as atavistic reversions to ancestral "ape" ways.

Extending the umbrella of our ethics, or morals, or even politics, to the chimpanzee meets with no better success than dismissing human warfare as glorified chimpanzee brutality. Both deny the chimpanzee's sovereign existence by totally misconstruing Darwinian nature. Man is no longer the measure of Creation.

Bibliography

A short list – for extensive coverage of source
material, see Notes and References.

Ayala, Francisco J. and Theodosius Dobzhansky (Eds.), *Studies in the Philosophy
of Biology* (London, Macmillan, 1974).

Bloom, Lois and Margaret Lahey, *Language Development and Language
Disorders* (New York, Wiley, 1978).

Boden, Margaret A., *Artificial Intelligence and Natural Man* (Hassocks, Sussex,
The Harvester Press, 1977).

Bourne, Geoffrey H. (Ed.), *Progress in Ape Research* (New York, Academic
Press, 1977).

Brown, Roger, *A First Language: The Early Stages* (Cambridge, Mass.,
Harvard University Press, 1973).

Curtiss, Susan, *Genie: A Psycholinguistic Study of a Modern-Day "Wild Child"*
(New York, Academic Press, 1977).

Dawkins, Richard, *The Selfish Gene* (Oxford University Press, 1976; London,
Paladin, 1978).

Gould, Stephen Jay, *Ontogeny and Phylogeny* (Cambridge, Mass., Harvard
University Press, 1977).

Griffin, Donald R., *The Question of Animal Awareness* (New York, The
Rockefeller University Press, 1976).

Harnad, Stevan R., Horst D. Steklis and Jane Lancaster (Eds.), "Origins and
Evolution of Language and Speech", *Annals of the New York Academy of
Sciences*, 280 (1976).

Harris, Marvin, *Cannibals & Kings* (London, Collins, 1978).

Leakey, Richard E. and Roger Lewin, *Origins* (London, Macdonald & Jane's,
1977).

Lieberman, Philip, *On the Origins of Language* (New York, Macmillan, 1975).

Linden, Eugene, *Apes, Men, and Language* (New York, Dutton, 1975; Harmondsworth, Penguin, 1976).

Montagu, Ashley, *The Nature of Human Aggression* (New York, Oxford University Press, 1976).

Popper, Karl R. and John C. Eccles, *The Self and its Brain: An Argument for Interactionism* (Berlin, Springer International, 1977).

Premack, David, *Intelligence in Ape and Man* (New Jersey, Lawrence Erlbaum, 1976).

Rumbaugh, Duane M. (Ed.), *Language Learning by a Chimpanzee: The Lana Project* (New York, Academic Press, 1977).

Schrier, Allan M. and Fred Stollnitz (Eds.), *Behavior of Nonhuman Primates, 4* (New York, Academic Press, 1971).

Solecki, Ralph S., *Shanidar: The Humanity of Neanderthal Man* (London, Allen Lane, 1972).

Teleki, Geza, *The Predatory Behavior of Wild Chimpanzees* (Lewisburgh, Bucknell University Press, 1973).

Temerlin, Maurice K., *Lucy: Growing Up Human* (Palo Alto, Science & Behavior Books, 1975; London, Souvenir Press, 1976; New York, Bantam, 1977).

Thorpe, W. H., *Animal Nature and Human Nature* (New York, Doubleday, 1974).

Turnbull, Colin, *The Forest People* (London, Picador, 1976).

Tuttle, R. H. (Ed.), *Socioecology and Psychology of Primates* (The Hague, Mouton, 1975).

van Lawick-Goodall, Jane, *In the Shadow of Man* (London, Collins, 1971; New York, Dell, 1972).

Washburn, S. L. and Phyllis Dolhinow (Eds.), *Perspectives on Human Evolution, 2* (New York, Holt, Rinehart and Winston, 1972).

Wilson, Edward O., *Sociobiology: The New Synthesis* (Cambridge, Mass., Harvard University Press, 1975).

Wilson, Edward O., *On Human Nature* (Cambridge, Mass., Harvard University Press, 1978).

I have neglected historical analyses from this list. The three most readable standard works dealing with Darwin's age are William Irvine, *Apes, Angels and Victorians* (New York, McGraw-Hill, 1955; Cleveland, Meridian, 1959); Loren Eiseley, *Darwin's Century* (New York, Doubleday, 1958; New York, Anchor Books, 1961); and John C. Greene, *The Death of Adam: Evolution and Its Impact on Western Thought* (Ames, Iowa State University Press, 1959; New York, Mentor, 1961). However, they are all beginning to show signs of ageing, largely because science history as a discipline has undergone such tumultuous changes since the Darwin centenary celebrations in 1959. For an analysis of the transcendental and materialist ideologies at play within the Victorian evolutionist debate, as well as a study of the ape-man question, see Adrian Desmond, *The New Reformation: Darwin and the Reign of Law* (London, Blond & Briggs, in preparation).

Notes and References

"I wonder what a chimpanzee would say to this?" – Charles Darwin in a letter to J. D. Hooker, 5 July 1857: Francis Darwin and A. C. Seward (Eds.), *More Letters of Charles Darwin* (London, Murray, 1903), I, p. 237.

1. Man's Crisis of Identity?

1 Gordon G. Gallup, Jr., James L. Boren, Gregg J. Gagliardi and Larry B. Wallnau, "A Mirror for the Mind of Man, or Will the Chimpanzee Create an Identity Crisis for *Homo sapiens?*", *Journal of Human Evolution*, 6 (1977), p. 311.
2 Mary-Claire King and A. C. Wilson, "Evolution at Two Levels in Humans and Chimpanzees", *Science*, 188 (1975), pp. 107–16. King & Wilson, "Our Close Cousin, the Chimpanzee", *New Scientist*, 3 July 1975, pp. 15–18. A similar analysis extended to the protein of other apes confirmed King's & Wilson's results and showed, as expected, that the pygmy chimpanzee approaches man still more closely. Elizabeth J. Bruce and Francisco J. Ayala, "Humans and Apes are Genetically Very Similar", *Nature*, 276 (1978), pp. 264–5. Expectations are running high that the first extended field studies of pygmy chimpanzees will uncover cultural traits and iconic gesturing of a degree not seen in other wild apes; the likelihood of this is increased by the recent observation of spontaneous signing in a group of captive pygmy chimpanzees. E. Sue Savage-Rumbaugh, Beverly J. Wilkersons and Roger Bakeman, "Spontaneous Gestural Communication among Conspecifics in the Pygmy Chimpanzee (*Pan panicus*)", in Geoffrey H. Bourne (Ed.), *Progress in Ape Research* (New York, Academic Press, 1977), pp. 97–116.
3 H. Reemtsma *et al.*, "Renal Heterotransplantation in Man", *Annals of Surgery*, 160 (1964), pp. 384–410.

4 See my forthcoming book *The New Reformation: Darwin and the Reign of Law* (London, Blond & Briggs, in preparation).

5 D. J. Merrell said "If I were a fruit fly working on primate taxonomy, I might consider humans and chimpanzees sibling species. Apart from minor differences in size, brain size, hairiness, and opposability of the great toe, they are, after all, quite similar." D. J. Merrell, "In Defence of Frogs", *Science*, 189 (1975), p. 838. For a reply see Lorraine M. Cherry, Susan M. Case and Allan C. Wilson, "Frog Perspective on the Morphological Difference between Humans and Chimpanzees", *Science*, 200 (1978), pp. 209–11.

2. Do Ape Words Make Sense?

1 The Duke of Argyll, *The Reign of Law* (London, Strahan, 1868), p. 265. His Grace was complaining about the skeletal procession in T. H. Huxley, *Man's Place in Nature*, republished in Huxley's Collected Essays (London, Macmillan, 1910), vol. VII, p. 76.

2 "Professor Huxley on Man's Place in Nature", *Edinburgh Review*, 117 (1863), p. 567.

3 "Evidence as to Man's Place in Nature", *The Athenaeum*, 28 February 1863, p. 288.

4 W. C. Watt, *Behavioral Science*, 19 (1974), p. 70.

5 John Limber, "Language in Child and Chimp?", *American Psychologist*, 32 (1977), p. 280.

6 R. Allen Gardner and Beatrice T. Gardner, "A First Language: The Early Stages. By Roger Brown", *American Journal of Psychology*, 87 (1974), p. 734.

7 Roger Fouts, "Discussion" in R. H. Tuttle (Ed.), *Socioecology and Psychology of Primates* (The Hague, Mouton, 1975), p. 407. See also Fouts' article in this volume: "Capacities for Language in Great Apes", pp. 371–90. Also Eugene Linden, *Apes, Men, and Language* (Harmondsworth, Penguin, 1976), pp. 6–8.

8 Francine Patterson, "Conversations with a Gorilla", *National Geographic*, 154, No. 4 (1978), p. 456.

9 H. S. Terrace, personal communication, 24 October 1978. I am also indebted to Dr. Terrace for showing me the unpublished ms. "Can an Ape Create a Sentence" by H. S. Terrace, L. A. Petitto, D. J. Sanders, J. W. Tynan, J. E. Butler, and T. G. Bever, which also mentions Nim's use of "dirty".

10 Georges Mounin, "Language, Communication, Chimpanzees", *Current Anthropology*, 17 (1976), p. 6.

11 Philip Lieberman, Edmund S. Crelin and Denis H. Klatt, "Phonetic Ability and Related Anatomy of the Newborn and Adult Human, Neanderthal Man, and the Chimpanzee", *American Anthropologist*, 74 (1972), pp. 287–307.

12 F. Max Müller, *The Science of Thought* (London, Longmans, 1887).

13 A. L. Kroeber, "Sub-Human Culture Beginnings", *Quarterly Review of Biology*, 3 (1928), p. 329.

14 R. Allen Gardner and Beatrice T. Gardner, "Teaching Sign Language to a Chimpanzee", *Science*, 165 (1969), p. 666.

15 Beatrice T. Gardner and R. Allen Gardner, "Comparing the Early Utterances of Child and Chimpanzee", in Anne D. Pick (Ed.), *Minnesota Symposia on Child Psychology* (Minneapolis, University of Minnesota Press, 1974), vol. 8, pp. 20–1.

16 Lois Bloom and Margaret Lahey, *Language Development and Language Disorders* (New York, Wiley, 1978), p. 123.

17 Ludwig Wittgenstein, *Philosophical Investigations*, trans. G. E. M. Anscombe (Oxford, Blackwell, 1972), p. 223.

18 E. Sue Savage and Duane M. Rumbaugh, "Communication, Language, and Lana", in Duane M. Rumbaugh (Ed.), *Language Learning by a Chimpanzee: The Lana Project* (New York, Academic Press, 1977), p. 305. The same sentiment is expressed more strongly by Rumbaugh in "The Emergence and State of Ape Language Research", *Progress in Ape Research*, p. 80, where he concedes "It is highly improbable that their [word] meanings are identical . . ." By 1978, the Rumbaughs had become fully conscious of this problem, and their recent attempts to teach new recruits (Sherman and Austin) the use of lexigrams suggested that they might have been a little hasty in assuming Lana's initial comprehension. They discovered that while they had glossed a symbol as referring to a food type, Sherman understood it to refer to the specific container holding the food. But the real difficulty arises when man and ape finally agree on the referent, and then try to understand one another's appreciation of it. E. Sue Savage-Rumbaugh and Duane M. Rumbaugh, "Symbolization, Language and Chimpanzees: A Theoretical Reevaluation Based on Initial Language Acquisition Processes in Four Young *Pan troglodytes*", *Brain and Language*, 6 (1978), pp. 286, 289.

19 Zenon W. Pylyshyn, "What the Mind's Eye Tells the Mind's Brain: A Critique of Mental Imagery", *Psychological Bulletin*, 80 (1973), pp. 1–24.

20 David Premack, *Intelligence in Ape and Man* (New Jersey, Lawrence Erlbaum, 1976), p. 25.

21 Laura Petitto, pers. comm., 24 October 1978.

22 Keith J. Hayes and Catherine H. Nissen, "Higher Mental Functions of a Home-Raised Chimpanzee", in Allan M. Schrier and Fred Stollnitz

(Eds.), *Behavior of Nonhuman Primates*, 4 (New York, Academic Press, 1971), pp. 59–115.

23 Roger S. Fouts, "Language: Origins, Definitions and Chimpanzees", *Journal of Human Evolution*, 3 (1974), p. 479.

24 Mark S. Seidenberg and Laura A. Petitto, "On the Evidence for Linguistic Abilities in Signing Apes", *Brain and Language* (in press); "What Do Signing Chimpanzees Have to Say to Linguists?", Papers from the 14th Regional Meeting, Chicago Linguistic Society (in press); "Signing Behavior in Apes: A Critical Review", *Cognition* (in press). I should like to thank Laura Petitto for allowing me to preview these papers.

25 Maurice K. Temerlin, *Lucy: Growing Up Human* (London, Souvenir Press, 1976), p. 120.

26 For a checklist, see Beatrice T. Gardner and R. Allen Gardner, "Evidence for Sentence Constituents in the Early Utterances of Child and Chimpanzee", *Journal of Experimental Psychology: General*, 104 (1975), pp. 244–67.

27 Beatrice T. Gardner and R. Allen Gardner, "Two-Way Communication with an Infant Chimpanzee", in *Behavior of Nonhuman Primates*, 4, p. 182.

28 R. Allen Gardner and Beatrice T. Gardner, "Early Signs of Language in Child and Chimpanzee", *Science*, 187 (1975), pp. 752–3.

29 Roger S. Fouts, "Acquisition and Testing of Gestural Signs in Four Young Chimpanzees", *Science*, 180 (1973), p. 979.

30 Linden, *Apes, Men, and Language*, p. 103.

31 Roger Brown, *A First Language* (Cambridge, Mass., Harvard University Press, 1973), pp. 186, 215. For the Gardners' critique of this book see Note 6.

32 Roger S. Fouts, "Ameslan in Pan", in *Progress in Ape Research*, pp. 1, 12

33 Bloom & Lahey, *Language Development and Language Disorders*, p. 204.

34 Seidenberg & Petitto, "Evidence for Linguistic Abilities".

35 Gardner & Gardner, "A First Language", pp. 735–6.

36 Seidenberg & Petitto, "Signing Behavior in Apes"; details of Nim's sign combinations were kindly made available to me in Terrace *et al*, "Can an Ape Create a Sentence", and Project Nim "Progress Report I" (mss.).

37 Huxley, *Man's Place in Nature*, p. 147.

38 Patterson, "Conversations with a Gorilla", p. 465.

39 Robert M. Yerkes, "The Mind of the Gorilla", *Genetic Psychology Monographs*, 2 (1927), pp. 154, 182–3.

40 Francine G. Patterson, "The Gestures of a Gorilla: Language Acquisition in Another Pongid", *Brain and Language*, 5 (1978), p. 77.

41 Theodosius Dobzhansky, *The Biology of Ultimate Concern* (London, Fontana, 1971), p. 68.

42 Karl R. Popper and John C. Eccles, *The Self and Its Brain: An Argument for Interactionism* (Berlin, Springer, 1977).

3. "Humanizing the Ape"

1 Müller defied Darwinians to teach English to an ape. Language, he insisted angrily in *The Science of Thought* (London, Longmans, 1887), "is our Rubicon, and no brute will dare cross it", (p. 160). Then the challenge:

> it becomes our duty to warn the valiant disciples of Darwin that, before they can claim a real victory, before they can call man a descendant of a mute animal, they must lay a regular siege to a fortress which is not to be frightened into submission by a few random shots, the fortress of language, which as yet stands untaken and unshaken on the very frontiers between the animal kingdom and the kingdom of man (p. 177).

Since words were "the very wings of thought", one was clearly impossible without the other, and this led inevitably to a classic Catch 22 situation, as one critic realised. "If man could not think without language, and could not have language without thinking, he would have had neither except by a miracle" (*Nature*, 23 June 1887, p. 173). Müller was not working miracles. Apparently, he imagined that man's ancestry by-passed the apes and indeed the entire brute kingdom completely, as though we had a direct line back to Creation. Certainly, according to Müller's canons, man's ancestors must *always* have carried the potential for words and thought. Thus his challenge: to vindicate Darwin *prove* that apes have that potential. Before Müller acquiesced, he demanded "complete evidence that whatever we find in man exists in the ape, either really or potentially". Convinced the fortress was impregnable and philosophically sound, he charged "Only if we can produce a speaking ape, should we have fulfilled the conditions which our problem necessarily involves and that has never been done, nay, for some reason or other, has never been attempted" (p. 116).

Once it was the ape's hippocampus, now a potential for language settled the question of man's ape ancestry. But only an old-fashioned Aristotelian like Müller could have reduced it to this. For Darwinism, the very terms of the challenge were incomprehensible. After all, "potential" implies some future and unavoidable "actual" state; the acorn grows to a mighty oak and nothing else. Its development is rigidly pre-programmed. Darwin's wonderful spread of life made a mockery of "potential" states, acorns *will* ultimately mutate into tomorrow's genetically distinct and less oak-like trees. Evolution was continuing Creation. Thus for Darwinians apes without language potential proved absolutely nothing. If chimps never learned to read, man and ape could still have had a joint Miocene ancestor. One line of descent (leading to man) would have evolved a language, the other (leading to chimps) would not. But this does demand a truly *creative* evolution, a fact which outraged many Victorians who accused Mr. Darwin of arrogantly assuming God's role: cartoons depicted the gentle naturalist like some blessed Olympian deity, bidding the worm rise out of chaos and begin his ascent to a top-hat-and-tailed Victorian gentleman. On the other hand, a great many natural theologians swung into the Darwin camp after 1860 – not imagining he was God, but sensing that evolution was the means of Creation.

2 Quoted in Harold T. P. Hayes, "The Pursuit of Reason", *The New York Times Magazine*, 12 June 1977, p. 22.

3 William H. Furness, "Observations on the Mentality of Chimpanzees and Orang-Utans", *Proc. Am. Phil. Soc.*, 55 (1916), pp. 281–90 (my emphasis). Furness was not the first to try coaxing speech from an ape, and in fact he had probably read R. L. Garner's account of a similar attempt in his book *Gorillas and Chimpanzees* (London, Osgood, 1896). Garner was an explorer cast in a wonderfully Victorian mould. In 1892 he sailed for the French Congo specifically to study wild apes. Here he built himself a stout cage, in which he lived for 112 days like some zoological specimen marked 'Victorian *Homo sapiens*', recording on the latest wax-cylinder phonograph the bewildered reactions of a wealth of animals (including gorillas) who trooped up to inspect him. Jules Verne, not one to miss the latest scientific shenanigans, immortalised these proceedings in *The Village in the Tree Tops*. Garner became convinced that apes *already* possessed a natural language, which drove other primatologists into paroxysms of despair ("his publications", moaned Yerkes in *The Great Apes*, "indicate serious lack of scientific competence"). Chimpanzee vocabulary was limited, Garner conceded, still it was enough to express simple desires; and he went on to crack the 'words' for "love", "thanks", "danger", "cold", "drink", "illness", "death", and so on, about twenty in all. This led him to try to teach an ape to talk "human" (only five years after Max Müller had goaded Darwinians to do just this). Garner did not try the obvious, and teach them human words as translations of the natural words he imagined them already possessing. Instead he acquired an infant chimpanzee as a cage-companion, and after weeks of labour and untold tins of corned beef bribes taught him to mouth the French word *feu* (fire), although he had appalling difficulty with the German *wie* (how) and the universal *mama*. (He even tried the native Nkami word *nkgwe* or "mother"). Any success must have been a matter of mimicry, painful at

that, because – with the dubious exception of *feu* – Moses the chimp had
no idea what the word could have referred to. Garner was nonetheless
jubilant that Moses managed *feu*. "If he had only learned one word in a
whole lifetime, he would have shown at least that the race is capable of
being improved and elevated in some degree."

4 Lightner Witmer, "A Monkey with a Mind", *The Psychological Clinic*, 3
   (1909), p. 179.
5 Robert M. Young, "Darwin's Metaphor: Does Nature Select?", *The
   Monist*, 55 (1971), pp. 442–503.
6 See my book *The New Reformation: Darwin and the Reign of Law* (London,
   Blond & Briggs, in preparation) for a longer discussion of Tyndall,
   Mivart and the diametric ways of interpreting nature in Darwin's day.
7 Witmer, "A Monkey with a Mind", p. 205.
8 Furness, "The Mentality of Chimpanzees", p. 290.
9 See the short but warmly perceptive biography of Kroeber in Abram
   Kardiner and Edward Preble, *They Studied Man* (New York, Mentor,
   1963), pp. 163–77.
10 A. L. Kroeber, "The Superorganic", first published (1917) in *American
   Anthropologist* and reprinted in A. L. Kroeber, *The Nature of Culture*
   (University of Chicago Press, 1952), p. 49. All other quotes from this
   source.
11 T. H. Huxley, in a letter to Herbert Spencer, 3 August 1861: Leonard
   Huxley (Ed.), *Life and Letters of Thomas Henry Huxley* (London, Macmillan, 1900), I, p. 231.
12 Edward O. Wilson, *Sociobiology: The New Synthesis* (Cambridge,
   Harvard University Press, 1975), p. 575.
13 I. C. McManus, in a letter to *The Times Literary Supplement*, 10 March
   1978, p. 285.
14 A. L. Kroeber, *Anthropology* (New York, Harcourt, Brace, 1948), p. 71.
15 Clifford Geertz, "The Transition to Humanity", first published in Sol Tax
   (Ed.), *Horizons of Anthropology* (Chicago, Aldine, 1964) and reprinted
   in Noel Korn and Fred W. Thompson (Eds.), *Human Evolution* (New
   York, Holt, Rinehart and Winston, 1967), p. 115.
16 Sir Arthur Keith, *A New Theory of Evolution* (Gloucester, Mass., Peter
   Smith, 1968; first published 1947), p. 206.
17 Charles Darwin, *The Descent of Man* (New York, A. L. Burt, 1874?),
   p. 205.
18 Genie was rescued from her tragic and inhuman imprisonment in November 1970. An adolescent girl, thirteen and a half years old, she looked a
   pitiful six or seven, weighed only 59 lbs and remained resolutely dumb
   (it turned out she had been thrashed whenever she made a noise, an ordeal
   that lasted twelve years and understandably led to her active repression

of any sound; when therapy began, she suffered appalling difficulty juggling breathing and speaking, having never had any practice). For most of her life, she had been straitjacketed by night in an infant's crib covered by chicken wire, and strapped to a high-chair by day, with only a bare room and beating stick for perceptual stimulation – and because that room was so tiny, she was short-sighted, never having needed to see beyond ten feet. Some of the cruelties were only learned from Genie after she began speaking telegraphically, as when she first revealed *Father hit arm. Big wood. Genie cry.* Day in, day out, through the twelve years of her mind's formation, she endured the indescribable horrors of total isolation. She had been refused human contact except at meal times, and what contact she received was not altogether human, for her unbalanced father growled at her like a dog if she uttered the slightest noise (which led to an obsessive fear of dogs or even pictures of wolves after her rescue, although she made heroic efforts to conquer this fear). Her mother had gone blind, and lived in terror of the father: he committed suicide not long after Genie was found.

When intensive therapy was initiated, by Susan Curtiss of UCLA among others, Genie's cerebral cortex, including the late-developing left hemisphere angular gyrus, had long since matured anatomically. This led to a whole host of critical questions; was it too late for her to learn language? indeed, had her brain already language lateralised? or was that dependent on actual language input before puberty?

After four years of intensive schooling and the stimulation of a foster home, Genie's speech was still telegraphic, although by 1975 she *could*, if pushed, form quite complex sentences, such as *I am thinking bout Miss J. at school in hospital*, which is way beyond the present capability of the best educated ape. Curtiss briefly compares the chimpanzee's linguistic development with Genie's, and concludes that in some ways the ape excels. For example, Genie has enormous difficulty with Wh-type questions (*where, what, why, when*), and in fact rarely formulated one of her own accord – though she understands them perfectly; but again if forced she will utter such quaint unanswerables as *Where is tomorrow Mrs. L?* Since Lana, at least, now asks for the name of objects she craves, Curtiss concludes that chimpanzees possess "at least one syntactic element absent in Genie's grammar". But specific Wh-type questions are uncommon in apes other than Lana, although in ASL questions can (and are) indicated in apes either by freezing the final gesture or by facial expression. Overall, Curtiss thinks Genie's performance generally resembles a chimpanzee's, though in a review Susan Goldin-Meadow questions the validity of the comparison, suggesting that there is no "reason to believe that a chimp's cortex is comparable to a human 'nonlanguage' cortex". Goldin-Meadow, also, is inclined to see Genie's language as "much richer" than anything yet attributed to an ape. "A Study in Human Capacities", *Science*, 200 (1978), p. 650.

Quite surprisingly, what Genie most resembles are left-hemisherecto-mised humans, who as adults have had to reacquire the rudiments of language in the right hemisphere. And this is rarely, if ever, completely achieved, leading Curtiss *et al.* to gloomily wonder whether Genie's language learning "will cease at some point in the near future". (S. Curtis, V. Fromkin, S. Krashen, D. Rigler and M. Rigler, "The Linguistic Development of Genie", *Language*, 50 [1974], p. 544.) Curtiss' conclusions in this respect are important. She had undertaken Genie's language tuition with one eye firmly on Eric Lenneberg's well-known belief that lateralisation of 'higher' mental functions is complete by puberty, by which time "cerebral plasticity is lost". In other words, it may be too late to acquire language after cortical maturation. But what Curtiss suspects has happened in Genie's case is this: true enough, the left (language) hemisphere matured in the absence of any language input, and perhaps the language region itself atrophied or failed to fully develop thus losing its plasticity for language. But in Genie that function has been apparently taken over by the right hemisphere, already specialised for other (holistic or Gestalt) functions. Moreover, the right hemisphere, far from being stunted, had undergone a spectacular cognitive growth. Contacting the hemisphere directly (via earphones, speaking into one ear at a time, and thus reaching the opposite hemisphere: the dichotic listening test), it was discovered that her left ear (*i.e.* right hemisphere) responded with 100 per cent accuracy to such instructions as "point out the [object]", while whispering into the right ear produced results that fell below chance. During her imprisonment, Genie apparently developed her right hemisphere functions beyond the norm. Visuo-spatial tests, tests to determine her ability to grasp the whole from an isolated part, and other gestalt perception tests proved her heightened ability – in one remarkable case, she scored the highest known marks. Thus it appears that this developed and active hemisphere took over partial language function once the input resumed after her rescue. Genie was, Curtiss declares, a "right hemisphere thinker". Susan Curtiss, *Genie: A Psycholinguistic Study of a Modern-Day "Wild Child"* (New York, Academic Press, 1977).

For a detailed discussion of Victor's predicament, see Harlan Lane, *The Wild Boy of Aveyron* (London, George Allen & Unwin, 1977; London, Paladin, 1979).

19 Bruce Chatwin, "The Quest for the Wolf Children", *The Sunday Times Magazine*, 30 July 1978, p. 10.

20 W. N. Kellogg and L. A. Kellogg, *The Ape and the Child* (New York, McGraw-Hill, 1933), p. 11. This book was subtitled "A Study of Environmental Influence upon Early Behavior".

21 Keith J. Hayes and Catherine Hayes, "The Intellectual Development of a Home-Raised Chimpanzee", *Proc. Am. Phil. Soc.*, 95 (1951), p. 108.

22 Keith J. Hayes and Catherine Hayes, "The Cultural Capacity of Chimpanzee", *Human Biology*, 26 (1954), p. 296.

23 Robert M. Yerkes, *Almost Human* (London, Cape, 1925), p. 180.

24 B. F. Skinner, *Verbal Behavior* (New York, Appleton–Century–Crofts, 1957), p. 3.

25 Noam Chomsky, "Verbal Behavior. By B. F. Skinner . . .", *Language*, 35 (1959), p. 30. In 1957, the same year as Skinner's book, Chomsky published his *Syntactic Structures*. Whatever the truth in Chomsky's genetic programme for human language, nothing is more dramatic than that untutored children, unlike chimpanzees, will spontaneously invent their own personal language (so long as the home environment is rich enough). This unprompted emergence of a private lexicon and rudiments of grammar suggest that the linguistic basics are programmed to break surface at the critical time, requiring an adult's example largely to mould the language into a conventional form. Child psychologists Susan Goldin Meadow and Heidi Feldman confirmed this when investigating six infants (aged from seventeen to forty-nine months) who were deprived of a language model; not feral or semi-mythical wild children, but those in normal American homes – only these were deaf children whose parents, fearing their being ostracised by the community, were determined the infants should speak, and thus refused to teach them sign language. Consequently, the children could say little, despite intensive speech therapy, yet they manually babbled in idiosyncratic signs. Wrote Goldin-Meadow and Feldman:

> we found that each of our deaf subjects developed a structured communication system that incorporates properties found in all child languages. They developed a lexicon of signs to refer to objects, people, and actions, and they combined signs into phrases that express semantic relations in an ordered way.

Thus man's "natural inclination" to encode the world in arbitrary signs can triumph against the most appalling odds, and a crude language emerges in the absence of an explicit model. "This achievement is cast into bold relief by comparison with the meagre linguistic achievements of chimpanzees", conclude Goldin-Meadow and Feldman with chauvinistic glee. "While chimpanzees seem to learn from manual language training, they have never been shown to spontaneously develop a language-like communication system without such training – even when the chimp is lovingly raised at a human mother's knee." Susan Goldin-Meadow and Heidi Feldman, "The Development of Language-Like Communication Without a Language Model", *Science*, 197 (1977), pp. 401–3.

26 R. Allen Gardner and Beatrice T. Gardner, "A First Language: The Early Stages. By Roger Brown . . .", *American Journal of Psychology*, 87 (1974), pp. 734–5.

4. A Metalinguistic Leap

1 Quoted in Frank Anders, "If you can teach an ape to read, can you do something for my retarded child?", *The New York Times Magazine*, 1 June 1975, p. 52.

2 David Premack and Arthur Schwartz, "Preparations for Discussing Behaviorism with Chimpanzee", in Frank Smith and George A. Miller (Eds.), *The Genesis of Language* (Cambridge, Mass., The M.I.T. Press, 1966), pp. 295 et seq.

3 Ann James Premack and David Premack, "Teaching Language to an Ape", *Scientific American*, 227 (1972), p. 95.

4 *Ibid.* See also David Premack, "On the Assessment of Language Competence in the Chimpanzee", in A. M. Schrier and F. Stollnitz (Eds.), *Behavior of Nonhuman Primates 4*, (New York, Academic Press, 1971), pp. 185–228.

5 Philip Lieberman, "Comments" on Mounin's paper, *Current Anthropology*, 17 (1976), p. 14.

6 Duane Rumbaugh, "Discussion", in R. H. Tuttle (Ed.), *Socioecology and Psychology of Primates* (The Hague, Mouton, 1975), p. 405.

7 Beatrice T. Gardner and R. Allen Gardner, "Evidence for Sentence Constituents in the Early Utterances of Child and Chimpanzee", *Journal of Experimental Psychology: General*, 104 (1975), p. 255.

8 "A Neuropsychological Comparison Between Man, Chimpanzee and Monkey", *Neuropsychologia*, 13 (1975), p. 125.

9 David Premack, "Language and Intelligence in Ape and Man", *American Scientist*, 64 (1976), pp. 681–2. For a longer discussion of methods and results, read David Premack, *Intelligence in Ape and Man* (New Jersey, Lawrence Erlbaum, 1976).

10 Premack & Premack, "Teaching Language to an Ape", p. 97.

11 William A. Mason, "Environmental Models and Mental Modes", *American Psychologist*, 31 (1976), p. 288.

12 Roger Brown, *A First Language* (Cambridge, Harvard University Press, 1973), p. 44.

13 Timothy V. Gill and Duane M. Rumbaugh, "Mastery of Naming Skills by a Chimpanzee", *Journal of Human Evolution*, 3 (1974), p. 485.

14 *Ibid.*, p. 484.

15 Duane M. Rumbaugh and Timothy V. Gill, "Lana's Acquisition of Language Skills", in Duane M. Rumbaugh (Ed.), *Language Learning by a Chimpanzee: The Lana Project* (New York, Academic Press, 1977), p. 168.

16 Georges Mounin, "Language, Communication, Chimpanzees", *Current Anthropology*, 17 (1976), p. 7.

17 Rumbaugh & Gill, "Lana's Acquisition of Language Skills", p. 176.

18 *Ibid.*, p. 173.

19 Duane M. Rumbaugh and Timothy V. Gill, "The Mastery of Language-Type Skills by the Chimpanzee (*Pan*)", *Ann. N.Y. Acad. Sci.*, 280 (1976), p. 575.

20 Charles Lyell, in a letter to Charles Darwin, 5 May 1869: Mrs. Lyell (Ed.), *Life, Letters and Journals of Sir Charles Lyell* (London, Murray, 1881), 2, p. 442.

21 Stephen Jay Gould, "Darwin's Untimely Burial", in his collected essays published under the title *Ever Since Darwin* (New York, Norton, 1977), p. 44.

22 R. Allen Gardner and Beatrice T. Gardner, "Comparative Psychology and Language Acquisition", in Kurt Salzinger and Florence L. Denmark (Eds.), Psychology: The State of the Art, *Ann. N. Y. Acad. Sci.*, 309 (1978), p. 37. The Gardners are quoting Noam Chomsky, *Language and Mind*: **70** (New York, Harcourt Brace Jovanovich, 1972).

23 Gardner & Gardner, *ibid.*, p. 61.

24 E. Sue Savage-Rumbaugh, Duane M. Rumbaugh and Sally Boysen, "Linguistically-Mediated Tool Use and Exchange by Chimpanzees (*Pan troglodytes*), *The Behavioral and Brain Sciences*, 1 (1978): Special Issue on Cognition and Consciousness in Nonhuman Species. I should like to thank Duane Rumbaugh for showing me a ms. of this paper.

25 *Ibid.* See also E. Sue Savage-Rumbaugh and Duane M. Rumbaugh, "Symbolization, Language, and Chimpanzees: A Theoretical Reevaluation Based on Initial Language Acquisition Processes in Four Young *Pan Troglodytes*, *Brain and Language*, 6 (1978), pp. 265–300.

5. Stretching Between Worlds

1 Richard K. Davenport, "Cross-Modal Perception: A Basis for Language?", in Duane M. Rumbaugh (Ed.), *Language Learning by a Chimpanzee: The Lana Project* (New York, Academic Press, 1977), p. 81.

2 Norman Geschwind, "Disconnexion Syndromes in Animals and Man", *Brain*, 88 (1965), p. 273.

3 *Ibid.*, p. 275. See also Norman Geschwind, "The Development of the Brain and the Evolution of Language", in C. I. J. M. Stuart (Ed.), *Monograph Series on Languages and Linguistics* (Washington D.C., Georgetown University Press, 1964), pp. 155–69.

4 Pers. comm., 1 November 1978.

5 For an analysis of the Huxley-Owen ideological perspectives and some social and political causes of their antagonism, see my forthcoming book *The New Reformation*.

6 Richard K. Davenport and Charles M. Rogers, "Intermodal Equivalence of Stimuli in Apes", *Science*, 168 (1970), p. 280.

7 R. K. Davenport and C. M. Rogers, "Perception of Photographs by Apes", *Behaviour*, 39 (1971), p. 320.

8 David Premack, *Intelligence in Ape and Man* (New Jersey, Lawrence Erlbaum, 1976), p. 346.

9 William A. Mason, "Environmental Models and Mental Modes", *American Psychologist*, 31 (1976), p. 293.

10 Lawrence Weiskrantz and Alan Cowey, "Cross-Modal Matching in the Rhesus Monkey Using a Single Pair of Stimuli", *Neuropsychologia*, 13 (1975), pp. 257–61. R. C. Elliot, "Cross-Modal Recognition in Three Primates", *ibid.*, 15 (1977), pp. 183–6. But see G. Etlinger and M. J. Jarvis, "Cross-Modal Transfer in the Chimpanzee", *Nature*, 259 (1976), pp. 44–5.

11 Georges Louis Leclerc, Comte de Buffon, "The Nomenclature of Apes", originally published 1749–67; reprinted in Theodore D. McCown and Kenneth A. R. Kennedy (Eds.), *Climbing Man's Family Tree* (Englewood Cliffs, Prentice-Hall, 1972), p. 50.

12 Norman Geschwind and Walter Levitsky, "Human Brain: Left-Right Asymmetries in Temporal Speech Region", *Science*, 161 (1968), pp. 186–7.

13 Albert M. Galaburda, Marjorie LeMay, Thomas L. Kemper, and Norman Geschwind, "Right-Left Asymmetries in the Brain", *Science*, 199 (1978), p. 852.

14 M. LeMay and N. Geschwind, "Hemispheric Differences in the Brains of Great Apes", *Brain Behav. Evol.*, 11 (1975), p. 51.

15 Pers. comm., 2 March 1978. Even in monkeys, the neocortical area that in man has become the angular gyrus is certainly worth investigating. Dr. Deepak Pandya in Geschwind's department has begun the task; as Geschwind said, "although it was obvious that the human angular gyrus was very large and that of the monkey was very small, it seemed to me because of my Darwinian tendencies that some forerunner should be present. I thought it was rather important to study this, since this might

give us some clues as to what later became human language." Results look promising, "the monkey certainly has a small area which I believe has the same properties as the human area", says Geschwind; and perhaps more importantly, "Dr. Pandya's work certainly shows it to have the right type of connections – it's on the right track but small." Pers. comm., 1 November 1978.

16 John Macnamara, "Cognitive Basis of Language Learning in Infants", *Psychological Review*, 79 (1972), p. 1.

17 Ann James Premack and David Premack, "Teaching Language to an Ape", *Scientific American*, 227 (1972), p. 95 (my emphasis).

18 Duane M. Rumbaugh and Timothy V. Gill, "The Mastery of Language-Type Skills by the Chimpanzee (*Pan*)", *Ann. N. Y. Acad. Sci.*, 280 (1976), pp. 574–5.

19 Lyn W. Miles, "Discussion Paper: The Communicative Competence of Child and Chimpanzee", *ibid.*, p. 596.

20 David Premack, "Language and Intelligence in Ape and Man", *American Scientist*, 64 (1976), p. 680.

21 Philip Lieberman, in R. H. Tuttle (Ed.), *Socioecology and Psychology of Primates* (The Hague, Mouton, 1975), p. 406.

22 Premack, "Language and Intelligence in Ape and Man", pp. 680–1.

23 Charles Darwin, *The Descent of Man* (New York, A. L. Burt, 1874?), p. 142.

24 David Premack, "On the Assessment of Language Competence in the Chimpanzee", in A. M. Schrier and F. Stollnitz (Eds.), *Behavior of Nonhuman Primates*, 4 (New York, Academic Press, 1971), p. 212.

25 Philip Lieberman, "Comments" on Mounin's paper, *Current Anthropology*, 17 (1976), p. 14.

26 Gordon G. Gallup, "Book Reviews: Rumbaugh, D. M. (Ed.) *Language Learning by a Chimpanzee*", *The Psychological Record*, 27 (1977), p. 795.

27 Mason, "Environmental Models", p. 293.

6. Cries and Whispers

1 William A. Malmi, "Discussion Paper: Chimpanzees and Language Evolution", *Ann. N. Y. Acad. Sci.*, 280 (1976), p. 598.

2 T. H. Huxley, in a letter to Joseph Fayrer, 14 June 1866: Leonard Huxley (Ed.), *Life and Letters of Thomas Henry Huxley* (London, Macmillan, 1900), 1, p. 274.

3 Quoted in Robert J. Joynt, "Paul Pierre Broca: His Contribution to the Knowledge of Aphasia", *Cortex*, 1 (1964–5), p. 209. For a scholarly analysis of phrenology, its history and the matrix within which it was

embedded, see Robert M. Young, *Mind, Brain and Adaptation in the Nineteenth Century* (London, Oxford University Press, 1970).

4 Charles Darwin, in a letter to Max Müller, 3 July 1874: Francis Darwin and A. C. Seward (Eds.), *More Letters of Charles Darwin* (London, Murray, 1903), 2, p. 45.

5 Norman Geschwind, "The Organization of Language and the Brain", *Science*, 170 (1970), pp. 940–1.

6 Bryan W. Robinson, "Limbic Influences on Human Speech", *Ann. N.Y. Acad. Sci.*, 280 (1976), p. 761.

7 Raimund Apfelbach, "Electrically Elicited Vocalizations in the Gibbon *Hylobates lar* (*Hylobatidae*), and their Behavioral Significance", *Z. Tierpsychol.*, 30 (1972), pp. 420–30.

8 Malmi, "Chimpanzees and Language Evolution", p. 601.

9 Bryan W. Robinson, "Anatomical and Physiological Contrasts between Human and Other Primate Vocalizations", in S. L. Washburn and Phyllis Dolhinow (Eds.), *Perspectives on Human Evloution*, 2 (New York, Holt, 1972), p. 440.

10 *Ibid.*, p. 442.

11 Dale W. McAdam and Harry A. Whitaker, "Language Production: Electroencephalographic Localization in the Normal Human Brain", *Science*, 172 (1971), p. 502.

12 See Juhn Wada's own story of how he came by this test, in Juhn Wada and Theodore Rasmussen, "Intracarotid Injection of Sodium Amytal for the Lateralization of Cerebral Speech Dominance", *Journal of Neurosurgery*, 17 (1960), p. 266. This test is not 100 per cent risk-free, since the very act of placing a needle in the carotid artery can very occasionally lead to a blood clot. Says Geschwind: "The study is therefore justified only if the patient's medical problems warrant doing a procedure with a small but definite risk of serious damage." Since apes are "not capable of giving informed consent", Geschwind implies that we could be faced by an ethical dilemma. I therefore think we should desist until risk-free tests are available. Pers. comm., 1 November 1978.

Today, sophisticated techniques exist for cerebral mapping. Consider the use of the radioactive isotope xenon 133, which emits gamma rays and can thus be tracked through the body. The isotope in saline solution is injected into the carotid (again, with some risk, so its use has to be medically justifiable). In the body, it can be used to pick out regions of high blood concentration, which in the brain indicates activation of a cerebral site. Some results have been unexpected. According to this technique, in man both left and right homologous areas function during speech; while silently counting to oneself activates neither Broca's nor Wernicke's area. In light of this, whatever results were achieved with "reading" apes, it would be difficult to know quite what they proved. See Niels A. Lassen, David H. Ingvar and Erik Skinhøj, "Brain Function and Blood Flow", *Scientific American*, 239 (1978), pp. 62–71.

13 R. W. Sperry, "Forebrain Commissurotomy and Conscious Awareness", *Journal of Medicine and Philosophy*, 2 (1977), p. 107.

14 For a longer discussion of preadaptation and the evolution of birds from small, active dinosaurs, see Adrian J. Desmond, *The Hot-Blooded Dinosaurs* (London, Blond & Briggs, 1975; New York, Dial Press, 1976) Ch. 6.

15 Norman Geschwind, pers. comm., 1 November 1978.

16 H. S. Terrace and T. G. Bever, "What Might be Learned from Studying Language in the Chimpanzee? The Importance of Symbolizing Oneself", *Ann. N.Y. Acad. Sci.*, 280 (1976), pp. 579–611.

17 M. R. Petersen, M. D. Beecher, S. R. Zoloth, D. B. Moody, and W. C. Stebbins, "Neural Lateralization of Species-Specific Vocalizations by Japanese Macaques (*Macaca fuscata*)", *Science*, 202 (1978), p. 326.

18 Ralph L. Holloway, "Culture: A *Human* Domain", *Current Anthropology*, 10 (1969), p. 395.

19 A. W. R. McRae, "Comments" on above paper, *ibid.*, p. 409.

20 Gordon W. Hewes, "Primate Communication and the Gestural Origin of Language", *Current Anthropology*, 14 (1973), p. 11. Hewes, "The Current Status of the Gestural Theory of Language Origin", *Ann. N.Y. Acad. Sci.*, 280 (1976), see pp. 488–99.

21 For Dart's own accounts of his *Australopithecus* discoveries, enlivened by a wealth of background details, read Raymond A. Dart, *Adventures with the Missing Link* (New York, Viking, 1959). Many suspected bludgeons and matching crushed crania are illustrated in this book.

22 Alfred Carpenter, "Monkeys opening Oysters", *Nature*, 36 (1887), p. 53.

23 Benjamin B. Beck, "Primate Tool Behavior", in R. H. Tuttle (Ed.), *Socioecology and Psychology of Primates* (The Hague, Mouton, 1975), pp. 413–47.

24 A. Kortlandt and M. Kooij, "Protohominid Behaviour in Primates", in J. Napier and N. A. Barnicot (Eds.), *The Primates*, Symposium, Zoological Society of London, 10 (1963), pp. 61–88.

25 Jane van Lawick-Goodall, *In the Shadow of Man* (New York, Dell, 1972), p. 109.

26 *Ibid.*, pp. 51–2.

27 Geza Teleki, "Chimpanzee Subsistence Technology: Materials and Skills", *Journal of Human Evolution*, 3 (1974), p. 585. For a recent discussion on nonhuman tool use and an attempt to distinguish and categorise tool-using behaviours according to a Piagetian framework, see

Sue Taylor Parker and Kathleen R. Gibson, "Object Manipulation, Tool Use and Sensorimotor Intelligence as Feeding Adaptations in Cebus Monkeys and Great Apes", *ibid.*, 6 (1977), pp. 623–41.

28 Teleki, "Chimpanzee Subsistence Technology", p. 588.
The chimpanzee evidence opens up new options for the history of man/ape tool using. Teleki believes that object manipulation might stretch back to the Oligocene, since it is now known to be common to apes, men and monkeys. Rudimentary tool-making and transportation could have existed in the Miocene man-ape ancestor, with the earliest hominids learning to dig for roots using sticks. Because they were perishable, we fail to find these fossil tools. But of course this is conjecture, however plausible, and debates over it are liable to rage for years. Still, Teleki repeats, "the likelihood that some extinct Primates once possessed technological capabilities – expressed for perhaps millions of years only in the manipulation, modification and transportation of 'soft' materials – is at least circumstantially strengthened by the chimpanzee evidence". *Ibid.*, pp. 581, 592. Beck strongly concurs, concluding on the basis of his study of tool use in baboons and other monkeys (where it may be quite striking, and even socially orientated, as in holding up a baby to stop an attacking male in its tracks) that "complex, learned tool behavior may have been present before the hominid grade was attained". Beck, "Primate Tool Behavior", p. 440. Parker and Gibson likewise suggest that intelligent tool use arose "in the common ancestor of the great apes and hominids". Parker & Gibson, "Object Manipulation", p. 634.

29 See also Benjamin B. Beck, "Baboons, Chimpanzees, and Tools", *Journal of Human Evolution*, 3 (1974), pp. 509–16.

30 Kenneth P. Oakley, "A Definition of Man", in M. F. Ashley Montagu, *Culture and the Evolution of Man* (New York, Oxford University Press, 1962), p. 6.

31 J. Buettner-Janush, *Origin of Man* (New York, Wiley, 1966), p. 290. Goodall's original notice was published as "Tool-Using and Aimed Throwing in a Community of Free-Living Chimpanzees", *Nature*, 201 (1964), pp. 1264–6.

32 Kenneth P. Oakley, *Man the Tool-Maker* (London, British Museum [Natural History], 1972), p. 3 and notice H. W. Ball's "Preface to Sixth Edition".

33 R. V. S. Wright, "Imitative Learning of a Flaked Stone Technology – The Case of an Orangutan", *Mankind*, 8 (1972), p. 296.

7. Is Romance Really Dead?

1 Francine G. Patterson, "The Gestures of a Gorilla: Language Acquisition in Another Pongid", *Brain and Language*, 5 (1978), p. 95.

2 David Premack, pers. comm., 15 November 1978.

3 R. Allen Gardner and Beatrice T. Gardner, "Teaching Sign Language to a Chimpanzee", *Science*, 165 (1969), pp. 671–2.

4 Charles Darwin, letter to Charles Lyell, 4 January 1860: Francis Darwin (Ed.), *The Life and Letters of Charles Darwin* (London, Murray, 1887), 2, p. 262.

5 J. Bronowski and Ursula Bellugi, "Language, Name, and Concept", *Science*, 168 (1970), pp. 669–73.

6 For a gentle criticism of Linden's heroes-and-villains approach, see Roger Wescott's review in *Man*, 11 (1976), p. 630.

7 Richard Owen, "Ape-Origin of Man as Tested by the Brain", *The Athenaeum*, 21 February, 1863, p. 262. For more on this debate see *The New Reformation*.

8 "Professor Huxley on Man's Place in Nature", *Edinburgh Review*, 117 (1863), pp. 563–4.

9 Charles Lyell, letter to Principal Dawson, 15 May 1860: Mrs. Lyell (Ed.), *Life, Letters and Journals of Sir Charles Lyell* (London, Murray, 1881), 2, p. 333.

10 M. J. S. Hodge, "The Universal Gestation of Nature: Chambers' *Vestiges* and *Explanations*", *Journal of the History of Biology*, 5 (1972), pp. 127–51.

11 [Robert Chambers], *Vestiges of the Natural History of Creation* (London, Churchill, 1844), pp. 274–5. For the social and theological setting of Chambers' ideas, see Charles Coulston Gillispie, *Genesis and Geology* (New York, Harper Torchbook, 1959), Ch. 6.

12 John Marshall, "On the Brain of a Bushwoman; and on the Brains of Two Idiots of European Descent", *Phil. Trans. Roy. Soc. London*, 154 (1864), p. 546. Compare this to Carl Vogt's advocacy of the "idiot" as a stand-in ape ancestor in *Lectures on Man* (London, Longman, 1864).

13 *The Times*, 22 August 1878, p. 8.

14 Letters from Charles Darwin to George John Romanes, 20 August 1878 and 2 September 1878: Mrs. Romanes (Ed.), *The Life and Letters of George John Romanes* (London, Longman, 1896), pp. 75, 78.

15 Cited by Loren Eisely in *Darwin's Century* (New York, Anchor, 1961), p. 303.

16 Marvin Harris, *Cannibals and Kings* (London, Collins, 1978), p. 110.

17 Charles Darwin, *The Descent of Man* (New York, A. L. Burt, 1874?), p. 708.

18 Adam Sedgwick, in a letter to Charles Lyell, 9 April 1845: John Willis Clark and Thomas McKenny Hughes (Eds)., *The Life and Letters of the Reverend Adam Sedgwick* (Cambridge-University Press, 1890), 2, p. 85.

19 Francis Darwin and A. C. Seward (Eds.), *More Letters of Charles Darwin* (London, Murray, 1903), 1, p. 114.

20 [Adam Sedgwick], "Objections to Mr. Darwin's Theory of the Origin of Species", *The Spectator*, 24 March 1860, p. 285.

21 Sir Gavin de Beer (Ed.), "Darwin's Notebooks on Transmutation of Species", *Bull. Brit. Mus. (Nat. Hist.)* Historical Series, 2 (1959–63), p. 50.

22 George John Romanes, *Mental Evolution in Man* (London, Kegan Paul, 1888), p. 2. Incidentally, Romanes had little first-hand knowledge of apes, though he was quite familiar with the cebus monkey, which he (or rather his put-upon sister) installed as a pet for study. Although he dutifully trotted out Locke's dictum that "Beasts abstract not", Romanes was a perceptive and able psychologist, encouraged by Darwin, who had no qualms about flouting convention. Hence, encouraged by the antics of his cebus monkey – who took to unscrewing everything in sight – he speculated *very* tentatively (remember this is 1888) that apes "if specially trained" might "display greater aptitude in the manner of sign-making than is to be met with in any other kind of brute". Adding curtly "But I do not want to press this point." *Ibid.*, p. 364.

23 [St. George Mivart], "Darwin's *Descent of Man*", *Quarterly Review*, 131 (1871), p. 89. For Mivart's collected essays on evolution see *Essays and Criticisms* (London, Osgood, 1892), vol. 2.

24 Louis Agassiz, "A Period in the History of Our Planet", *The Edinburgh New Philosophical Journal*, 35 (1843), p. 6.

25 Charles Darwin, *The Origin of Species* (New York, Mentor, 1958), p. 331. This is a republication of the sixth edition.

26 C. H. Waddington, *The Nature of Life* (London, Unwin, 1963), p. 104. Some evolutionary theorists have no qualms about introducing value judgments, recognising them explicitly as such. Ayala writes that "Progress occurs when there is a directional change towards a *better* state or condition. The concept of progress, then, contains two elements: one descriptive – that directional change has occurred; the other axiological – that the change represents an improvement or betterment. The notion of progress requires that a value judgment be made of what is better and what is worse, or what is higher and what is lower..." Francisco J. Ayala, "The Concept of Biological Progress", in F. J. Ayala and Theodosius Dobzhansky (Eds.), *Studies in the Philosophy of Biology* (London, Mac-

millan, 1974), p. 341. The most interesting question in this respect is "Why do we so desperately need to discover 'progress' in the fossil genealogy?". Does it say more about us than the way evolution works?

The battle rages on under its least sophisticated guise in psychology. In 1969 William Hodos and C. B. G. Campbell denounced the infamous "phyletic scale" psychologists forever invoke, which is too often a hierarchy of cheap and expendable minds: frog-rat-cat-pigeon-man. This laboratory sequence has little evolutionary meaning, tending only to simulate the preDarwinian ascent to manhood at its crudest level. Each of these creatures is specialised for a remarkably distinct life-style. As George Gaylord Simpson says, "the anatomical differences among these organisms are in large part ecologically and behaviorally determined, are divergent and not sequential, and do not in any useful sense form an historical series". See William Hodos and C. B. G. Campbell, "*Scala Naturae*: Why there is No Theory in Comparative Psychology", *Psychological Review*, 76 (1969), pp. 337–50. This paper was recently and, to my mind, none too convincingly answered by Matthew Yarczower and Lenis Hazlett, "Evolutionary Scales and Anagenesis", *Psychological Bulletin*, 84 (1977), pp. 1088–97. How is one to reprieve a science hell-bent on sitting man atop a motley assortment of lab pets of increasing 'subhumanity'? The obvious answer is to dismantle the preDarwinian edifice, liberate its chained members, then using ecology and consequent behavioural specialisation, explain their mental predispositions. This will spotlight psychological divergence without reference to which creature scores higher on some fixed scale.

27 C. G. Jung, *The Undiscovered Self*, trans. R. F. C. Hull (London, Routledge & Kegan Paul, 1974), pp. 43–4.

28 Theodosius Dobzhansky, "Chance and Creativity in Evolution", *Studies in the Philosophy of Biology*, p. 333.

8. Reflections and Ripples

1 Gordon G. Gallup, Jr., "Towards an Operational Definition of Self-Awareness", in R. H. Tuttle (Ed.), *Socioecology and Psychology of Primates* (The Hague, Mouton, 1975), p. 335.

2 David Lack, *Evolutionary Theory and Christian Belief* (London, Methuen, 1961), p. 115.

3 Robert Ardrey, *African Genesis* (New York, Dell, 1972), p. 34.

4 Gordon G. Gallup, Jr., "Self-Recognition in Primates", *American Psychologist*, 32 (1977), p. 335.

5 Croora Robertson, quoted in George John Romanes, *Animal Intelligence*

(London, Kegan Paul, 1882), p. 479. For infant (human) self-recognition, see Beulah Amsterdam, "Mirror Self-Image Reactions Before Age Two", *Developmental Psychobiology*, 5 (1972), pp. 297–305.

6 Robert M. Yerkes, "The Mind of the Gorilla: Part II. Mental Development", *Genetic Psychology Monographs*, 2 (1927), p. 519.

7 Pers. comm., 18 January 1978.

8 Gordon G. Gallup, Jr., "Chimpanzees: Self-Recognition", *Science*, 167 (1970), p. 86.

9 Gallup, "Towards an Operational Definition of Self-Awareness", p. 325.

10 William A. Mason, "Environmental Models and Mental Modes", *American Psychologist*, 31 (1976), p. 293.

11 Gallup, "Self-Recognition in Primates", p. 334. Gallup, "Absence of Self-Recognition in a Monkey (*Macaca fascicularis*) Following Prolonged Exposure to a Mirror", *Developmental Psychobiology*, 10 (1977), pp. 281–4.

12 W. Lynn Brown, A. A. McDowell, and E. M. Robinson. "Discrimination Learning of Mirrored Cues by Rhesus Monkeys", *The Journal of Genetic Psychology*, 106 (1965), pp. 123–8.

13 Gallup, "Self-Recognition in Primates", p. 334.

14 Pers. comm., 29 August 1978.

15 E. Sue Savage and Duane M. Rumbaugh, "Communication, Language, and Lana", in Duane M. Rumbaugh (Ed.), *Language Learning by a Chimpanzee: The Lana Project* (New York, Academic Press, 1977), p. 307.

16 Gordon G. Gallup, Jr., "Book Reviews", *The Psychological Record*, 27 (1977), p. 796.

17 Geza Teleki, "Group Response to the Accidental Death of a Chimpanzee in Gombe National Park, Tanzania", *Folia Primatologica*, 20 (1973), p. 84.

18 Ralph S. Solecki, *Shanidar: The Humanity of Neanderthal Man* (London, Allen Lane, 1972), p. 194.

19 Arlette Leroi-Gourhan, "The Flowers Found with Shanidar IV, a Neanderthal Burial in Iraq", *Science*, 190 (1975), pp. 562–3.

20 Ralph S. Solecki, "Shanidar IV, a Neanderthal Flower Burial in Northern Iraq", *Science*, 190 (1975), pp. 880. Solecki, "The Implications of the Shanidar Cave Neanderthal Flower Burial", *Ann. N.Y. Acad. Sci.*, 293 (1977), pp. 114–24. For the evidence that Neanderthal man probably cared for his sick and injured, see T. Dale Stewart, "The Neanderthal Skeletal Remains from Shanidar Cave, Iraq: A Summary of Findings to Date", *Proc. Am. Phil. Soc.*, 121 (1977), pp. 121–65.

21 F. M. Bergounioux, " 'Spiritualité' de l'Homme de Néanderthal", in G. H. R. von Koenigswald (Ed.), *Hundert Jahre Neanderthaler* (Utrecht, 1958), pp. 151–66. Contrast this with Marcellin Boule's "brutal" Neanderthal, introduced in "L'Homme Fossile de la Chapelle-aux-Saints", *Annales de Paléontologie*, 8 (1913), pp. 209–70.

22 Biruté M. F. Galdikas, "Orangutan Death and Scavenging by Pigs", *Science*, 200 (1978), pp. 68–70. Of course, the Bornean climate (which speeds up decomposition of a corpse) and forest ecology may not parallel that of man's prehistory; still, it demonstrates how rapidly a large primate carcass can be scavenged under favourable conditions.

23 The literature on this debate is massive and still growing. What sparked it off was a paper by Philip Lierberman and Edmund S. Crelin, "On the Speech of Neanderthal Man", *Linguistic Inquiry*, 2 (1971), pp. 203–22. Using only a (perhaps) poorly reconstructed Neanderthal skull, Lieberman and Crelin traced the vocal apparatus, suggesting that the modulating air passages were as ineffectual as a baby's. After feeding the data into a computer, they deduced that the "Neanderthal phonetic repertoire is inherently limited"; in fact, that he was incapable of generating the vowels *u, i, a,* and *ɔ* (as in "brought"). This implied that Neanderthal man was limited to some nasal consonants plus a few vowels, indeed that his speech was severely impaired. And anyway they argued that he probably lacked the neural means of comprehending the full range of quick-fire speech. Tumultuous criticism was heaped on Lieberman's and Crelin's heads, ranging from the ideological (they were arch-reactionaries trying desperately to brutalise Neanderthal) to the anatomical (their Neanderthal cranium was improperly restored) to methodological (their figures were incorrect). For a sample of the response (few aligned themselves with the heretics), see R. C. Carlisle and M. I. Siegel, *American Anthropologist*, 76 (1974), pp. 319–25. M. LeMay, *Am. J. Phys. Anthrop.*, 42 (1975), pp. 9–14. Dean Falk, *ibid.*, 43 (1976), pp. 123–32. The debate rages on.

24 Henry de Lumley, "A Paleolithic Camp at Nice", *Scientific American*, 220 (1969), pp. 42–50.

25 Alexander Marshack, "Implications of the Paleolithic Symbolic Evidence for the Origin of Language", *American Scientist*, 64 (1976), pp. 136–45.

26 David Premack, "Language and Intelligence in Ape and Man", *ibid.*, p. 674.

27 See Philip Rieff's introduction to Charles Horton Cooley, *Social Organization* (New York, Schocken, 1962), p. vi.

28 Robert Cooley Angell, "Introduction", in Albert J. Reiss (Ed.), *Cooley and Sociological Analysis* (Ann Arbor, University of Michigan Press, 1968), p. 12.

29 George H. Mead, *Mind, Self and Society* (University of Chicago Press, 1934), p. 140.

30 John Dewey, "George Herbert Mead", *Journal of Philosophy*, 28 (1931), p. 310. See also T. V. Smith, "The Social Philosophy of George Herbert Mead", *American Journal of Sociology*, 37 (1931), pp. 368–79. For Mead's

appreciation of Cooley, see Mead, "Cooley's Contribution to American Social Thought", *ibid.* 35 (1930), esp. pp. 704–5.

31 Mead, *Mind, Self and Society*, p. 183.

32 Anselm Strauss, *The Social Psychology of George Herbert Mead* (University of Chicago Press, 1956), p. xvi.

33 Smith, "The Social Philosophy of G. H. Mead", p. 368.

34 Pers. comm., Jan. 18, 1978.

35 Gordon G. Gallup, Jr., Michael K. McClure, Suzanne D. Hill, and Rosalie A. Bundy, "Capacity for Self-Recognition in Differentially Reared Chimpanzees", *Psychological Record*, 21 (1971), pp. 69–74.

36 Maurice K. Temerlin, *Lucy: Growing Up Human* (New York, Bantam, 1977), p. xiv.

37 Gallup begs to differ on the pivotal point of the distinction (or lack of) between chimpanzee and human selves. He takes a pragmatic line; and in order to give some idea of the complexity and subtlety of the problem, I quote his rejoinder in full:

"If I were to accept your proposition that as long as societies differ then selves must be adaptively distinct, I might be forced to view the differences between some human societies (e.g., aborigines vs. the industrialized west) as perhaps being sufficiently separate to justify enslavement. Conversely, what would you say about chimpanzees reared in human homes? Differences in societies are not necessarily enduring or even fundamental, and in spite of these differences it is becoming increasingly apparent that chimpanzees and people share basically the same conceptual equipment in common. How then do we justify keeping them behind bars?" (Pers. comm., 29 August 1978)

Humanised apes are the major problem, since they do *prima facie* seem to have absorbed our social life and aspects of our culture; but is this totally true? Are there not *innate social tendencies* or expectations that man, ape or for that matter wolf are born with? It seems so, and it may well be that the dominance patterns manifested in Gombe ape society re-emerge somewhat distorted in humanised apes. Lucy Temerlin, for example, immediately dominates some humans and submits to others, almost on first encounter, a fact which Maurice Temerlin has exploited in his psychotherapy sessions. But the point needs urgent further examination.

In so far as this boils down to disagreements over facts, the problem can be resolved. Personally, I think that chimpanzee society does differ to some degree from human society, which has emerged in its characteristic form as a result of reciprocal altruism (see my final chapter), and this has forged the human mind in its own peculiar mould. But the underlying reason for my divergence from Gallup is our opposing metaphysics, since in this instance I owe allegiance to the "purist" Darwin, as I called him; hence I am reluctant to perjure myself by denying all adaptive distinctions between our two species. I am the first to uphold the chimpanzee's sovereign 'self', but consider that I would be insulting (if not untrue to Darwin) if I equated this with the 'self' of another species.

38 Terrace and Tom Bever at Columbia, believing that the ability to symbolise one's *self* might be the crucial spur to syntactic development (which begins by mapping the self's relation to the world at large), expected Project Nim to throw some light on this. By tempting Nim to forge a symbolic fortress round his self-concept, they had hoped to accelerate his acquisition of human-style syntax. They suggested "that a concept of self whereby a chimpanzee is able to conceptualise its feelings, intentions, and so on, in relation to other individuals in its environment, may be a crucial step in motivating the chimpanzee to acquire the syntactic competence characteristic of human language". This proved overly ambitious. H. S. Terrace and T. G. Bever, "What Might be Learned from Studying Language in the Chimpanzee? The Importance of Symbolizing Oneself", *Ann. N.Y. Acad. Sci.*, 280 (1976), p. 586.

9. Introspection

1 Francine Patterson "Conversations with a Gorilla", *National Geographic*, 154, No. 4 (1978), p. 438.

2 N. K. Humphrey, "The Social Function of Intellect", in P. P. G. Bateson and R. A. Hinde (Eds.), *Growing Points in Ethology* (Cambridge University Press, 1976), p. 303.

3 Nick Humphrey, "Nature's Psychologists", *New Scientist*, 79 (1978), p. 900.

4 Jane van Lawick-Goodall, *In the Shadow of Man* (New York, Dell, 1972), p. 131.

5 Wolfgang Köhler, *The Mentality of Apes* (London, Kegan Paul, 1927), pp. 287, 298.

6 Benjamin B. Beck, "Cooperative Tool Use by Captive Hamadryas Baboons", *Science*, 182 (1973), pp. 594–7.

7 E. W. Menzel, "Spontaneous Invention of Ladders in a Group of Young Chimpanzees", *Folia Primatologica*, 17 (1972), pp. 87–106.

8 Goodall, *In the Shadow of Man*, p. 107.

9 "It is not very illuminating, perhaps, to describe a chimpanzee as 'figuring out' how to proceed, while it sits and stares at the problem before it. Certainly such an assertion lacks originality, as well as precision. But we

cannot escape the inference that some such process is at work . . ."
William A. Mason, "Environmental Models and Mental Modes",
American Psychologist, 31 (1976), p. 293.

10 Patterson, "Conversations", p. 465.

11 Mark S. Seidenberg and Laura A. Petitto, "Signing Behavior in Apes:
A Critical Review", *Cognition* (in press); "On the Evidence for Linguistic
Abilities in Signing Apes", *Brain and Language* (in press).

12 R. Allen Gardner and Beatrice T. Gardner, "Teaching Sign Language
to a Chimpanzee", *Science*, 165 (1969), p. 668; "Evidence for Sentence
Constituents in the Early Utterances of Child and Chimpanzee", *Journal
of Experimental Psychology: General*, 104 (1975), p. 266.

13 Francine G. Patterson, "The Gestures of a Gorilla: Language Acquisition
in Another Pongid", *Brain and Language*, 5 (1978), pp. 78, 80.

14 Patterson, "Conversations", p. 459.

15 Humphrey, "Social Function of Intellect", p. 312.

10. The Gombe: From Hunting to Holocaust

1 Glynn Isaac, "The Food-Sharing Behavior of Protohuman Hominids",
Scientific American, 238 (1978), pp. 90–104, 106, 108.

2 Figures from David Pilbeam and Stephen Jay Gould, "Size and Scaling
in Human Evolution", *Science*, 186 (1974), pp. 892–901.

3 S. L. Washburn and C. S. Lancaster, "The Evolution of Hunting", in
Richard B. Lee and Irven DeVore (Eds.), *Man the Hunter* (Chicago,
Aldine, 1968), pp. 293–303.

4 For a recent restatement of his thesis, see Arthur Koestler, *Janus: A
Summing Up* (London, Hutchinson, 1978).

5 Geza Teleki, "Primate Subsistence Patterns: Collector-Predators and
Gatherer-Hunters", *Journal of Human Evolution*, 4 (1975), p. 127.

6 Jane van Lawick-Goodall, *In the Shadow of Man* (New York, Dell, 1972),
p. 49.

7 Teleki, "Primate Subsistence Patterns", p. 127.

8 Geza Teleki, "The Omnivorous Chimpanzee", *Scientific American*, 228
(1973), p. 42.

9 See C. R. Carpenter's foreword to Geza Teleki's *The Predatory Behavior
of Wild Chimpanzees* (Lewisburg, Bucknell University Press, 1973), p. 10.

10 Akira Suzuki, "The Origin of Hominid Hunting: A Primatological
Perspective", in R. H. Tuttle (Ed.), *Socioecology and Psychology of Primates*
(The Hague, Mouton, 1975), p. 268.

11 Morris and Goodall rightly call it "complex, multifaceted and often
perplexing". Kathryn Morris and Jane Goodall, "Competition for Meat

Between Chimpanzees and Baboons of the Gombe National Park", *Folia Primatologica*, 28 (1977), p. 118.

12 Konrad Lorenz, *On Aggression* (London, Methuen, 1966), pp. 19, 206–36.

13 Adriaan Kortlandt, "Discussion" in Tuttle, *Socioecology*, p. 302.

14 Roger Peters, *ibid.*, pp. 303–4.

15 J. D. Bygott, "Cannibalism among Wild Chimpanzees", *Nature*, 238 (1972), pp. 410–11. A slightly different version is given by Goodall (albeit based on Bygott's field notes), suggesting that more of the infant was eaten. Even so, she records that in each of the cases of infant cannibalism, "relatively little had been consumed". Jane Goodall, "Infant Killing and Cannibalism in Free-Living Chimpanzees", *Folia Primatologica*, 28 (1977), pp. 262–4, 279.

16 Teleki, "Primate Subsistence Patterns", pp. 169–72.

17 Jane Goodall, "Watching, Watching, Watching", *The New York Times*, 15 September 1977, p. A27.

18 Judging by the response, Goodall's Leakey Lecture (given on 11 January 1978) caused a considerable stir; and the great bulk of questions following concentrated on the recent murders in the Gombe.

19 Ashley Montagu, "Of Chimpanzees and Men", *The New York Times*, 2 May 1978, p. 34, replying to the *Times'* editorial, "A Theory of Devolution", 22 April 1978, p. 18.

20 Richard W. Wrangham, "Artificial Feeding of Chimpanzees and Baboons in their Natural Habitat", *Anim. Behav.*, 22 (1974), p. 85. On the basis of Wrangham's figures (which suggest that aggression rose steeply as banana provisioning increased), Reynolds attacks Teleki's conclusions, and suggests that ape predation on baboons might be unnaturally high in this artificially contrived study region. Vernon Reynolds, "How Wild are the Gombe Chimpanzees?", *Man* (N.S.), 10 (1975), pp. 123–5. But this is something of a minor criticism, despite an element of truth: the Gombe chimpanzees were simply cashing in on the fresh meat supply, but switched back to their old targets after the provisioning stopped. Teleki's work has led to some valuable insights, and a new picture of the origin of primate predation is slowly emerging. For an overview, see M. D. Rose, "The Roots of Primate Predatory Behavior" *Journal of Human Evolution*, 7 (1978), pp. 179–89. Yet there is still a deep division on the question of the antiquity of chimpanzee hunting: some see it as comparatively recent, Teleki imagines it more deeply rooted, hinting at the possibility that the man-ape ancestor had omnivorous habits which evolved into both chimpanzee and human hunting.

11. The Mechanics of Morality

1 A. Kortlandt, "Comments" on Hewes' paper, *Current Anthropology*, 14 (1973), p. 13.

2 Frederick Engels, *Dialectics of Nature* (New York, International Publishers, 1963), p. 283.

3 Robert M. Yerkes, *Chimpanzees: A Laboratory Colony* (New Haven, Yale University Press, 1943), pp. 190–1.

4 Emil Menzel, "Natural Language of Young Chimpanzees", *New Scientist*, 65 (1975), p. 130. See also Emil W. Menzel, "Chimpanzee Spatial Memory Organization", *Science*, 182 (1973), pp. 943–5.

5 E. Sue Savage-Rumbaugh, Duane M. Rumbaugh, and Sally Boysen, "Symbolic Communication Between Two Chimpanzees", *Science*, 201 (1978), p. 643.

6 T. H. Huxley, "Evolution and Ethics. Prolegomena", in T. H. Huxley, *Evolution and Ethics* (London, Macmillan, 1925), p. 31. This is vol. IX of Huxley's Collected Essays.

7 Robert L. Trivers, "The Evolution of Reciprocal Altruism", *The Quarterly Review of Biology*, 46 (1971), pp. 35–57.

8 Richard Dawkins, *The Selfish Gene* (London, Paladin, 1978), pp. 198–202.

9 S. C. Strum, "Primate Predation: Interim Report on the Development of a Tradition in a Troop of Olive Baboons", *Science*, 187 (1975), pp. 755–57. For a critique of this paper, and Shirley Strum's rejoinder, see Steven J. C. Gaulin and Jeffrey A. Kurland, "Primate Predation and Bioenergetics", *Science*, 191 (1976), pp. 314–15; and pp. 315–17 for Strum's answer.

10 Savage-Rumbaugh, Rumbaugh & Boysen "Symbolic Communication", pp. 643–4.

11 Colin Turnbull, *The Forest People* (London, Picador, 1976), pp. 95–6.

12 Trivers, "The Evolution of Reciprocal Altruism", p. 49.

13 *Ibid.* p. 54.

Index